D1326820

The Letters of
Denis Devlin

Denis Devlin in his twenties.
PHOTOGRAPH COURTESY OF HELEN O'CONNOR

The Letters of
Denis Devlin
Edited by SARAH BENNETT

CORK **cup** UNIVERSITY PRESS

First published in 2020 by
Cork University Press
Boole Library
University College Cork
Cork T12 ND89
Ireland

Library of Congress Control Number: 2020934708

Distribution in the USA Longleaf Services, Chapel Hill, NC, USA.

British Library Cataloguing in Publication Data
A CIP catalogue record for this book is available from the British
Library.

ISBN 9781782054092

Printed by BZ Graf in Poland

Design and typesetting by Alison Burns at Studio 10 Design, Cork

Front cover: Denis Devlin in his twenties, photograph courtesy of
Helen O'Connor

Credits for other images in this edition can be found on page xi

CONTENTS

My dear Sheila, We have been thinking of doing a play at Christmas one of W. B. Yeats "Plays for Dancers." They are short and in verse and there is some dancing to be done. Masks have to be worn and coloured silk, the action is artificial, every gesture emphasised by a drum tap. If the nuns have a copy you might read them and see if you like the plan. They are lovely plays. I hear you are learning lots of music there so we shall have some good playing at Christmas. I am going to the concerts here, next Saturday a young Russian called Horovitz is playing, he is said to be original. I gave a lecture to the French Society the other day which was a success. I hope you are practising your writing Sheila because I believe you have a talent there which you ought to cultivate. And besides it's a priceless relief from life. — Mr. Madden was here telling funny stories and, as usual, till 4 o'clock in the morning. We are having hard bright weather in Dublin, this frosty winter sun is pleasant. But we get tired often of the darkness and long for the country. So write and tell me what your country is like

Yours (ha! ha!) with love Denis.

Facing page and above: Letter from Denis Devlin to Shiela Devlin, [November 1933].

ACKNOWLEDGEMENTS

This project got off the ground with a generous award from Oxford's John Fell Fund, and a research allocation from Oriel College, Oxford. Oriel has provided a supportive and congenial environment throughout, granting a research sabbatical in 2019, which allowed me to bring the edition to a close. I'd like to thank my colleagues for their conversation, counsel and good cheer, in particular Kathryn Murphy, Gonzalo Rodriguez-Pereyra, Bruno Currie, Marion Turner, Richard Scholar, Francesco Manzini and Moira Wallace. Long periods working in Dublin libraries and archives have been enabled by the Godfrey-Walkers: for their generous hospitality and generally fabulous company I am deeply grateful.

My thanks go to Maria O'Donovan and the team at Cork University Press for taking an interest in the project, working with startling efficiency during a period of lockdown, and providing me with practical help and encouragement throughout. Especial thanks are owed to Aonghus Meaney for his brilliantly scrupulous copy-editing.

These letters have been gathered from archives across Europe and North America, and my work would not have been possible without the cooperation, guidance and practical assistance of librarians and archivists across the world. The following people deserve particular thanks: Reid Echols at the Harry Ransom Center; Gregory O'Connor, Ken Robinson and the rest of the staff at the National Archives of Ireland in Dublin; Romain Mari at the Fondation Saint-John Perse; Timothy Murray and Valerie Stenner at the Morris Library, University of Delaware; Alison Clemens, Rebecca Aldi and the Reading Room team at the Beinecke Rare Book and Manuscript Library; Avice-Claire McGovern and the wider staff at the National Library of Ireland; Jane Maxwell and the the team at the Manuscript Library, Trinity College Dublin; Dean Smith and Lorna Kirwan at the Bancroft Library, UC Berkeley; Brianna Cregle at Princeton University Library; Aaron Michael Lisec at Southern Illinois University; Edith A. Sandler at the Library of Congress; Kris Kinsey at the University of Washington Libraries; Diana Harper and Christine Colburn at the University of Chicago Library; Mary Haegert and Susan J. Halpert at the Houghton Library, Harvard; Nicole Potter at Syracuse University Libraries; the Reference Department at the American Heritage Center, University of Wyoming; Jonathan Jeffrey at the Department of Special Collections, Western Kentucky University; Lindsay G. Bright at the Archives of American Art, Smithsonian Institution.

From the start of this project, a correspondence with various people who have personal or scholarly connections to Devlin, his close friends and the wider community he corresponded with, has fortified my research. Alex Davis and Jim Mays have been with this project from the beginning, lending it their support, experience and expertise, and often guiding my research in productive ways. It could not have been produced without their help. John Coffey, Ann Brewer Fischer (who generously provided a photograph of her father on holiday with Devlin in their student days), John Deane and John Lucas were all generous with their time and information, supplying important biographical and bibliographical details. It was a joy to finally locate members of the Devlin family in the middle of this research, and to discover their interest in continuing the legacy of Denis' life and work. I am particularly indebted to Denyse Woods and John Healy for their insight, warmth and encouragement. Helen O'Connor and Caren Farrell did tremendous work in uncovering material by and relating to their Uncle Denis.

My translations from French and Italian were reliant upon the careful reading and correction of Francesco Manzini and Roger Little; the Irish was brought to light in consultation with Bernard O'Donoghue and John and Eavan Healy. For their time, patience and advice I am extremely grateful.

To the Bennetts – a large, active and loving family like the Devlins and very far from 'inconvenient' – I owe a great deal, especially to Mum and Dad. Thanks to Carys Anne for giving me an occasional break and much to look forward to. And thanks, above all, to Michael Molan, my first and most trusted reader and my favourite companion.

PERMISSIONS

Letters, manuscripts and poems by Denis Devlin are included by permission of the Dedalus Press, acting for the Denis Devlin Estate, and with the support and assistance of the Devlin family. The cover photograph is reproduced with the kind permission of Helen O'Connor. Other images used in this edition are reproduced courtesy of Ann Brewer Fischer, the University of Delaware Library, and Library Collections, Western Kentucky University.

While every effort has been made to contact the estate holders for the archives containing Devlin's letters, and the copyright holders for quotations used, this has not always been possible. The editor and publishers would be very grateful to hear of any copyright holders who have not been found and acknowledged.

Publication of Devlin's diplomatic letters from the Department of Foreign Affairs Papers is made possible with the permission and generous assistance of the National Archives of Ireland.

Quotations from the poetry of Brian Coffey are included with the permission of the Dedalus Press, acting on behalf of the Brian Coffey Estate. Material from the Brian Coffey Papers is included with permission of the University of Delaware Library, and with the generous cooperation of the late John Coffey. Quotations from the poetry of Thomas MacGreevy appear with the kind permission of Clíona Uí Thuama and Robbie Ryan. Material from the Thomas MacGreevy Papers is included with permission from the Board of Trinity College, the University of Dublin. Letters to Shiela Devlin are included with the kind permission of Caren Farrell; correspondence between Denis and Caren Devlin and Robert Penn Warren and Eleanor Clark is included with the kind permission of Rosanna and Gabriel Warren; material from the Niall Montgomery Papers is included with the kind permission of James Montgomery, Rose Mary O'Brien, Ruth Bourke and Christine O'Neill; material from the George Reavey Papers is included with the kind permission of Susan Bullowa; material from the Allen Tate Papers is included with the kind permission of Helen Tate; letters to Alexis Leger are included with permission of the Fondation Saint-John Perse, Aix-en-Provence; lines from A. M. Blackmore and E. H. Blackmore's translations of Mallarmé are reproduced with permission of Oxford Publishing Limited, through PLSclear.

ABBREVIATIONS

ARCHIVES, LIBRARIES AND INSTITUTIONS

AHC, UWy	American Heritage Center, University of Wyoming
Beinecke, YU	Beinecke Rare Book and Manuscript Library, Yale University
FSJP	Fondation Saint-John Perse, Aix-en-Provence
HRC, UTx	Harry Ransom Center, University of Texas at Austin
HU	Houghton Library, Harvard University
LoC	Library of Congress, Washington
NAI	National Archives of Ireland, Dublin
NLI	National Library of Ireland, Dublin
PU	Department of Rare Books and Special Collections, Princeton University Library
TCD	Manuscript Department, The Library of Trinity College Dublin
UCB	Bancroft Library, University of California, Berkeley
UChi	Special Collections Research Center, University of Chicago Library
UDel	University of Delaware Library

BOOKS

BCPV	*Poems and Versions 1929-1990* (Brian Coffey)
CPDD	*Collected Poems of Denis Devlin*
CPTM	*Collected Poems of Thomas MacGreevy: An Annotated Edition*
LSB	*The Letters of Samuel Beckett*
OC	*Oeuvres Complètes* (Paul Eluard)
SLRPW	*Selected Letters of Robert Penn Warren*
TOT	*Thorns of Thunder* (Paul Eluard)

CHRONOLOGY

DEVLIN'S EARLY LIFE

1908

DD born in Greenock, Scotland, to Liam and Margaret Devlin. He was the eldest of nine children.

1919

The Devlins relocate from Scotland to Dublin. Liam Devlin purchases a pub in Parnell Square, which becomes a meeting place and unofficial headquarters for republican activity during the War of Independence.

DD attends O'Connell School, a Christian Brothers School on North Richmond Street in Dublin.

1923

DD moves to Belvedere College.

1926

DD begins training for the priesthood at All Hallow's College, Clonliffe, and enrols at University College Dublin (UCD) for a degree in modern languages.

1927

DD leaves Clonliffe and pursues a BA in English and French at UCD.

1928

DD enrols as a law student at Dublin's King's Inns, but does not sit examinations.

1929

DD awarded first-class honours in English and French.

Remains at UCD to pursue an MA in French.

INTRODUCTION

Devlin the correspondent

A MODESTY, FELT OR AFFECTED, regarding the incapacities of the letter-writer is a common topos in even the most energetic and prolific of correspondences. Robert Louis Stevenson, whose published letters number 2,800, made repeated apologies for his inadequacy as a correspondent, a 'vice' which predisposed him to leniency in the face of a poor return.[1] Samuel Beckett, whose published correspondence is similar in length to Stevenson's, and represents a mere fraction of the 15,000 letters found by his editors, complained persistently about the difficulty of writing letters. For Beckett, this difficulty had to do with the emotional cost of intimacy, a concern for intellectual honesty, and a sense of obligation to what began as a narrow circle and became a wide and dauntingly international public. Denis Devlin's struggle with letter-writing was different in nature and consequence, but no less legendary to those who knew him. Beckett wrote through the difficulty; Devlin more often did not. When his old friend and early collaborator Brian Coffey remarks bluntly, in a reminiscence written after Devlin's death, that 'Denis was not a good correspondent', it is with regret at a friendship poorly documented: only six letters and postcards from Devlin are preserved in Coffey's University of Delaware archive, compared to around thirty from Samuel Beckett. We know of the existence of at least one more letter from Devlin, mentioned in an essay by Coffey, but the archive is probably not far from representative. The dearth of early correspondence between Devlin and his Dublin friends can in part be explained by the way these friendships were conducted. Despite their international study, travel and professional obligations in the 1930s and '40s, Devlin, Coffey and Beckett had family homes in Dublin and its suburbs in common. Lunch dates in Dublin were arranged by telephone, and meetings often happened by chance in a city of that size. Stevenson, an only child, recognised that '[t]he presence of people is the great obstacle to letter-writing'. [2] Devlin, brought up in a family of nine siblings with parents who were renowned for a courageous hospitality (his father Liam ran a Dublin hotel that became a safe haven for republican activity during the War of Independence), thrived in company, and sought out society in every city he lived in. But there were other obstacles to letter-writing, of which Devlin was very aware.

His wife Caren, who occasionally took up the slack in her husband's correspondence with mutual friends, joked that Devlin's bad habit was a sickness: '[i]t seems to be his "maladie", not writing letters.'[3] With greater earnestness, as the young Devlin attempts to assuage any offence caused to his close friend Thomas MacGreevy by an irregular correspondence, he pleads:

> Must I repeat that if I don't write often, it is not that I am forgetful, but that writing is of extreme difficulty to me. What makes material for letter-writing with most intelligent people: i.e., I suppose, "what they are thinking" does not exist in me because I never think except à rebours of someone else.[4]

It is no coincidence that this urgent appeal is made in a letter to MacGreevy, who was a peculiarly scrupulous correspondent, and a dextrous thinker, able to discourse freely on people, art, music and literature. As we have seen in the first volume of Beckett's correspondence, MacGreevy's letters demanded the rich and considered response they tended to receive, and despite Devlin's professed shortcomings, the letters he writes to MacGreevy in the 1930s bring out a vivacity and intellectual ambition we see in only the very best of his published work. For Devlin, this effort took time and application, and his letters to MacGreevy were often written across a long period, in discrete instalments, or sections marked as continuations. Devlin struggled, it seems, to call these letters to a decisive end. One that was begun on 5 October 1935, and continued on 22 October with no greater explanation than 'I am a wretched hound, I admit, about letters', closes abruptly with the sentence: 'I'm sealing this now to send, otherwise it would lie around.' It is postmarked the following day.

Devlin's correspondence with MacGreevy waned during his years in America in the 1940s, as physical distance increased and professional responsibilities in the Washington legation mounted, although his concern for MacGreevy's wellbeing and position in Dublin's cultural life remained. In 1950, as Devlin took up his position as minister plenipotentiary in Rome, MacGreevy was made director of the National Gallery of Ireland. The correspondence revived in more official circumstances, as both friends recognised the mutual advantages of the connection: we see Devlin using MacGreevy's short monograph on Jack Yeats as he energetically (and ultimately unsuccessfully) negotiates space for Jack Yeats at the 1952 Biennale Festival in Venice, a move MacGreevy was pushing for along with officials in the Arts Council and the civil service. Devlin later provides his friend with a reassuring point of contact in Rome when he sends paintings from the gallery to Italy for exhibition or restoration. Read after the intimacy of the 1930s' correspondence, there is a strange formality to these last letters, which are part of an official and recorded diplomatic dialogue between institutions. Perhaps as a consequence of the more burdensome role letters play in Devlin's diplomatic life in the 1950s, or an anxiety about transgressing beyond his professional remit in official communication, Devlin finds it difficult to deviate from the bureaucratic mode: 'I have your letters of the 6th and 8th of December. Thank you most kindly for your goodness in writing to the Secretary of my Department ....'[5] While MacGreevy initially seems to indulge in the new ceremony of the exchange ('His Excellency ... My dear Minister'), a more familiar mode takes possession in the continued correspondence, as the typed missives are finished with handwritten and personal greetings: '[Your family] tell me you will be home. Let's have a spree with me.'[6]

Devlin's plea for mercy over his letter-writing malady should not be dismissed as an affectation. Aspects of his own diagnosis can help us make sense of both the limitations and the value of his correspondence. Behind the inferiority complex which leads him to assume that 'most intelligent people' are able to set down in letter form an auto-generated discourse of 'what they are thinking', is an idealised perception of what the letter *should*, or *could* be. Devlin often seems to feel constrained by a sense of the letter's potential as a vessel for criticism. The expectation that might be aroused by a letter responding to the gift of a friend's latest book, for example, will often cause him to balk, or defer the proper treatment for a later occasion. A few months after receiving Brian O'Nolan's first novel, *At Swim-Two-Birds*, a transparent satire of student life at their *alma mater*, University College Dublin, he writes:

> I have been very keen on writing at length about it and so kept putting off a letter. […] It might have been better just to say it was a grand or a swell book but that seemed inadequate, although you might have preferred it, but I would like to say what interested me from chapter to chapter. It wld. be dangerously near taking on the pomposity of a critic which I dislike myself so why shld. I want to do it with others? I don't know but I "feel impelled to" try; it may be no damn use whatever. […] I will send on what I have to say.[7]

The promised letter, with the fuller exegesis, never comes – or if it did it has not been preserved in O'Nolan's papers. Years later, in response to the poem 'Seasons of the Soul' in an inscribed copy of Allen Tate's *The Winter Sea*, Devlin is similarly reluctant to offer extended critical thoughts in epistolary form: 'I notice the reviewers, though they praise it, are being rather wary of tackling it head on and I won't try to yet, or in a letter, but I should think it will be recognised as one of the major poems since the last war.'[8] The letter in this volume which presented the most acute transcription challenges is one uncomfortably poised between the informal missive and the functional document; not insignificantly, this is a letter responding to a request for criticism. George Reavey, an acquaintance in Paris as well as (an often negligent) publisher to Devlin, Coffey and Beckett, tended to elicit a tonal uncertainty in his publishing correspondence with friends. In this letter Devlin answers Reavey's request for a few lines of dust-jacket blurb on the poems that make up *Intercessions*. '[W]ith some diffidence', he offers critical reflections, and evidently struggles to make them cohere on the page:

> The poems are metaphysical ?though and their mode is a sort of sensorialism, near animism, and so not <u>referring</u> to their realisation in ethics. To bring the mind from the frozen mallarmean lake to movement with The logical counterpart of the modern dialectical movement in practical ethics & politics.[9]

The 'clear copy' transcription provided for this letter is, of necessity, more interventionist than anywhere else in the volume, and sense is only made of Devlin's crossings out and orphaned phrases with some labour and interpretive licence. In this awkward drafting process there is no feeling for the letter form as a safe space for the dry run of ideas. The encroachment of purposeful prose – prose destined for publication – on the intimate space of letter-writing evidently oppresses him. We have access to some of Reavey's answering correspondence over the publication of *Intercessions*, but not the response to this letter. Needless to say the blurb was not published, and perhaps it was Devlin's intention to force Reavey's hand on this issue. His summary reflection shows that he knows the inadequacy of what he has provided: 'That is vague & pompous but it's the best I can do.'

Devlin's letters do, however, provide critical insight into his own work and the work of others, and that insight will often come in the way he described to MacGreevy, 'à rebours of someone else'. If there is an *ars poetica*, it does not come in the form of the grand statement of literary practice, but rather through the exchange of ideas. What comes through very vividly is a sense of the letter as conversation: a warm, humorous, energetic, vociferous forum for discourse between friends. Or an opportunity to resume old arguments, as we see more than once in this volume. In a letter to MacGreevy that begins with tender talk about love and loss following the death of MacGreevy's mother, the conversation switches to some remarks the older poet has made in a recent letter about Devlin's work. An unwelcome comparison with AE ('that awful Methodist illuminé hot-gospeller AE!'), and some advice Devlin must have heard often before, that he should say things more simply in his poetry, sparks this impassioned defence of his practice:

> I say poems that way because there is no other way of saying what my poems are. I who am so scrupulous about every single word [,] who examine for months whether I have put the verse in all its original impression, it is hard to be called a dauber. You have a fallacy with your 'saying things simply' unless you mean saying them integrally.[10]

In a more benign mood, and in the framework of an intimate and gossipy conversation with MacGreevy, Devlin helps us understand what has perplexed many critics who have tried to describe the terrain of Irish poetic modernism: the heterogeneity of practice that coexists with a shared cultural purpose in the stifling atmosphere of Ireland in the 1930s. Flattered and exhilarated at the fallout from Beckett's claim that he and Coffey were the members of the new generation of Irish poets most worthy of attention in 'Recent Irish Poetry' (1934), Devlin reports excitedly on the reaction of those who come off less favourably. He then offers this measured reflection on Beckett's endorsement:

> But I don't know. I don't think I shall make a poetry that Beckett would approve of. The exquisite shock of contradictions tires me now – or at least either I'm not spiritually taut enough or I think that swordblade too limited enjoyment. I was about to tell you what I think about poetry but it would bore us both and besides I can't link one moment with another intellectually.[11]

In a typical and conversational move, Devlin checks himself before entering too far into literary profundity in a letter. His preliminary reflections show us, however, that Beckett's generous essay may reveal more about Beckett's own aesthetic priorities at this point than any 'movement' in contemporary Irish poetry. The modernity he diagnoses – the expression of fractured lines of communication, and interrogation of the ideal forms and 'objects' of poetry – is not the modernity Devlin feels. This tension perhaps anticipates Devlin's move in the 1940s towards a less frenetic, more evenly tempered poetry, and more conservative forms. Importantly, the divergence between the public expression of artistic solidarity and the private statement of aesthetic disagreement reveals that such unity in difference was an urgent necessity in a culture hostile to experiment. This is evident in Devlin's eager effort to drum up subscriptions in Dublin for *Echo's Bones* in order to mitigate the effect of Beckett's unpopularity 'on account of the pundits': the Dublin literary establishment.[13] In Beckett's published letters we have already seen the contrast between his public endorsement of Devlin's work and his private reservations. On the publication of *Intercessions* he remarks upon 'lovely fragments' which appear 'adventitious' in the larger context of the collection, and offers a grim judgement on Devlin's turn to the metaphysical.'[14] In this volume, the arguments and disagreements between Devlin and MacGreevy, Coffey and Beckett that are performed at first- and second-hand in the informal and genial space of the letter, give us a keener insight into Devlin's aesthetic priorities than anywhere else in his published work.

Through conversation, argument, passion and affection, these letters characterise a man whose biography has until now been in large part obscure. Will a fuller knowledge of Devlin the man aid the understanding and appreciation of his poetry? This was, fascinatingly, something he himself contemplated in the 1930s, as he struggled to gain the attention of influential literary figures like W.B. Yeats and T.S. Eliot:

> I have noticed that people who know me invariably like my poetry, whereas those that don't know me do not invariably do. Does that mean that the interesting thing is I + my poetry? You see whatever the answer, it must be pleasant to me.[15]

Devlin certainly inspired great loyalty, affection and appreciation in those who knew him well. The coda at the end of this volume shows Caren Devlin's correspondence with friends soon after her husband's early death from lung cancer in 1959, regarding the establishment of the Denis Devlin Memorial Award Fund, a summons taken up with energy and ardour by friends in Europe and America.[16] In the years following his death, the high regard in which Devlin was held extended to an effort to preserve the legacy of his poetry. Caren wrote to Brian Coffey that it was Devlin's 'last wish' that Coffey should look over his unfinished and unpublished poems.[17] Coffey brought together Devlin's *Collected Poems* in an *Irish University Review* special issue (1964), and a Dolmen Press volume the following year. *The Heavenly Foreigner*, a long poem which had been in gestation since the 1930s, and published in various forms, was issued in a 'variorum' edition from Dolmen in 1967. Robert Penn Warren and Allen Tate had a manuscript of Devlin's poems in hand before his death, and had been investigating the possibility of placing it with the English publisher Eyre & Spottiswoode. After negotiations with various American publishers the posthumous *Selected Poems*, co-edited by Penn Warren and Tate, came out with Holt, Rinehart & Wilson in 1962. The preface to this edition takes great pains to animate the man. An astonishingly detailed verbal portrait of Devlin's face begins to reveal a shrewd, compelling and generous social personality:

> His head gave an impression of compactness; hair somewhat wavy, very dark, profuse but lying close to the skull; ears close-set to the skull [...] this general impression of compactness and inwardness was modified by a large aquiline nose and extraordinarily, piercingly blue eyes that peered inquiringly out from under strong black eyebrows.[18]

Gaiety and generosity are qualities repeatedly remarked upon in the tributes that followed Devlin's death, and for Penn Warren and Tate they are the 'words that linger longest [...] His openness to life quickened the sense of life in those around him.' In the reminiscences of Devlin's UCD friend Niall Montgomery there is a more determined effort to draw the personality and the poetry together; he describes a 'secret, special fellow', and rues the inadequate flatness of words in conveying 'the sense of magic which Denis Devlin as a young poet communicated, the sense in which dionysiac suggested Devlin'.[19] If Devlin was guilty of being a bad correspondent to his friends, he was evidently a cherished and affecting friend to his correspondents, and these letters provide testimony to the conviviality he was known for. Whether or not Devlin's conjectural equation ('Does that mean that the interesting thing is I + my poetry?') is true, the reader now has better resources with which to judge.

The letters and the working life

These letters begin in 1932, when Devlin was twenty-four and a graduate student in Paris. On his return to Dublin in 1933 a transitional period began, in which Devlin was pursuing poetry, publication and a literary lifestyle, and deliberating over whether to follow a career in academia (he took up a short-lived 'assistanceship' in English at UCD in August 1934) or a career in the civil service (he first attempted the exams in February 1934, and failed). His work in the diplomatic service, which began with a cadetship in 1935 and matured to his first foreign posting to Rome in 1938, gave him less time to devote to personal correspondence, and less time to devote to creative writing of any kind. He had been sending out a manuscript of his first volume of poems without success before he was appointed to the Department of External Affairs; the invitation from George Reavey came in March 1935, shortly after the appointment. Devlin submitted a version of the manuscript for what was to become *Intercessions* in July of that year, and was subjected to a two-year delay, in which the operation of Reavey's Europa Press moved to London, a partnership with Stanley Nott failed, and Reavey's involvement in the International Surrealist Exhibition took precedence over other projects. As the letters reveal, the delay weighed upon Devlin for converging reasons. It caused him some social embarrassment – '[p]eople here think I'm hoaxing' – and the rarity of stretches of professional calm in which he could revise the poems distressed him: 'I have a little free time now at night, I want to use it; if you delay I shall find myself near September and in the devil of a flurry as I shall be going to Geneva then.'[20] The possibility of a swift removal to another country was an ever-present anxiety, as Devlin wanted to consummate his years in Dublin with the release of his poems, and to experience the reception of his poems among his family, friends and colleagues. *Intercessions* was eventually published in August 1937, and Devlin was posted to Rome in May of the following year – he had nine months to appreciate the release of his poems in Dublin, give or take a trip to London for the Anglo-Irish Trade Agreement talks. His initial delight at the appearance of the book and its immediate reception ('I am hearing nice things about my book; the make-up is making a very favourable impression') was somewhat dampened by the personal effort involved in getting copies on display in bookshops ('I happened to be at Combridge's, Grafton St, and to mention the book which is not displayed. The manager got very indignant …').[21]

The early years in America were remarkably industrious; Devlin seems to have found the encounter with a new literary scene, first in New York, then in Washington, rejuvenating. He was received into American poetry circles quickly and enthusiastically. While a downbeat Devlin, recently arrived in New York, remarked to Niall Montgomery in a letter of January 1940 that, in a political sense, 'Eire doesn't cut any ice as a sensation now nor North Eire either', a fortnight later he was declining an invitation to join the table of poet and journalist Amy Bonner (a representative of Chicago's *Poetry* magazine) at the

Poetry Society of America dinner. It was not long before *Poetry* accepted Devlin's 'Farewell and Good' for publication. In his first months in America he was fortunate to meet the poet-editor Norman Macleod, who established the Poetry Center at the YMHA on 92nd Street. Macleod provided Devlin with his first American publishing, and reading, opportunity, giving him space alongside William Carlos Williams, Marianne Moore and W.H. Auden in *The Calendar: An Anthology* (1940), and inviting him to read at the 'Y'. In a letter of March 1940, by which time Devlin had been moved to Washington, he writes to Macleod with gratitude and excitement of 'how glad [he is] for the chance of becoming better known'.[22] We catch a glimpse here of Devlin's disappointment at the lack of impact his poems had made in Dublin, as he confesses that 'if you have no signs of being believed, your belief in yourself slips away without noticing and that was happening to me'. He also acknowledges that the move to New York had given him the time and space to finish poems which had long been in gestation in Dublin, but which had been 'let drift'.

The correspondence from 1941–2 is dominated by a collaborative venture Devlin had taken on with Macleod: an anthology of Celtic poetry, intended for the Colt Press in San Francisco, a small fine-printing venture run by the typographer Jane Grabhorn and the shipping heir and literary enthusiast (later turned trade ambassador and activist) William M. Roth. Devlin's correspondence with Roth concerning the anthology charts an increasing intimacy, as the formal 'Dear Mr. Roth' yields to 'My dear Bill Roth'. On learning that the Colt Press was to cease operations without issuing the anthology, as Roth took up a position in the Office of War Information, Devlin's response is warm, gracious and sincere: 'Without being sentimental, I am sure that books [are] one of the few reliefs in the foul shrieking of the war. And your press meant more to you than the anthology to me, so you have my full sympathy.'[23] In a published memoir Roth reveals that nascent discussions over the possibility of a Colt Press volume of Devlin's poems sharpened his regret at having to abandon the Celtic anthology. America's participation in the war put a strain on other publishing ventures Devlin was involved with in the early 1940s. *The Southern Review* announced its intention to suspend publication at a time when Devlin's 'Lough Derg' was under submission – the poem made it into the final wartime issue. The literary friendships and associations Devlin formed in New York and in his early years in Washington, and this early burst of American productivity, proved vital to sustaining his literary reputation across the decade. *Lough Derg and Other Poems* was published by the New York firm Reynal & Hitchcock in 1946. The reception of that volume was almost inevitably cordial in the influential southern journals in which Devlin had published; the critic Vivienne Koch, a friend and the wife of Norman Macleod, declared in *The Sewanee Review* that *Lough Derg* stood up to the 'half-dozen most notable books of postwar poetry'.[24] It was not inconsequential that Devlin had earned the admiration and support of Allen Tate and Robert Penn Warren, two of the closest friends he made in Washington, and among America's most prominent critics. Tate and Penn Warren had been responsible for steering the creative orientation of the *Sewanee* and the *Southern Review* respectively.

In Devlin's later letters to Roth, as the anthology project looked to be coming to fruition, he writes: 'I hope to goodness priorities are'nt [*sic*] going to catch me in poetry too. It's becoming a nightmare with me at my office.' The old complaints, which for a youthful Devlin were directed at the burden of regular, office-based employment in Dublin, return as his legation duties expand. Where his work gives him unexpected pleasure, at the International Civil Aviation Conference in Chicago for example, which he finds 'one of the most interesting I've attended', he nonetheless regrets that such commitments leave him 'so loaded with work that I've not read a poem for weeks'.[25] At this time Devlin had embarked upon the creative task that was to preoccupy his writing life in the late 1940s: translations of the long poems of Alexis Leger, who wrote under the pen name Saint-John Perse, which were published together as *Exile and Other Poems* (1949). Devlin and Leger had poetry and diplomacy in common. Leger was in Washington as an exile from Nazi-occupied

France, receiving institutional support from the Library of Congress in a literary consultant role secured by Archibald MacLeish (then Librarian of Congress). The letters to Leger are largely written after Devlin had moved to take up a position as counsellor in the Office of the High Commissioner in London, accompanied by his new wife Caren. They resume the intimate and productive collaboration which had begun in Washington. A set of notes included in one letter provides an abundant insight into Devlin's translation principles with regard to 'Exil', the instances of firm conviction as well as those areas of latitude. Of Leger's 'l'ossuaire des saisons', he writes: 'I preferred "bone-heap" to "ossuary" both for the sound and clarity. "Ossuary" wld. not sound well here and, besides being archaic, conveys nothing of the meaning, since "os" as "bone" is not present to the English ear.'[26] Of Leger's 'l'échéance d'un mot pur': '"Pure statement fallen due" – I am not sure of this. Would the following be closer: "for a chance fall of pure statement"[?] If so, wld. you amend?' The *Exile* translations are perhaps Devlin's most highly regarded work, and Leger evidently held Devlin in high esteem as a translator; in Koch's review of *Lough Derg* she had declared the fact that 'M. Perse considers Mr. Devlin to be his most successful transcriber' as an 'open secret'.[27] Devlin is sincere and emphatic in asserting the pleasure of the enterprise. The despatch containing the corrected version of 'Exil' is underlined with '[i]t has been hard & lovable work; I shall never forget'. In a Christmas card sent that year, the Gallimard edition of Leger's *Vents* provokes the reflection: 'en me félicitant d'avoir été votre collaborateur' ['I congratulate myself on having been your collaborator'].[28]

Caren Devlin remarks, in that same Christmas card, that Devlin was approaching the end of the first poem he had worked on since completing 'Exil'. This was *The Heavenly Foreigner*, versions of which were to appear in journals in Dublin, Cork, Tennessee, London and Rome over the next years. The idea for the poem had been in process since the 1930s, but time spent with Leger's work perhaps tells in its long form, ambitious autobiographical vision, and its concern with travel and place. In 1950 Devlin took up an appointment as minister plenipotentiary to Italy, which was raised to ambassador when the Irish legation was granted embassy status in 1958. The letters Devlin wrote in his Roman years are more reticent about his writing life, and Caren often took on the responsibility of informing their mutual friends of the creative projects he was involved with. In a letter to the author Eleanor Clark, a friend of long standing and Penn Warren's second wife, he refers offhandedly to having written 'poetry during the winter, some of which will be in the next <u>Botteghe Oscure</u> as well as translations of René Char, who is the great passion with the Principessa these days. After that, no more translation for me.'[29] The poem was 'The Colours of Love', published later that year in *Botteghe Oscure*, the journal run by the literary patroness Marguerite Caetani (née Chapin, cousin to T.S. Eliot and wife of the Italian composer Roffredo Caetani, prince of Bassiano) in Rome. Devlin collaborated with the American poet Jackson Mathews on the Char translations, which appeared in the same number of *Botteghe Oscure*, and did indeed prove to be his last published translation venture.

The letters show that Devlin discussed his ambitions for one of his final poems, 'The Passion of Christ' (1957), with the poet and classicist Robert Fitzgerald, who was based in Italy in the 1950s while working on a translation of the *Odyssey*. Dedicated to Allen Tate, this was a further foray into the fragmentary long form of *The Heavenly Foreigner*, meditating on faith and the individual. Fitzgerald sent him a copy of George Santayana's *The Idea of Christ in the Gospels* (1946), to which Devlin responds with diffidence in June 1956 – 'I have merely glanced at it so far but I think it will help me. God knows I shouldn't be writing this poem at all' – and with a creeping, if no less self-deprecating, sense of its significance in August: 'It was extremely kind of you to send me Santayana's IDEA OF CHRIST IN THE GOSPELS, which I am just beginning to read. It will either help or totally befuddle me; if the latter, I'll just read the Gospel afterwards.'[30] In both letters Devlin asks eagerly for news of Fitzgerald's poetic activity aside from the Homer. The solicitation of poetry conversation in letters is a feature throughout Devlin's correspondence, but it perhaps takes on a greater urgency in the last decade in Rome, as his official duties take greater hold, and bursts of time spent in the company of his closest American and Irish friends are rarer and more precious. 'How is the poem coming?' he asks of Penn Warren, engaged in the long narrative poem *Brother to Dragons* after an extended period of prose immersion: '[y]ou haven't sent me the proof and I hope it's not because of my culpable but insignificant epistolary scarcity'.[31]

As Devlin's professional circumstances increasingly affect his writing life, physical circumstances exert an impression on the writing hand in the 1950s. Devlin's letter-writing hand at full strength is more generous to his correspondents, not to mention his transcribers, than that of many of his peers: Beckett's acute slant and Coffey's minisculity are forbidding comparisons. The legibility of his cursive script can vary according to the occasion, the length of the letter, and the thickness of the nib. His letters are overwhelmingly written by hand, although the ratio of handwritten to typewritten letters evens out in the 1940s and '50s. This may be a result of official correspondence becoming more habituated in the working life, although Devlin remained a wayward typist despite a youthful boast of dexterity ('I've been rolling off Hugo too on the typewriter …').[32] The diplomatic correspondence would have been largely dictated ('the typing's mine, unfortunately', he makes a point of noting in a typed letter to Roth), just as a slew of Devlin's personal and literary correspondence in the particularly busy period of the move from Washington to London in the late 1940s is dictated, in Caren's hand.[33] His handwriting noticeably degrades during the Roman years, revealing the ailing health that dogged him throughout that decade far more plainly than the content of the letters themselves. If a young Devlin was capable of good-humouredly indulging his illnesses ('I have been in bed with 'flu for the last few days. Half Dublin is affected and in bed but a doctor told my sister that this is pure imagination & laziness on its part … Dublin has only got a bad cold'), he never matched the startling deliberateness of Samuel Beckett's medical self-analysis, and in his mature years was not prone to divulging his physical weakness. Writing to his sister Shiela from a nursing home in June 1951, only a year after moving to Rome, Devlin remarks dismissively: '[t]his is a very temporary address. It's me stummick. How is your leg?'[34] Deflecting discussion of his own health with a concern for the health of others is a persistent trope in these letters. Robert Penn Warren's arm, which was causing him trouble at the time of a prospective visit to Rome, preoccupies a letter sent later in 1951: 'couldn't you drop into Switzerland and get it "cut" there? [...] be careful with that arm because noialtri are certainly watching out for you all' [noialtri: all of us].[35]

It is not through personal correspondence with friends, but through his private correspondence with the department, and the letters of Devlin's friends to others, that we piece together the debilitating setbacks that Devlin endured with apparent sanguinity in his final decade. During an extended stay in Italy in 1956 Penn Warren writes from Rome that 'Denis [...] is in the hospital with a variety of ailments including a slipped disk', and a few months later he reports an upward curve: 'Denis is in great shape, and seemed to have survived a cocktail party at the Swedish Embassy with the usual aplomb.'[36] Two years later, and less than a year before Devlin's death, the news is tentative: 'He is in better health now but still wobbly, I guess.'[37] Devlin's letter to Seán Murphy in the department, supporting the earlier provision of medical certificates, confirms that in 1957 he was recovering from 'a haemorr[h]age followed by pneumonia when I was apparently in the best form'.[38] The heat in Rome, a city he and Caren were settled in and enamoured with, did provide a habitual cause for complaint, and it had been raised by Devlin's doctors as a factor exacerbating his lung trouble. Devlin's final letter was written, appropriately enough, to his oldest friend Brian Coffey in the intensity of a Roman summer and shortly before he left the city for Dublin for the last time. Devlin finds himself in the familiar position of apologising for a delayed response to more than one letter from Coffey, and staving off misinterpretation: 'No, my failure to write to you did not mean that I did not like the poem. In fact, I like it very much.'[39] The poem in question is one of Coffey's finest, 'Missouri Sequence', written after a long and difficult period of poetic absence. In a gesture of friendship, Devlin does what we know did not come easily to him in letters and sets out his thoughts on the work, a process helped by the evidently specific questions Coffey had posed: 'though I have no reserves about parts 2, 3 and 4, I think part 1 should be shortened considerably – though I do not agree with your shortening of the passage "how casual the fall of seed". I would not touch your Chinese philosopher who is very attractive.' Raising the possibility of a detour to London (where Coffey and his family were based at that time) *en route* to Dublin, a wearily curmudgeonly line couches a genuine affliction: 'I am eager to get away from all this Italian screaming & really debilitating heat.'

Principles of editing and selection

SELECTION AND REPRESENTATION

A few years before I began work on this project, the last of Devlin's sisters, Raphael, had died, along with his son Stephen, to whom the estate had passed. Devlin's literary papers are held in the National Library of Ireland; an archive was donated by Devlin's sister Moya Lindsay and an additional instalment later given by Raphael McMullen. The archive contains drafts and typescripts of Devlin's published and unpublished poems, translation work, and prose fragments, but no correspondence to or from Devlin.[40] A note from Caren to Devlin's sister Shiela after his death reveals that this limited archive may have been his own design. Returning a letter Shiela had written Denis some years previously, Caren writes: 'I thought you might like it back as a souvenir. Tore up (as I promised him) all other letters.'[41] From the beginning, therefore, this was a project circumscribed by what was available in public archives. The archival reach of these letters is fully international as a consequence of Devlin's diplomatic career: I have consulted correspondence to, from and concerning Devlin in archives in Dublin, Aix-en-Provence, Rome and across the United States. The challenges involved in gathering the correspondence have meant that the letters in this edition are, to a degree, self-selecting, and my principle has been inclusive. There are very few personal letters for which slightness and functionality (notes arranging meetings) or repetition (pro forma letters of introduction sent to American colleagues on the occasion of a visit by George Reavey) have recommended exclusion.

The absence of a private archive of papers has limited the family dimension in the range of correspondents represented. Devlin's immediate family, based in Upper Mount Street near Merrion Square before moving to Dún Laoghaire in the final decade of his life, was, by his own description, 'large' and 'active'.[42] Devlin was the eldest of nine children, in an overwhelmingly female household (all but one of his eight siblings was a sister). Shortly before this volume was completed, a small cache of letters between Devlin and his sister Shiela, and to Devlin from his mother, was uncovered by Shiela's daughter Caren Farrell. These letters reveal a fun and intimate family dynamic, and testify to the excitement with which Devlin's international missives were received at home in Dublin. 'Do please write as soon as possible,' writes Shiela, '[w]e go mad when a letter comes with those big foreign stamps on the envelope, and the illegible writing of the good old you. Don't forget.'[43] It is regrettable that more of these letters did not survive.

As Devlin rose through the diplomatic ranks from cadet to ambassador in Rome, the burden of professional correspondence intensified. The letters from 1940 onwards, whether engaged in private and literary business or diplomatic affairs, are almost exclusively written on paper with the delegation or embassy letterhead. Devlin was also sending personal mail through the office's postal service: Caren writes to Robert Penn Warren in 1952, apologetically enclosing a letter that has been opened by one of the secretaries, presumably confusing outgoing for incoming mail. Personal and literary correspondence is increasingly composed and channelled along official lines.

The Department of Foreign Affairs Papers held at the National Archives in Dublin are vast, and described in paper catalogues that offer brief and variably instructive file summaries. Predictably, the catalogues relating to the 1950s are better organised than those covering the 1930s, and Devlin's letters from the Rome legation (later embassy) were easier to identify. The available letters reveal the gradual transition in the volume and nature of correspondence that fell under Devlin's professional remit. The few letters I found from his early years as cadet relate largely to expense claims for trips to Zürich as personal secretary to President de Valera, who was undergoing specialist eye treatment. In Washington in the 1940s, when Devlin was secretary to the Irish legation (working under Minister Robert Brennan), his responsibilities included gathering newspaper summaries and clippings relating to Irish domestic and international policy, and testing the opinion of the Irish-American community and the wider American public on issues such as Irish neutrality. The volumes of *Documents in Irish Foreign Policy* (1998–), published by the Royal Irish Academy in conjunction with the Department of Foreign Affairs (DFA) and the National Archives of Ireland, contain memoranda of meetings written by Devlin during his time in Washington. He occasionally communicated with the department in lieu of the minister, but his main correspondence is a series of brief covers for enclosures ('I desire to enclose herewith for your information the program of a Feis held on the 9th instant by the St. Brendan Society of Boston …').[44]

When Devlin was made minister plenipotentiary to Italy in 1950, and minister to Turkey the following year, his duties proliferated. He sent the secretary of the department regular, and detailed, political reports on Italian and Turkish relationships with the international community, territorial disputes, elections and crises. He corresponded with the department's Cultural Relations Committee and the Arts Council regarding Ireland's participation in Italian festivals of the arts (notably the Biennale), the Catholic Stage Guild award, and the loan and transportation of works of art. He reported on the Italian trade and agricultural fairs at which he was most often the Irish representative.

He was also writing letters on behalf of the legation to the wider public: to Irish citizens in Rome who needed assistance in matters relating to citizenship, scholarships and travel, and to Italian citizens looking to learn more about Ireland (educational enquiries range from Class V of Palidano Elementary School wanting to learn more about Ireland, to a University of Trieste student working on citizens' rights to compensation). The DFA Papers shed light on another side to diplomatic life, in the folders containing personal correspondence with the secretary. These letters, which also date from Devlin's time as minister and ambassador to Italy, raise salary queries, express anxieties over rumoured transfers, and disclose the health issues that necessarily impinged on his duties. In this edition I have selected a representative range of the diplomatic correspondence in the National Archives, including letters from each stage of his career. The form and functionality of these letters does not recommend the majority for inclusion in what I hope to be a readable edition. My selections have been made based on a judgement of the cultural, political or personal insight afforded by the letter. Taken together, they provide a broad and varied picture of Devlin's diplomatic life.

TRANSLATION

Devlin studied English and French as an undergraduate at UCD, pursued French literature at master's level (with a thesis on Montaigne), and then began doctoral study at the Sorbonne in France. In his two years in Paris he was mainly reading French poetry (Eluard and Breton in particular). Devlin's wife Caren, whom he met in Washington, was an American with a French father; her services as a translator are at one stage enlisted by the department, as these letters show. The French language, therefore, had an important role in Devlin's life and his relationships. The letters to MacGreevy and Coffey will often slip playfully between English and French. Devlin's correspondence with Alexis Leger concerning the 'Exil' translation is conducted in two languages, the earlier letters largely written in French and the more substantive description of word choice and idiomatic usage written in English.

Devlin's translation endeavours extended to Irish, German and Italian literature, and as minister to Italy he was regularly conversing and corresponding in Italian. It is difficult to assess Devlin's comfort with the Italian language from the evidence of these diplomatic letters, which are largely formulaic documents, lacking the verbal ambition of his French letters to Leger. While Devlin's French is not always perfectly correct, he seems to have felt intellectually at ease with the language. The only letter in Irish was written to his sister Shiela, in return for an Irish letter of hers. If this was an exercise in keeping the language up, it was also evidently a fun recreational activity for the siblings: an opportunity to experiment in verse and baroque hybrid constructions ('spaghettiouchtána' springs to mind). Devlin had spent the summer of 1930 in the Blasket Islands improving his Irish, and his grasp of the written language seems to have been sound. In this edition, where a phrase appears which is not in the primary language of the letter, I have included a translation in the notes. Letters in a language other than English appear in their original form, followed by a translation.

ANNOTATION

Devlin's dual existence as poet and diplomat, resident in five countries across his career, means that his correspondence relates, directly or indirectly, to a fascinating variety of cultural and historical situations, places and people. While it is anticipated that the majority of readers of this edition will be interested in Devlin in a literary capacity – as an Irish modernist poet emerging in a decade of censorship and cultural polarity, an accomplished translator, and a close associate of the Southern Agrarian poet-critics in America – the volume is designed to be accessible and informative to readers without a literary background, readers who are approaching Devlin, for example, with an interest in the history of the emerging Irish Free State, or in Irish diplomacy. The annotations are designed to illuminate connections between people, places and events. The sections of letters are organised by place, broadly corresponding to each decade of Devlin's adult life, and I have provided chronologies for each section as easy reference points. Short biographies of the correspondents represented in the edition can be found at the end of the volume. For all other people I have provided brief notes of biographical identification at first mention, including dates (where possible), and some indication of their contemporary significance in relation to Devlin, or the particular cultural moment. I have indicated, too, those people who have not been identified in my research. The notes demonstrate the connections between letters within the volume, where a conversation is resumed or an important context supplied. One of the ambitions of this edition is to encourage further scholarship on Devlin's work and this period in Irish cultural history. The annotations, therefore, make substantial outward gestures. I have identified the literary works Devlin refers to, or suggested possible candidates where less information is supplied, and provided cross-references to corollary and parallel correspondences, both published (the letters of Samuel Beckett and Robert Penn Warren) and unpublished (the letters of Brian Coffey, Thomas MacGreevy and George Reavey).

---

1. Robert Louis Stevenson to Edmund Gosse, 26 September 1883, *The Letters of Robert Louis Stevenson*, vol. 4, ed. Bradford Booth and Ernest Mehew (New Haven: Yale University Press, 1994), p. 162.

2. RLS to Mr and Mrs Thomas Stevenson, 1 January 1886, *The Letters of Robert Louis Stevenson*, vol. 5. (1995), p. 169.

3. CD to Robert Penn Warren, 2 February 1952.

4. DD to Thomas MacGreevy, 28 April 1934.

5. DD to Thomas MacGreevy, 15 December 1955.

6. MacGreevy's letters are contained in the Department of Foreign Affairs Papers in the National Archives of Ireland, Dublin (DFA/Rome Embassy/129K).

7. DD to Brian O'Nolan, 1 June 1939.

8. DD to Allen Tate, 28 February 1945.

9. DD to George Reavey, 24 March 1937.

10. DD to Thomas MacGreevy, 15 March 1936.

11. DD to Thomas MacGreevy, [31] August 1934.

12. Samuel Beckett, 'Recent Irish Poetry' (1934), reprinted in *Disjecta: Miscellaneous writings and a dramatic fragment*, ed. Ruby Cohn (London: John Calder, 1983), p. 70.

13. DD to George Reavey, 22 October 1935.

14. SB to Thomas MacGreevy, 21 September [1937]. *The Letters of Samuel Beckett*, vol. I, ed. Martha Dow Fehsenfeld and Lois More Overbeck (Cambridge: Cambridge University Press, 2009), p. 549.

15. DD to Thomas MacGreevy, 26 [April] 1934.

16. See Robert Penn Warren Papers, Yale Collection of American Literature (MSS 51), Box 21, Folder 409 (Caren Devlin Correspondence), Beinecke Rare Book and Manuscript Library, Yale University.

17. CD to Brian Coffey, [September 1959].

18. Robert Penn Warren and Allen Tate, Introduction to *Selected Poems* (New York and Chicago: Holt, Rinehart & Winston, 1963), p. 9.

19. Niall Montgomery, 'Farewells Hardly Count', *Éire-Ireland: Weekly bulletin of the Department of External Affairs*, no. 494, 5 September 1960; enclosure in letter from NM to RPW, 23 July 1960, Robert Penn Warren Papers, Box 21, Folder 409, Beinecke, YU.

20. DD to George Reavey, [May 1936]; DD to George Reavey, 10 July 1936.

21. DD to George Reavey, [October 1937]; DD to George Reavey, 12 November 1937.

22. DD to Norman Macleod, 30 March 1940.

23. DD to William M. Roth, 20 June 1942.

24. Vivienne Koch, 'Poetry Chronicle', *The Sewanee Review*, vol. 54, no. 4, Oct–Dec 1946, p. 699.

25. DD to Allen Tate, 12 November 1944.

26. DD to Alexis Leger, 14 February 1948.

27. Koch, *The Sewanee Review*, 1946, p. 699.

28. CD and DD to Alexis Leger, [Christmas 1948].

29. DD to Eleanor Clark, 9 May 1942.

30. DD to Robert Fitzgerald, 7 June 1956; DD to Robert Fitzgerald, 5 August 1956.

31. DD to Robert Penn Warren, 3 March 1953.

32. DD to George Reavey, 5 December 1938.

33. DD to William Roth, 16 April 1942.

34. DD to Shiela Devlin, 8 June 1951.

35. DD to Robert Penn Warren, 1 October 1951.

36. RPW to Albert Erskine, 5–12 June 1956; RPW to Brainard Cheney, 15 October 1956, in *Selected Letters of Robert Penn Warren*, vol. 4, ed. Randy Hendricks and James A. Perkins (Baton Rouge: Louisiana State University Press, 2008), pp. 124, 152.

37. RPW to Brainard Cheney, 1 October 1958, *SLRPW*, vol. 4, p. 240.

38. DD to Seán Murphy, 3 August 1957.

39. DD to Brian Coffey, 21 July 1959.

40. As of March 2020. Family letters recently uncovered by Devlin's nieces and nephews may be added to the NLI archive.

41. CD to Shiela Healy (née Devlin), 24 October 1959. Private collection, Caren Farrell.

42. DD to Thomas MacGreevy, 18 February 1936.

43. SD to DD, 23 July 1942. Private collection, Caren Farrell.

44. DD to Joseph P. Walshe, 15 October 1941, DFA/219/3A, NAI.

The Letters

Devlin (left) pictured with Sam Pope Brewer on holiday in Spain at Easter 1932.

Prologue:
Paris and the Continent,
1932–3

CHRONOLOGY

1930

Summer   DD visits the Blasket Islands to improve his Irish.

September   DD and Brian Coffey publish a co-authored and
                  self-funded volume, *Poems*, while graduate students
                  at UCD.

1930–1

DD uses German exchange scholarship to study at
Munich University.

1931

Submits MA thesis on Michel de Montaigne.

Uses a further travel grant to study towards a
doctorate at the Sorbonne, joining Coffey in Paris.

1932

March–April DD travels to Spain with American journalist Sam
             Pope Brewer.

1933

January   DD makes his first broadcast on 2RN, reading an
                  essay on 'The Christian Reaction in Modern French
                  Literature'. During his time in Dublin he broadcasts
                  occasional poetry review shows and readings of his
                  own poetry and the work of others.

To Brian Coffey
[2 April 1932]

C'est bien ton gout?[1]

Denis

[*in Sam Pope Brewer's hand* [2]]

Surrealistic view of Barcelona induced by consumption of ten bottles of pinard shortly before driving.[3] Further and more detailed reports later.

Sam

> Co-authored postcard, signed. Recto image is colour photograph from the 'Exposición Internacional de Barcelona 1929'. *Dating*: Postcard is postmarked twice, with an erroneous '2nd April 1926' and a corrected '2nd April 1932'. Brian Coffey Papers (MSS 382), Box 30, Folder 22, Special Collections, University of Delaware Library.

---

1. c'est bien ton gout? (Fr.): this is to your taste?

2. Sam Pope Brewer (1909–76), American journalist who was foreign correspondent for *The New York Times* from 1945. A graduate student at Yale, Brewer was granted a fellowship to spend a year at the University of Paris, where he met Coffey and Devlin.

3. Pinard is a French term for wine, associated with soldiers' rations during the First World War.

To Mervyn Wall

[Autumn 1932–Spring 1933]   Hotel de l'avenir, Paris

Dear Mervyn,

Various things have helped to make me a bit homesick this evening. First, having passed the afternoon with a disagreeable American, having walked too much on the hard stone of the boulevards, eaten with a French poet who wanted to be praised more than is decorous, I am out of humour; and then another whom I like very much talked about his country among the mountains in the South of France so well that I was tempted to write a poem about the rivers & mountains of my own country – and why shouldn't I? But I decided to write to you instead.

Did you get Brian's poems and what do you think of them? Brian and I have been thinking about that review. We find it can be printed & edited fairly cheaply here. The following are the tentative plans: –

1)   Format: about Dublin Opinion[1] size 16 pages double column[.]

2)   Intention: by a complete and thorough examination of the problems of the day, to enable young Irishmen, after this examination of conscience, to take definite directions[.]

3)   Contributors: Wall, O'Malley, Farrell, Sheridan, [?Conversey,] Donnelly, McHugh, Cusack, Brian, me & any others who write well & have opinions.[2] These will have to furnish the mass of the material.

Possible Irish contributors: Myles Dillon, Hogan, Delargey [for Delargy], Mac T[h]omáis, a mathematician, O'Faolain[.][3]

Possible French contributors: Breton & Eluard (if they would), Bonheur, Folain [*for* Follain], Fondane, Miailhe.[4]

Possible English contributors: Auden & Spender two new young poets exceedingly good.[5]

4) Texts:

(i) Poems by Brian [Coffey], Sheridan, Donnelly, [?Conversey], Cusack, Mac Donagh and others[.][6]

(ii) Short stories & Sketches by you[,] O'Malley, Farrell[,] Donnelly, Sheridan, Donnelly [*sic*][.]

(iii) Articles: a) Series by me on the poet's criticism of English poetry, the direction of Irish poets & the equipment necessary for a young poet.

b) Series by J.J. Hogan on the Academic criticism of English poetry[.]

c) Series by Brian on French poets.

d) Articles by you on Drama [and] its future in Ireland[,] by Farrell on Irish licensing rules[,] by [Ó] Nualláin on freedom of opinion in Ireland, by [?Conversey] on Irish puritanism and music, by x on Einstein[,] by x on Communism[,] by x on Catholicism[,] by x on the humanist position[,] by Delargey on folklore[,] by Thomson on the Gaelic question[,] by Breton on Surrealism[,] by me attacking Joyce & Eliot etc.[7]

e) <u>Translations</u> of poems by those last four young Frenchmen I mentioned and what they think poetry is. These are already promised. Of poems by famous living poets if they give us permission.

f) A page of translation from all the great philosophers on the nature of poetry or art.

g) A page of attack on epigrams, insults and innuendo of those manifestations of Irish life which merit disapproval.

h) drawings[.]

i) well chosen photographs representing symbolically the actual state of society e.g. in the same number confronting each other St Thomas and Lenin; or a queue outside a Dublin cinema & a beautiful naked girl on a hill under moon; or Chartres cathedral & a handsome German or Russian factory[.]

There would be six monthly numbers with a different coloured cover each month, only the name and the number on the cover, something like this

	Editors: Coffey & I
question	
	Dublin editor: Niall Sheridan
①	

WHAT DO YOU THINK OF IT ?

Question.

If all fails, I wish you & O'Malley would come over here & we might start a movement. When are you coming[?] You'd better before [d]e Valera breaks away from the Bank of England otherwise your money will be worth damn all.[8] How is your play going?[9] I am writing a revolutionary poem.[10] I [?wish] you would write a Surrealist play. Indeed I wish you would write poetry as I am convinced there is a lot of your imagination that is denied expression. It's good here. Come over. And for the Lord's sake, don't take months to write to me as I want to know what you think of the review. I can't get my knees under my rickety table so I've written this on the bed which is why.

> Yours,
> Denis.

Autograph letter signed. 2 leaves, 4 sides. *Dating:* Devlin was in Paris Autumn 1931– Autumn 1933. The mention of the 'revolutionary poem', 'Bacchanal' (drafted 1931–3), de Valera's new government and plans to break away from the Bank of England would put this in late 1932 at the earliest. Samuel Beckett is notably excluded from the roster of Irish writers he wishes to assemble for this new journal project; Devlin was first made aware of Beckett in the summer of 1933, through MacGreevy, and first met him in September 1933 (see DD to Thomas MacGreevy, [23 September] 1933). Mervyn Wall Collection, Harry Ransom Center, University of Texas at Austin.

---

1. *Dublin Opinion* was a monthly Irish satirical magazine, running from 1922 to 1968.

2. Ernie O'Malley (1897–1957), Irish writer and revolutionary. James T. Farrell (1904–79), Irish-American novelist and short-story writer, who was in Paris in 1931. Niall Sheridan (1912–98), UCD contemporary who collaborated with Devlin on various literary projects, and became a renowned broadcaster for Irish radio and television. Conversey has not been identified. Charles Donnelly (1914–37), Irish poet and political activist who studied at UCD in 1931, and died fighting for the Republicans in the Spanish Civil War in 1937. Roger McHugh (1908–87), Irish academic and politician, studied English and history at UCD at the same time as Devlin.

3. Myles Dillon (1900–72), Irish historian, philologist and Celticist, taught Sanskrit and comparative philology at UCD in the 1930s. Jeremiah Joseph Hogan (1902–82), Irish academic, taught in the UCD English department in the late 1920s, becoming professor of English in 1934, and president in 1964. See DD to Thomas MacGreevy,

[31] August 1934. Séamus Ó Duilearga (born James Hamilton Delargy) (1899–1980), Irish folklorist, lectured in UCD's Department of Modern Irish in the 1920s, becoming professor of folklore in 1946. George Derwent Thomson (Irish name Seoirse Mac Thomáis) (1903–87), English classicist who co-edited and translated a best-selling memoir of growing up in the Blasket Islands, Maurice O'Sullivan's *Twenty Years a-Growing* (1933). Thomson was lecturer in classics at University College Galway in 1931, teaching through the medium of Irish. Seán O'Faolain (born John Francis Whelan) (1900–91), Irish writer, critic and editor. Between 1928 and 1933 he was senior lecturer

4. André Breton (1896–1966) and Paul Eluard (1895–1952), French surrealist poets. Devlin was immersed in the work of Breton and Eluard in his two years in Paris. It is not clear if he ever met Breton, but in a letter to MacGreevy he enthusiastically recalls Samuel Beckett's account of meeting those writers (see DD to Thomas MacGreevy, [23 September] 1933). Gaston Bonheur, pseudonym for Gaston Tesseyre (1913–80), French poet and journalist. He met Devlin in Paris as a teenager, already involved in surrealist publishing networks. Jean Follain (1903–71), French poet associated with the 'Sagesse' group that emerged in the 1920s in a series of pamphlet editions, offering an alternative to surrealism. Devlin includes a copy of Follain's 'Soir d'époque' in DD to Thomas MacGreevy, 26 April 1934. Benjamin Fondane (1898–1944), Romanian-French poet-critic, philosopher, theatre producer and screenwriter, who moved to Paris in the 1920s. Miailhe is unidentified.

5. W.H. Auden (1907–73) and Stephen Spender (1909–95), English poets who in the early 1930s were making their names as part of a generation of *engagé*, leftist intellectuals.

6. Donagh MacDonagh (1912–68), Irish writer, broadcaster and judge, son of the executed leader of the Easter 1916 Rising, Thomas MacDonagh. He studied English at UCD in the early 1930s and spent his second undergraduate year at the Sorbonne.

7. Brian O'Nolan (see Correspondents' Biographies) sometimes used the Irish form of his surname, Ó Nualláin; James Joyce (1882–1941) was the leading Irish prose modernist of the generation prior to Devlin's; Thomas Stearns Eliot (1888–1965), American poet, critic and editor, and perhaps the most influential figure in English literary culture in the 1920s and '30s.

8. Éamon de Valera (1882–1975) was a commander in the Easter 1916 Rising, the first president of the Irish Republic, and the founder and leader of the Fianna Fáil party that was in government from 1932 to 1948. Seán Lemass, minister for industry and commerce of the newly elected Fianna Fáil, had proposed a break with sterling and the establishment of a state bank in November 1932, but such a radical departure from the British currency was not attempted until Ireland joined the European Monetary System in 1978.

9. Wall's debut play, *Alarm Among the Clerks*, premiered at the Peacock Theatre, a small stage space on the ground floor of the Abbey Theatre, in April 1937.

10. This poem is probably 'Bacchanal', which ran under the working title 'News of Revolution'. The NLI drafts of the poem are undated, but Brian Coffey notes that the poem was written from 1931 to '33 (see 'For the Record' and 'News of Revolution', *Advent VI: Denis Devlin special issue* (Southampton: Advent Books, 1976), pp. 21–4).

Dublin, 1933–9

CHRONOLOGY

1933

May	Gaston Bonheur, a Parisian friend, publishes a French translation of DD's 'Passerelle' in *14 rue du Dragon*.
Autumn	DD returns to Dublin.
	DD and Coffey first meet Samuel Beckett.

1934

February	DD fails civil service exam.
Autumn	Appointed to the UCD English department on an 'assistanceship'.
December	'The Gradual' is published in the final issue of *The Bookman*.

1935

Spring	DD takes up a cadetship in the Department of External Affairs.
March	Begins discussion with George Reavey on the publication of his poems.
May	Visits MacGreevy in London.
Sept–Oct	Travels to Geneva with Éamon de Valera as part of the Irish delegation to the League of Nations.

1936

Mar–May DD accompanies Éamon de Valera on a trip to Zürich to receive specialist eye treatment.

June DD's translations of five Eluard poems, 'She of Always, All of Her', 'Nakedness of Truth', 'Girls in Love', 'One for All' and 'They are Alike', appear in *Thorns of Thunder*, the first English-language edition of Eluard's poetry, published by Reavey's Europa Press to coincide with the International Surrealist Exhibition in London.

Makes a trip to London to attend exhibition.

August DD's versions of André Breton's poems 'Rather Life', 'The Plume', 'Allotropy' and 'The Vertebrate Sphinx' are published in *Contemporary Poetry and Prose*, nos. 4–5.

September Joins the Irish delegation to the League of Nations Assembly in Geneva.

October DD's 'You Don't Know a Good Thing When You See It' is published in *transition*, no. 25.

1937

January DD accompanies Éamon de Valera on another trip to Zürich, via London.

Jan–Mar Begins a relationship with Ria Mooney.

March Irish translations of the poetry of Baudelaire, Gerard de Nerval and Rimbaud, collaborations between DD and Niall Montgomery, are published in *Ireland Today*, vol. II, no. 1.

August	*Intercessions* is published in limited edition by Reavey's Europa Press.
October	Mooney leaves Dublin with the Abbey Theatre company on a tour of America.

1938

May	DD appointed secretary to the Irish legation in Rome.

To Thomas MacGreevy
[23 September] 1933

Dear Tom –

Maria Saal sounds quiet and retired, I have complications now, I should like to be there.[1] I am reading German again now and it happens that the conventional picture of Germany suited my own experience of three years ago; so it is a closed room in my memory with a limited number of sensations, but those very tender.[2] Is Karnten near Innsbruck?[3] [M]y just ecstatic day was there.

We have seen Sam Beckett twice in the last few days. He has been charming to us and we talked for hours about Paris and poetry; I was delighted to hear his account of the meeting with Breton and Éluard: Breton impressed him and Éluard inspires affection; which is proper: I think I shall like him, I am discovering him slowly; and according to his movement of course, which is hesitating like a shy horse. He likes using only the essential phrase which makes conversation between him and Brian very amusing. When I read the violent poem he offered us, I thought ruefully of your perfidious assurance that now as poor Sam's father was dead, Sam would surely write some thing so smooth and elegiac.[4] Do you remember saying that in Paris? Sam did promise us his quietest piece and gave it with an air of (and a phrase of) "There; I understand perfectly your difficulties. Commercial, Christmas, Holy Ireland."[5] What must the others be like! However I like it and we can publish it in perfect safety for its surprise is not sexual or theological.

I must go to Father Brown [*for* Browne] and get his poems.[6] And you must send Red Hugh at once.[7] Really at once because already we are starting the business far too late. I should be so pleased too if you would send me for myself when you can, copies of "The Cab", "Homage to Proust"[,] the little poem about your mother, and the one about Pompeii and ashes.[8]

I must ask you about your novel though I'm afraid you will not have gone ahead with it.[9] I shall be very disappointed if you don't publish; not personally, but I as an economic man. Besides, it would affect you very much for the good if you were a success. You must have had a wretched summer in Paris. Did you stay in the Cité?[10]

Brian is here in the profound dumps. I am reading St Augustine whom I find a greater [?blinder] of himself than any poet that tries to boast of metaphysical interest. Nothing holds against criticism – that's for you who believe in the Undercurrent Rhythm.

I am determined to marry Anitschka.[11] I have no money to go and get her and still the dreadful task of telling my people. I am also going for a civil service post because my father hasn't a sou for me. And I can't imagine my ever becoming reconciled to Dublin. What a shabby town! There is no use in giving you any news because there is none interesting. I saw O'Casey's "The Plough and the Stars" last night for the first time.[12] It is cheap melodrama.

Did you ever meet a hurly-burly mixture of theosophy and big-business and selfishness[?] I did last night and I'm very tired. So give my regards to the Churches and send me the poems and a letter and take my very best wishes yourself.[13]

Denis

Autograph letter signed. 2 leaves, 4 sides. *Dating*: postmark. *Address*: Herrn Thomas MacGreevy, Scholl Meiselberg, Karnten, Maria Saal, Austria. Thomas MacGreevy Papers (MS 7985-8190), 8112/1–16, Manuscript Department, The Library of Trinity College Dublin.

---

1. Maria Saal is a market town in southern Austria. MacGreevy found occasional work as a guide with a travel company that organised European tours.

2. In 1930–1, before arriving in Paris, Devlin had used a German exchange scholarship to study in Munich.

3. Innsbruck is the capital city of Tyrol, a state in western Austria; Kärnten is the southern Austrian state bordering East Tyrol.

4. William Frank Beckett, a quantity surveyor, died of a heart attack in June 1933.

5. In the summer of 1933, Devlin and Coffey devised a scheme to announce the arrival of a 'new movement' in Irish poetry by having poems by themselves, MacGreevy and Beckett printed on Christmas cards and sold in Dublin. The poem Beckett submitted was 'Enueg I' (see *LSB*, I, p. 166). The project was unrealised (see DD to Thomas

MacGreevy, 10 November 1933), but Coffey made copies of his Christmas poem-card, featuring the poem 'Yuki-Hira' (see Brian Coffey, *Poems and Versions 1929–1990* (Dublin: The Dedalus Press, 1991), p. 13).

6. Father Patrick Browne, or Pádraig de Brún (1889–1960), later monsignor, was an Irish cleric, classical and Irish scholar, professor of mathematics at St Patrick's College, Maynooth (1914–45) and president of University College Galway (1945–59). He was friends with W.B. Yeats, and a supporter of younger generations of Irish writers.

7. MacGreevy's 'Aodh Ruadh Ó Domhnaill' (first published in 1926) was a poem named after the Irish chieftain 'Red Hugh' O'Donnell, whose burial place in Valladolid, Spain, MacGreevy had visited with poet-dramatist Lennox Robinson (1886–1958).

8. 'The Cab' is the familiar name for one of MacGreevy's most renowned poems, 'Crón Tráth na nDéithe' ('Twilight of the Gods'), first published in 1929 as 'School of ... Easter Saturday Night'; 'Homage to Marcel Proust' (1931) is a poem remembering MacGreevy's mother, and his childhood in Tarbert; the poem 'about Pompeii and ashes' is MacGreevy's 'Nocturne', unpublished until the New Writers' Press edition of *Collected Poems* (1973), which closes with the lines 'I rake the fire./ Hearths in Pompeii/ Empty ...' (*CPTM*, p. 51).

9. In Paris in 1929, under the encouragement of poet, novelist and fellow war-veteran Richard Aldington, MacGreevy had begun work on a novel which he abandoned soon after his return to London in 1933.

10. Île de la Cité, an island in the Seine, in the centre of Paris.

11. Anitschka has not been identified. In Brian Coffey's notes and essays on Devlin we see mention of an early relationship with a woman he met in Munich, a relationship that had a profound effect on Devlin's poetry. See Coffey, 'Of Denis Devlin: Vestiges, sentences, presages', *University Review*, vol. II, no. 11, 1962, pp. 3–18, reprinted in *Poetry Ireland Review*, no. 75, Winter 2002/3, pp. 84–5. See also 'Introduction', in *The Heavenly Foreigner* (Dublin: The Dolmen Press, 1967), pp. 7–13.

12. Sean O'Casey's *The Plough and the Stars* premiered at the Abbey Theatre in 1926 and was part of the Abbey's annual schedule throughout the 1930s. The Abbey production Devlin would have seen, running from 18 to 24 September, starred F.J. McCormick and Shelah Richards as Jack and Nora Clitheroe, and was directed by Lennox Robinson.

13. MacGreevy met Henry (1880–1947) and Barbara (1879–1960) Church, an American couple devoted to the arts, when he was living in Paris. They remained close friends and correspondents, and later introduced MacGreevy to Wallace Stevens

To Shiela Devlin[1]
[November 1933]

My dear Sheila [*for* Shiela],

 We have been thinking of doing a play at Christmas[,] one of W.B. Yeats[’s] "Plays for Dancers."[2] They are short and in verse and there is some dancing to be done. Masks have to be worn and coloured silk, the notion is artificial, every gesture emphasised by a drum tap. If the nuns have a copy you might read them and see if you like the plan.[3] They are lovely plays.

 I hear you are learning lots of music there so we shall have some good playing at Christmas. I am going to the Concerts here, next Saturday a young Russian called Horowitz is playing, he is said to be original.[4] I gave a lecture to the French Society the other day which was a success.[5] I hope you are practising your writing Sheila because I believe you have a talent there which you ought to cultivate. And besides it's a priceless relief from life. – Mr. Madden was here telling funny stories and, as usual, till 4 o'clock in the morning. We are having hard bright weather in Dublin, this frosty winter sun is pleasant. But we get tired often of the drabness and long for the country. So write and tell me what your country is like[.]

Yours (ha! ha!) with love

Denis

Autograph letter signed. 1 leaf, 2 sides. *Dating:* Devlin gave his French lecture at UCD in autumn 1933; Horowitz's Dublin recital, part of the Celebrity Concerts series, was on 18 November 1933. Private collection, Caren Farrell.

---

1. Devlin's sister was named Sighle on her birth certificate, and took the irregular Anglicised form for personal and official purposes. Despite this, Devlin used the regular Anglicised form in his letters to her, as did their mother Margaret in referring to her.

2. Yeats's *Four Plays for Dancers* (1921) – containing *At the Hawk's Well* (1916), *The Only Jealousy of Emer* (1919), *The Dreaming of the Bones* (1919) and *Calvary* (1920) – brought together the legends of the Irish Heroic Age and the aesthetic influence of Japanese Noh theatre.

3. Shiela Devlin attended the Kylemore Abbey school in Connemara, run by Benedictine nuns.

4. In the 1930s the Theatre Royal in Dublin hosted a series of Celebrity Subscription Concerts, featuring international artists on tour. Vladimir Horowitz (1903–89), the young Russian virtuoso pianist, gave the second concert in the winter 1933 series.

5. The UCD French Society. See DD to Thomas MacGreevy, 10 November 1933.

To Thomas MacGreevy
10 November 1933

Dear Tom –

I can see that you were annoyed at my failure to publish the poems and probably on account of Father Brown [*for* Browne], was it not?[1] Did Brian not tell you my reasons? And after having talked with the printer I am quite convinced that publishing single poems in Dublin is [a] foolish waste of money. Your letter did not show any annoyance but I reasoned that you ought to feel some – I went down to Maynooth, Father Brown and I got on very well together and Sam and I are very friendly too. You were right about his father's death monseigneur; it was the cause of two or three 'lovely' poems. My sisters have cooed and gurgled over your poems, I had to read them carefully as your punctuation is very important. Won't Stephen's [*for* Stephens'] Irish anthology be absurd without us four?[2]

I gave a very good lecture in Earlsfort Terrace on modern French poetry and in addition successfully defended Picasso and Matisse.[3] And at a dance the other night a drunk poet came over to me and delivered a long[,] intricate and beautifully-phrased criticism of Brian's poems in our first book. I had not met him before but Brian has, he says. His name is [?Colm] Barry.[4] He is coming to see me tonight with his poems.

I am still waiting wearily for my examination.[5] I feel that it will never come off. Have you any plans? Give my regards to the Churches.

I miss Paris very much. I have not lost enthusiasm for poetry, I write a great deal and not by rule but I'm afraid I'm not building the poems properly. I need an atmosphere in which it is possible to believe that what I'm doing matters a great deal.

If you're coming back to Dublin don't forget to let me know beforehand. It's now between 5 & 7 in the afternoon, the time of day I love most. I had a most wonderful walk in the Mountains yesterday with O'Malley.[6]

I enclose a poem of which you suggested to me the preserving of the first line. Please show it to Brian.

Denis

Temple of the Spirit[7]

I have money to night [*sic*] and yet I am not happy.
Blots of laughter splash on the noise in the café.
Clients have fun and waiters make it snappy.

———

I could hire a cab and shut my eyes inside,
And as it took the corners on a skid,
Pretend it was a bird taking the wind.
Then I would dine and wine till I was blind.
Asparagus lobster and cream
And sauce on a chicken's wing
White wine in ice white cream
All served by silken men,
And pretend I was an Emperor of the Ming
Preserved in the Palace of the Sun.

———

Then I could have a painted girl
And pretend her anxious drivel
Was something novel.
I could amuse my mind by travel
Life full of eyes; life what a whirl!
I that live to realise the truth of the old adage
I that am the future dwelling place of old age.

Denis Devlin.

Autograph letter signed. 3 leaves, 6 sides. *Address*: Envelope originally addressed to MacGreevy at École Normale Supérieure, Paris 5, over-written with 15 Cheyne Gardens, London, SW3, Angleterre. Thomas MacGreevy Papers, 8112/1–16, TCD.

1. See DD to Thomas MacGreevy, [23 September] 1933, n. 6.

2. Susan Schreibman has noted that the Irish novelist and poet James Stephens (1880–1950) wrote to members of the newly formed Irish Academy of Letters in 1933 asking for contributions to an anthology of Irish writing intended for publication with New York's Methuen. See Schreibman, 'Irish Poetic Modernism: Portrait of the artist in exile', in *The Oxford Handbook of Modern Irish Poetry*, ed. F. Brearton and A. Gillis (Oxford: Oxford University Press, 2012), pp. 130–44. Stephens was in Paris in the late twenties, at the same time as Devlin and MacGreevy, and like MacGreevy he formed a close friendship with James Joyce (who declined Yeats's invitation to join the Irish Academy).

3. Earlsfort Terrace was the location of the majority of UCD teaching and accommodation buildings in 1933. Pablo Picasso (1881–1973), Spanish painter and sculptor, and Henri Matisse (1869–1954), French painter, draughtsman and sculptor. Both artists were at the forefront of radical art movements in the early twentieth century.

4. This poet has not been identified.

5. See DD to Thomas MacGreevy, 26 [April] 1934.

6. O'Malley joined the Irish Volunteers and served as an officer during the War of Independence, later fighting with the anti-Treaty republicans during the Civil War. He was in prison for the early years of the Free State, and spent the late 1920s and early 1930s touring North and Central America, during which time he wrote *On Another Man's Wound* (1936), one of the most renowned memoirs of the War of Independence.

7. This is an unpublished poem.

To Thomas MacGreevy

26 January 1934   39 Upper Mount Street, Dublin

My dear Tom –

I had word from Brian which made me so discontented not to have been in London. Very little fun here, there is no one whose conversation does not bore me after a short time. I say so without arrogance, a fault with which Brian has been taxing me lately – at your instance, I wonder? And I am not essentially pagan "as Tom says"; nor is the reference to Breton false "as Tom says". But here, if I want to talk poetry, they answer with Eliot and Pound and Auden, and on their account know Laforgue and not Rimbaud nor Mallarmé and think Proven[ç]al is important.[1] The most nauseating thing about litterateurs is that they can be taken in by a puny fool like Huxley. Imagine having Huxley quoted at you. Really I'm in bad humour because my examination is next week and there is always the possibility of failure. The emotions attendant upon communications – isn't that bien frappé?[2] – though they be uninteresting, never fail to annoy. I think there is going to be an outburst of verse from these jeunesses that I frequent. One of them you would like very much and another is like Joyce – I am weighing my words – except that he is … scrupulous or delicate or something. Another is like Jacques Rivière when young and another is a pleasant devil with a tender heart.[3]

Spinoza is helpful and Santa Teresa useful to someone even slightly unorthodox whom she would probably smile at.[4] She must have been a delightful woman to talk to. I don't like St. Augustine so much.[5] I am understanding Rimbaud better with practise [*for* practice]. Every one else is tiresome beside him. I'm afraid I don't read the philosophers in the right way, or do you think there is a right way? I hope you won't say that being a poet, I can only be expected to pick them rapaciously like a slug, for my own greedy purposes. I ought to give them their due. By the way, isn't English mental life EVINCED by the disgraceful lack of control they are showing with regard to this Whitehead …[6] On the fly-leaf it says comprehensively "The greatest philosopher since Descartes" and someone actually repeated that phrase to me with conviction ... The benefits of advertising. Is there anything I ought to read? I saw Denis Johnston's play last night: "The Moon on [*for* in] the Yellow River".[7] It's clever but a fake profundity.

I am very delighted to hear that your poems are being published; and Brian tells me that your two novels are being written.[8] I have never thanked you for the lovely Poussin and for this I now make amends.[9] I am writing to Eliot and enclosing some poems so as to extract a letter from him armed with which I shall with C.P. Curran's help try to intimidate Yeats into backing me.[10] Curran says a word of support from Eliot would impress Yeats. When are your poems coming out and in what house? And won't you send me a copy? How do you like London? And may we (Sheridan {the one you'd like} and I) use some of your conversation in a book we're writing against English culture in Ireland?[11] For instance your analysis of the gentleman-cad and Romeo & Juliet.

Are you coming over to Dublin some time? Sam Beckett seems to have disappeared. And he has books of mine. Well, good-bye. Blast this bloody exam. I hope I fail it.

amitiés les meilleures,[12]

Denis

Autograph letter signed. 2 leaves, 4 sides. *Address*: Thomas McGreevy, Esq., c/o Mrs Dowden, 15 Cheyne Gardens, London. Thomas Mac-Greevy Papers, 8112/1–16, TCD.

---

1. Jules Laforgue (1860–87), Franco-Uruguayan poet and pioneer of *vers libre*, whose ironic mode is recognised as a major influence on T.S. Eliot's poetry. Arthur Rimbaud (1854–91), prodigious French poet whose prose-poetry, symbolist experiment, and revolutionary aspirations exerted a profound influence on surrealist poets. Stéphane Mallarmé (1842–98), the foremost French symbolist poet, purveyor of a famously difficult, hermetic verse. American modernist Ezra Pound (1885–1972) had a long-standing relationship with the Provençal language and troubadour poetry, dating from his student days at Hamilton College. He translated the poems of Arnaut Daniel and others, and in critical works such as *The Spirit of Romance* (1910) promoted an understanding of Provençal and the troubadour tradition as vital to the reformation of the modern poetic idiom.

2. bien frappé (Fr.): well struck.

3. Jacques Rivière (1886–1925) was a French literary critic and editor of *La Nouvelle Revue Française*. His work was prominent in French intellectual culture after the First World War.

4. Baruch Spinoza (1632–77), Dutch rationalist philosopher who laid important groundwork for Enlightenment thought and modern biblical criticism. Saint Teresa of Ávila (1515–82), Spanish mystic and reformer of the Carmelite order. Saint Teresa and St John of the Cross, both important figures in the Counter-Reformation, are consistent points of reference in MacGreevy's essays and articles on religious art and architecture.

5. St Augustine of Hippo (354–430), early Christian philosopher and theologian.

6. Alfred North Whitehead (1861–1947), English mathematician and philosopher, appointed professor of philosophy at Harvard in 1924. Whitehead made a significant impact on Anglo-American intellectual life, and modernist literature specifically, in the early twentieth century. Works such as *Science and the Modern World* (delivered as the Lowell Lectures in Boston in 1925 and first published in Britain the following year) influenced the work and thought of T.S. Eliot and Gertrude Stein. The edition Devlin refers to may be *Adventures of Ideas* (Cambridge: Cambridge University Press, 1933).

7. Denis Johnston (1901–84), Irish playwright and critic. *The Moon in the Yellow River* premiered in Dublin's Abbey Theatre in April 1931, under Johnston's pseudonym E.W. Tocher.

8. See DD to Thomas MacGreevy, [23 September] 1933, n. 9.

9. This could be a print or an essay on Nicolas Poussin (1594–1665), French baroque painter, on whose work MacGreevy was later to publish a monograph, *Nicolas Poussin* (Dublin: The Dolmen Press, 1960).

10. William Butler Yeats (1865–1939) was the foremost Irish poet of the revolutionary generation, a feature of London's modernist landscape, and a significant cultural force in the newly established Irish Free State, serving as a senator from 1922 to '28. Constantine Peter Curran (1880–1972), lawyer, architectural historian, was a contemporary of James Joyce at UCD. He remained a friend and advocate of Joyce's work, publishing a memoir on their friendship, *James Joyce Remembered*, in 1968. Devlin's letter to Eliot has not been found, and there is no record of Eliot's unfavourable response (mentioned in DD to Thomas MacGreevy, 26 April 1934) in the published Eliot letters.

11. The book has not been identified.

12. amitiés les meilleures (Fr.): best regards.

To Thomas MacGreevy

26 [April] 1934   39 Upper Mount Street, Dublin

My dear Tom –

I have seen your name in various paper and reviews. I am glad and I hope it means you are getting on better. As for me, so little has been happening that it has been difficult to take account of anything except the immediate business of existing. I worked for some time for a Dip. Service exam. which never took place, then for a Civil Service exam. in which I failed. So I am living like a heavy log on the exiguous stream of my parents' bounty; watching, now almost without protest, the multiplication of the scarabs, the clergy, and listening now indifferently to the Sunday-morning pavements pattering with feet on the way to Mass. I remember how my heart sank the first time I heard that noise. How happy you that live in a pagan country! Here the weather has been delightful all year and the summer promises warm and fine and the prospect of spending it here doesn't please me at all. For one thing the countryside will be covered with bikers from Lancashire and the Lowlands and for another the most banal exotic excitements drive me almost to tears; I want away.

> "Je partirai. Steamer balançant ta mâture
> lève l'ancre pour une exotique nature"[1]

If not, I shall be driven to write that horror, an escape-poem, as the English call it. I'm tired of whingeing, too.

These eight months of quiet have let me finish my poems carefully; I have only 3 or 4 to touch up. Eliot wrote me a nice letter saying he didn't like them "quite enough". Besides, I had written him an idiotic letter not impertinent of course but pedantically laudatory and deviously beseeching. Yeats, whom Curran tried to interest, was vague and "could not understand these young men". Higgins I know and he is full of praise and I'm being published in the next Dublin Magazine.[2] And that leads me to an important question. I have noticed that people who know me invariably like my poetry, whereas those that don't know me do not invariably do. Does that mean that the interesting thing is I + my poetry? You see whatever the answer, it must be pleasant to me.

Brian sent me a postcard saying that your poems are coming out on Monday.[3] The card arrived this morning (Saturday) so I have very little time for collecting subscriptions. Why didn't you write to me directly and not through Brian? I met Skeffington last night; he said you were annoyed that I hadn't written lately.[4] Is that why? Really, Tom, it is very absurd of you. Must I repeat that if I don't write often, it is not that I am forgetful, but that writing is of extreme difficulty to me. What makes material for letter-writing with most intelligent people: i.e., I suppose, "what they are thinking" does not exist in me because I never think except à rebours of someone else. Therefore, if there are things I can do for you in Dublin, please write and ask me.

It is near the time when last year we had so many pleasant dinners and so much lovely wine. My God, the number of grandes fines à l'eau we drank! You can't drink cognac here, it's too dear and seldom good.

Have you met any of the Communist poets and what are they like? I disagree with you about Auden, I think he is a good poet. Of course there are obvious criticisms to be made. I enclose a poem by Jean Follain whom I knew in Paris. I forget whether you met him or not. Have you seen Salvador Dali since or [?Junior]?[5]

I hope your book sells well, I shall propagate it in Dublin. I have a couple of names which I am sending on to-day. I shall write again when I have read it.

(I met an old schoolteacher of mine, a Jesuit, to-day; we hadn't met for years. I asked him to guess my age. He said 30![6] Heigh-ho!)

(I think of breaking my marriage engagement. I don't love her, I forget her. I am not otherwise in love. Ought I?)

My affectionate regards.

Denis

[*enclosed poem*]

SOIR D'EPOQUE

Le p[è]re lisait la grande vie
dans les roman[s] salis
des bibliothèques de quartier;
la m[è]re jeune et pale
qui n'avait ri que le jour de ses noces
repr[é]sentait la douce mort;
l'arpette sur un pallier [*for* palier]
empli d'un sale couchant
attendait le bon vouloir
des princes et des rastaquouères;
la neige tombait
sur le Père-Lachaise;
les souteneurs en casquette de soie
r[é]unis sous la lyre a gaz
maniaient les dames et les rois;
l'athl[è]te contait au boucher
qu'un soir à Amsterdam
il avait vu passer la garde
avec les fifres et les tambours.
C'était une année d'abondance:
les froments avaient bien germ[é]
sur la terre de France,
on allait sur les fortifs
pour se souvenir de la guerre,
les jeunes gens embrassaient
des corsets roses et de bas noirs,
souvent mour[a]ient dans les villages
des filles en odeur de sainteté.

JEAN FOLLAIN[7]

Autograph letter signed. 3 leaves, 5 sides, including typed poem. *Dating*: Devlin dates the letter 26. 5. 1934, but it was probably written on 26 April, corresponding to an envelope postmarked 4 May 1934. MacGreevy's Poems – the upcoming release of which this letter refers to – were published on 1 May. *Address*: Thomas McGreevy, Esq., 15 Cheyne Gardens, London, SW3, Sasana. Thomas MacGreevy Papers, 8112/1–16, TCD.

---

1. 'Je partirai! Steamer balançant ta mature/Lève l'ancre pour une exotique nature!': 'Away! You steamer with your swaying helm,/raise anchor for some more exotic realm!' (Stéphane Mallarmé, from 'Brise marine', *Collected Poems and Other Verse*, ed. and trans. E.H. Blackmore and A.M. Blackmore (Oxford and New York: Oxford University Press, 2006), p. 81).

2. F.R. Higgins (1896–1941), Irish poet and friend of Yeats who became an Abbey Theatre director in 1935, and later its business manager. His most recent volume, *Arable Holdings*, had been published by Cuala Press the previous year.

3. MacGreevy's Poems were published on 1 May 1934.

4. Owen Sheehy-Skeffington (1909–70), son of the Irish nationalist Francis Sheehy-Skeffington, who was executed in the Easter Rising. Sheehy-Skeffington was a lecturer in French at Trinity College Dublin from 1933 until his death, and he served as a senator from 1954.

5. Salvador Dalí (1904–89), Spanish surrealist artist, who spent much of the late 1920s and '30s in Paris.

6. Devlin was twenty-six in May 1934.

7. 'Soir d'époque' was first published in *La Main Chaude* (1933) and reprinted in *Usage du temps* (Paris: Gallimard, 1983 [1943], pp. 31-2). See appendix for translation.

To Thomas MacGreevy
[31] August 1934

My dear Tom –

I am in a little seaside village in Wicklow – Kilcool [*for* Kilcoole] – for a fortnight's bathing which is ending now. I find with horror that even swimming is beginning to bore me. What shall I do? [I]t was only my correspondence with the cosmos – but such a piffling thought should not even occur to me. And why does it? Because I have been a year away from Paris. It's no use: all your admonitions and hopes for my having some beneficial influence here are exaggerated – I am not one to affect my surroundings but to be affected by them. Here is discouraging: the atmosphere, political, economic and therefore (il materialismo è la salvezza) literary is pre 1870.[1] Consider Higgins.[2] An estimable man soft breathing gentle cow. Quite content to look on his poetry as a job and to pick out suitable emotions now and again round which to write a charming lyric with experiments in assonance! He experiments in decking out a carcass. Willing to admit of course that the big world is worried about living, that the war may have made a change, but there are certain eternal values. But you know it all. Yeats is worse. [B]ullock bulwark of contented undereducation. None of these damned Irish writers has had even a conventional education. You know all this and I wonder how in God's name you can imagine anyone living here in interest or calm. Wasting my temper in objecting to things I rejected six years ago. I tell you I will turn English. I have no sympathy with the attempt to build up an Irish literature in English. Lucan is a Latin poet.[3]

I am still without a job, the Foreign Affairs exam has not come off yet. In the meantime there is a chance of my getting an Assistanceship in English in University College. The old professor, Donovan, is dead and by some extraordinary perversity his successor is a young and lively man who not only knows but likes literature, and who recogniz-es post-war poetry. He (J. J. Hogan) is reorganizing his faculty and is keen on having me join him.[4] He will succeed too unless political influence prevents. – Can you advise me what to do? You see, I must choose between the University and Foreign Affairs. I agree with the Church in being convinced that I can destroy or fortify my mind by choice; and having examined and compared examples of the Professorate and Diplomacy, I have concluded that the latter career would be more beneficial to me than the former. Professors are amusing and informing but their business is musty, diplomats (being a diplomat for Ireland is ridiculous) are stupid, there's a lot of nerveracking routine work, but there seems to be more contact with actuality. Of course pace O.[5] But I prefer the fairyland of the present to that of the past, death is too impressive a name for it. Pompous and young writing? You really ought to be flattered because I spin myself inside a haze for practically everyone – oh a golden haze. In the end I have no choice. I shall be driven to take the University by its coming first and I can't afford to refuse a job.

Brian is very lively but tired after his hard work of the last year. He got third place in the examination, "cum magna laude".[6] I was very glad, the more[ ]so as it has stopped some ill-natured gossip here. I find him changed, less fond of fantasticalness. Is he becoming a 'grown-up man'? He says so. He seems more really no longer interested in certain things. Give me your impression. He seems to be getting on well with Eliot who practically offered to publish his poems but Brian has still some ridiculous ogival objection to having it done – He had bought a number of 'An Phoblacht' about a fortnight ago.[7] You know that since the strike the 'Phoblacht' has increased its circulation enormously, it appears three times a week.[8] There was a virulent article attacking Dublin in this number, it was thus prefixed[:] '"How long is it since your last confession? Answer. Seven hundred years." McGreevy's Poems.'[9] So you see. If your sister has not already sent you a copy, let me know and I shall send you one.

Sam Beckett must be back in London now and I haven't got his address. Will you be so kind and give him this word from me when you see him? Tell him I got his books and thank him for them. And a succession of disasters prevented me from telephoning him as I said.

Also, his article in 'The Bookman' raised a storm.[10] It appears Yeats was furious; it appears that Austin Clarke is vindictive by nature and will pursue Sam to his grave; it appears Seamas [*for* Seumas] O'Sullivan thought he might have been mentioned at least; and my domestic bull Higgins[,] voyez-moi ce type[,] amazed me by being glad "he got off so lightly".[11] I was flattered by what he wrote of me and through his agency a poem has been taken by the Bookman (the weakbacks! they picked the one that's nearest the little ramp they are running on in England now.)[12]

But I don't know. I don't think I shall make a poetry that Beckett would approve of. The exquisite shock of contradictions tires me now – or at least either I'm not spiritually taut enough or I think that swordblade too limited enjoyment. I was about to tell you what I think about poetry but it would bore us both and besides I can't link one moment with another intellectually. Beckett is a bit like John the Baptist only if that would annoy him don't tell him.

Is your mother in good health? I'm sure she was charmed with your book.

You are disgustingly lazy: why don't you finish that novel? I suppose there's no sign of your coming to Dublin.

Affectionately yours,

Denis D.

Autograph letter signed. 3 leaves, 6 sides. *Dating*: Devlin dates the letter 'Last day of August, 1934'. Postmark 4 September 1934. *Address*: Envelope originally addressed to MacGreevy c/o Mrs Dowden in Cheyne Gardens, overwritten with 'Tarbert', Limerick, Ireland. Thomas MacGreevy Papers, 8112/1–16, TCD.

---

1. il materialismo è la salvezza (It.): materialism is the salvation.

2. See DD to Thomas MacGreevy, 26 [April] 1934, n. 2.

3. Marcus Annaeus Lucanus, or Lucan (39–65 AD), Roman poet, whose most renowned work is the epic poem *Pharsalia, or Bellum civili* (*c.* 61–5 AD), an account of the war between Julius Caesar and Pompey. Devlin's reference to Lucan's Latin is

unclear: Lucan was born in Corduba (now Córdoba, Spain), educated in Athens and was favoured by Emperor Nero in Rome before a feud divided them. He remained a staunch patriot and republican.

4. Robert Donovan (1862–1934) held the chair in English at UCD from 1910 until his death in 1934. Jeremiah Hogan was Donovan's successor. See DD to Mervyn Wall, [Autumn 1932–Spring 1933], n. 3.

5. The 'O' Devlin makes exceptions for, presumably a professor, has not been identified.

6. Coffey had been studying in Paris since 1930, transferring from physical chemistry to philosophy in 1933, when he entered the Institut Catholique de Paris to work under the renowned Thomist philosopher Jacques Maritain.

7. *An Phoblacht* ('The Republic'), newspaper published by Sinn Féin, founded in 1906. In 1934, under the editorship of Donal O'Donoghue, the paper was campaigning vigorously against Eoin O'Duffy's Blueshirt fascist organisation.

8. Regular newspaper publication was suspended in Dublin between July and September 1934 while compositors, linotype operators and machine hands went on strike. *An Phoblacht* had permission from the General Workers' Union to remain in print, and increased its circulation with midweek bulletins.

9. The article on Dublin, written by Donal O'Keefe, uses the question from MacGreevy's 'Crón Tráth na nDéithe' as its title and epigraph (in MacGreevy's poem the question reads '*How long since your last absolution?*/Answer: *Seven hundred years*' (*CPTM*, p. 15)). Just as MacGreevy's poem looks despairingly at post-Civil War Dublin, O'Keefe's article condemns the gombeen capitalism of the Fianna Fáil government.

10. In a polemical article in a 1934 special Irish issue of *The Bookman*, 'Recent Irish Poetry', Beckett, writing under the pseudonym Andrew Belis, divided Irish poets into 'antiquarians' (Yeats, James Stephens, F.R. Higgins) and 'others'. Devlin and Coffey, included in the latter camp, were credited above other poets of their generation. See *Disjecta: Miscellaneous writings and a dramatic fragment* (London: John Calder, 1983), pp. 70–6, 75.

11. Seumas O'Sullivan, born James Sullivan Starkey (1879–1958), Irish poet and editor of *The Dublin Magazine*. voyez-moi ce type (Fr.): look at this guy.

12. Devlin's 'The Gradual' was published in the final issue of *The Bookman*, in December 1934.

To George Reavey

25 March 1935   39 Upper Mount Street, Dublin

Dear Reavey,

Coffey wrote me such an illegible letter about your plan for publishing us that I am quite vague as to what I should send you. Is it to be a monthly review or an anthology or a volume each?[1] I could take any of these meanings from his letter. And when must you have my poems?

I'm of course tremendously delighted at being published, you are a goddesend [*for* godsend]. I'd pitched my poems in a drawer, I've got rejection slips long ago from every possible printsheet. The Dublin pundits, too, dislike poetry – Of course, if the series is well advertised, they might buy it here through spite.

I saw a poem of yours in the 'Review of Reviews' some time ago.[2] I liked it, it will be a good thing to open with. It ought to surprise the dull religiosity of the English communist group.[3]

Would you like me to do a little publicity here? If so, I'd have to know the titles, dates of publication etc. And the subscription, when must I send it, and how? (I can manage £10, I'm in a putrid job now, I mean it's putrid being in a job.)[4]

I should be grateful if you would let me know these particulars and thank you for asking me to join.

– What will the format be like?

Yours sincerely,

Denis Devlin.

Autograph letter signed. 2 leaves, 3 sides. George Reavey Papers (MS 3430), Container 49.5, Harry Ransom Center, University of Texas at Austin.

----

1. George Reavey (see Correspondents' Biographies) had set up the 'Bureau Littéraire Européen', a literary agency, with Marc Slomin in Paris in 1934. In 1935 he founded the Europa Press, which was initially run from Paris and transferred to London with Reavey the following year (see DD to Thomas MacGreevy, 15 March 1936).

Reavey's own *Nostradam: A sequence of poems* (1935) and *Signes d'adieu: Frailty of love* (1935) were listed as volumes 1 & 2 in what Reavey was at that point envisaging as the 'Europa Poets Series'; Beckett's *Echo's Bones: And other precipitates* (1935) was the last volume to issue from Europa in Paris.

2. Reavey's 'Quixotic Gas' appeared in the January 1935 issue of London's *Review of Reviews* (p. 44).

3. See DD to George Reavey, 23 June 1936, n. 2.

4. Devlin was appointed lecturer in English at UCD in autumn 1934; he resigned the lectureship early in the following year, when he took up a position as a cadet in the Irish Department of External Affairs. The date from which his cadetship began is unclear, but he is mentioned in foreign policy documents from April 1935 (Letter from Frederick H. Boland to Seán Murphy, 30 April 1935, *Documents on Irish Foreign Policy, Vol IV, 1932–1936* (2004), p. 342), so it is likely that he was already working in the department at this point.

* * * * *

To George Reavey

25 April 1935   39 Upper Mount Street, Dublin

Dear Reavey,

I put off answering your letters because I thought I should see you in Paris during Easter. I had all plans made for passing a week there when my leave was cancelled at the last minute.

Enclosed you will find £10 (2 £5 notes.) If it comes to more let me know. I shall send on my manuscript in about 2 weeks. Is that all right?

I have been telling people about the publication. If the "Irish Times" praised it, it wd. sell. Do you know them? I'm in bad water there. In general though, this is an extremely painful country to live in.

Yours sincerely,
Denis Devlin.

Autograph letter signed. 1 leaf, 2 sides. George Reavey Papers, Container 49.5, HRC, UTx.

To Thomas MacGreevy

1 June 1935   39 Upper Mount Street, Dublin

My dear Tom –

I am sending under separate cover the Easter number of An Phoblacht in which your poem appeared.[1] I am very sorry for having taken so long about it but, literally, I have no time. Finally I had to ask my sister to get it for me and finally I had to get her to help in typing out Brian's poems to comply with the hasty request of that same Paris poet. I work hard at the office[,] so hard that sometimes I have to go to bed when I come home, my nerves beating at me. My body is strong, but my nerves are weak. This, please note, is not due to contemporary literary neurasthenia but to the small stock of nerves I was born with. Also, I'm trying to get my rebellious poems in order.

All this I repeat so that you may have material for composing an explanation to Mrs. Dowden for my seeming remissness in not acquainting her of my gratitude for her charming company and gracious house and tranquil hieratic Pekingese.[2] Please acquaint her so.

I have to hurry on with Brian's stuff, so I must tell you that I really did enjoy being in London, and I had a good time with you – I think, by the way, that I disagree with your opinions more than you think and of conviction but the matter is tedious.

Good luck[.] In a hurry[.]

Denis

Autograph letter signed. 3 leaves, 5 sides. Thomas MacGreevy Papers, 8112/1–16, TCD.

---

1. MacGreevy's 'The Six Who Were Hanged' was published in the Easter issue of *An Phoblacht* (Saturday, 20 April 1935), p. 4. The journal regularly featured republican ballads and revolutionary poems. This is one of MacGreevy's most passionately political poems, responding to the execution of six republican prisoners at Mountjoy during the Irish War of Independence.

2. While MacGreevy was living in London for periods in the 1920s and '30s, his main address was Cheyne Gardens in Chelsea, where he lodged with Hester Dowden (1868–1949), daughter of Edward Dowden, Trinity professor of literature, and her daughter Dolly Travers-Smith (1901–77).

To George Reavey

18 June 1935   39 Upper Mount Street, Dublin

Dear Reavey –

Sorry haven't sent MS. Shall send it in a few days. Perhaps better issue Coffey's before mine?[1] – Good review of yours in 'Time & Tide'.[2]

For review Dublin: send to the Irish Times, Westmoreland St. & Dublin Magazine, 2 Crow St. I shall lend mine to a Univ. mag.[3] Circulars gone round.

Yours sincerely,

Denis Devlin

Autograph postcard signed. *Address*: M. George Reavey, Bureau Littéraire Européen, 13, rue Bonaparte, PARIS. VI. George Reavey Papers, Container 49.5, HRC, UTx.

---

1. Brian Coffey's *Third Person* was published by Europa in 1938, a year after Devlin's *Intercessions*.

2. In an issue of *Time and Tide* magazine, the literary reviewer Roderick Random wrote an enthusiastic response to Reavey's *Nostradam: A sequence of poems*, describing Reavey as 'one of the most considerable young poets writing today' (*Time and Tide*, 1 June 1935, vol. XVI, no. 22, p. 823).

3. The university magazine is possibly *Comhthrom Féinne*, a UCD student magazine in which many of Devlin's friends and contemporaries were publishing, named after one of the college's mottos ('comhthrom féinne' translates as 'fair play').

To George Reavey

13 July 1935   39 Upper Mount Street, Dublin

Dear Reavey,

Enclosed herewith you will find my MS. I regret very much to have kept you waiting so long, and I hope it has not deranged your plans regarding publication.

There is no consistency in the typing, I'm afraid. Some of the titles are in capitals, some in small characters, but I don't mind which way you print them [—] but I want Gobineau and Andre Breton and Breton capitalised in the Eiffel Tower, and the date of the latter only inserted.[1] The spacing is irregular, but I intend a uniform space to exist between the paragraphs everywhere.

I like your poems immensely.

The mistake of the ignorant fool in the "Irish Times" will be rectified. Or did you know that he had mentioned your book in Publications Received?[2] But you probably know already how little knowledge exists here. I expect there will be a few orders, at least, when the prospectuses have bee[n] spelled out.[3] I'm having it mentioned on the Radio.[4]

                    Yours Sincerely,
                    Denis Devlin

Typed letter signed. 1 leaf, 1 side. George Reavey Papers, Container 49.5, HRC, UTx.

---

1. Joseph Arthur, comte de Gobineau (1816–82), French ethnologist and novelist, is addressed in capitals in Devlin's surrealist poem 'Communication from the Eiffel Tower' (earliest draft dated 1932), transforming intermittently into 'GOBETHAU'. André Breton's name is summoned in the early drafts of the poem – 'I declaim that I, Andre Breton/Breton and I mixed like the play of mirrors/Make tabla rasa ready for new writing' (Denis Devlin Literary Papers (MSS 33,747-33,810), MS 33,765/7 (3), National Library of Ireland, Dublin) – but in the final published version his name is replaced by the 'BABEUF' of French political journalist and revolutionary Francois-Noel Babeuf (1760–97).

2. On 6 July 1935, *Nostradam* was listed in the 'Publications Received' column of *The Irish Times*. The error Devlin refers to has not been identified.

3. The practice of circulating book prospectuses among prospective clients to promote interest and gain subscriptions was still current in the early twentieth century.

4. Devlin's first literary broadcast on 2RN (another name for Radio Athlone, an early manifestation of RTÉ Radio, and an aural play on 'To Erin') was an essay on 'The Christian Reaction in Modern French Literature' in January 1933. He became a frequent contributor, presenting poetry review shows and reading his own work in a feature called 'A Poet Reads'; Devlin appreciated the opportunity to give a platform to his friends' work.

* * * * *

To George Reavey

14 August 1935   39 Upper Mount Street, Dublin

Dear Reavey,

Reference my MS. I should not like to take out any of the poems I sent for the book as they form a whole. At the same time, I should find it difficult to pay much more money.

I notice that the type is very large and the spacing wide in your book. Wld. it be possible to crush my MS into the same space by using small type and narrow spacing? It wld. not look so well, of course, but I don't mind that.

I shld. be glad if you wld. examine this plan & let me know whether it can be done.

– I have been on holiday, hence my delay in answering your letter. Please excuse it.

Yours Sincerely,
Denis Devlin

Autograph letter signed. 1 leaf (folded), 3 sides. George Reavey Papers, Container 49.5, HRC, UTx.

To George Reavey

2 October 1935   39 Upper Mount Street, Dublin

Dear Reavey,

I should be glad to know how the printing stands. You will remember my asking you whether it would be possible to include all the MS I sent you in the prescribed number of pages by using smaller type. Can this be done? If not, will you let me know how much extra it would cost me to have it all done in your size of type? I expect of course that cost would be increased by changeing [*sic*] to smaller type but probably not by much. If much more expense were to be involved, I should simply have to cut out some poems.

Has Beckett been brought out yet?[1] I have been away recently and out of touch – When am I due for publication?[2]

Yours Sincerely,

Denis Devlin

Autograph letter signed. 1 leaf, 2 sides. Reavey's costing calculations appear in the top left corner of the recto side, and at the bottom of the verso. George Reavey Papers, Container 49.5, HRC, UTx.

---

1. *Echo's Bones: And other precipitates* was published in December 1935.
2. See DD to Thomas MacGreevy, 5 October 1935, n. 2.

To Thomas MacGreevy

5 October 1935   39 Upper Mount Street, Dublin

My dear Tom,

I don't know whether you may have listened to 2RN last night (i.e. the 4th instant) and heard my marvellous recital of your Nocturne of the Self-Evident Presence.[1] It ran "… Mr. Thomas McGreevy, an Irishman, who has been most incomprehensibly neglected." I was delivering an attack in answer to F.R. Higgins, on Yeats and all his followers. Are you pleased? I am glad to have got the chance.

I have been to Geneva with the delegation.[2] I had an awful time, really working all day long from 7.30 in the morning till 12 at night. I am said to have done quite well. I felt a fool broadcasting rimery during a war. I have lost interest in Irish, I can barely understand the translations I did last year.

Oct 22

I am a wretched hound, I admit, about letters. I got a shock to day when a humble clerk in the office told me he had searched all the libraries in Dublin for your book[.] So I gave him the name of your publisher. My broadcasting you has really been of benefit, many people have enquired about you[.] I am chagrined that you did not hear me. The clerk (above) turned out to be quite well-read and I had known him before for an intelligent fellow. He does not like Whitman and is sceptical about E. Pound.[3] He loved the 'Lament for the Death of an Up. Class.'[4] He said "McGreevy must be a very scholarly man."

Nothing of me – except that I am very pro-Italian. I do not much care for being the ally of savages. And at present my work is the implementation of the sanctions agreed on at Geneva against Italy. Isn't it foul? Can you tell me any other way of making a lump sum of money? No, of course not[.]

Give my kindest regards to Sam. I enjoyed that day in London with you both. I was there the week after. I was with my friend then.

I'm sealing this now to send otherwise it would lie around. Rotten pen.

>Yours
>
>Denis.

Autograph letter signed. 2 leaves, 4 sides. *Dating*: Letter written in two instalments (5 and 22 October), postmarked 23 October. *Address*: Originally addressed to Thomas MacGreevy, Esq., 15 Cheyne Gardens, London, SW3, over-written with Tarbert, Co. Kerry, Ireland. Thomas MacGreevy Papers, 8112/1–16, TCD.

---

1. See DD to George Reavey, 13 July 1935, n. 4.

2. In his first major assignment as a cadet in the Department of External Affairs, Devlin travelled to Geneva with Éamon de Valera as part of the Irish delegation to the League of Nations Assembly, where international security was under scrutiny following the Italian invasion of Abyssinia. According to the Irish press the delegation left Ireland on Tuesday, 3 September (travelling via London), and returned on Tuesday, 1 October. For a history of Irish involvement in the League of Nations see Michael Kennedy, *Ireland and the League of Nations, 1919–46: International relations, diplomacy and politics* (Blackrock, Co. Dublin: Irish Academic Press, 1996).

3. Walt Whitman (1819–92), American poet and pioneer of the free verse tradition in English. Whitman's influence can be seen across Devlin's career, in early poems such as 'Communication from the Eiffel Tower', and the late elegy 'The Tomb of Michael Collins' (1954).

4. *Lament for the Death of an Upper Class* (London: John Miles, 1935) was Thomas MacGreevy's translation of Henry de Montherlant's best-known novel, *Les Célibataires* (1934).

To George Reavey

22 October 1935   39 Upper Mount Street, Dublin

Dear Reavey,

About my book – I agree to its being printed at the terms you state. When you have arranged with the printers, you can let me know and I shall send on the amount still due. If you think it better to sell it for 5/-, I agree.[1]

I am setting about drawing up a subscription list for Beckett's book. I'm afraid I mismanaged yours. I sent out your forms to about 50 people with a covering letter. Unfortunately I had got it into my head that Combridge (booksellers here) were about to stock them so I mentioned that copies were to be had there.[2] Of course when the people went to the shop, there was none to be had. So when arranging Beckett's list, I shall put down your book too. Apart his friends, Beckett is not popular here on account of the pundits (Higgins, F. O'Connor, O'Faoláin etc[.], + the Professor people)[.][3]
Can you tell me if many demands came direct from Dublin?

F.R. Higgins, Secretary, Irish Academy of Letters, c/o Thom + Co. 2 Crowe Street, Dublin.
                    Yours sincerely,
                         Denis Devlin.

P.S. On second thoughts I don't make out a list, but simply distribute the forms and let the subscribers write to you. Is this correct? Do you accept postal orders made out in English money? I don't think many people here wld. buy French money first & then send it on.

Can you let me have 35 forms for Beckett's book? And do you know if Beckett is circularising the people he knows in Dublin?
                    D.D.

Autograph letter signed. 2 leaves, 3 sides. George Reavey Papers, Container 49.5, HRC, UTx.

1. Once *Intercessions* was published it sold at the same price as *Echo's Bones*: 3s. 6d. for the regular edition, and 10s. 6d. for the signed edition.

2. Combridge's was a bookseller, print-seller, and picture-frame maker on Grafton Street in Dublin.

3. Frank O'Connor, born Michael Francis O'Donovan (1903–66), Irish short-story writer who along with Sean O'Faolain was crucially involved in Dublin periodical culture. The disdain in which Beckett held Dublin literary society at this time is evident in his 1930s' letters to MacGreevy, where O'Faolain is given the nickname 'All Forlorn' (see Beckett to Thomas MacGreevy, 16 January 1936, *LSB*, vol. I, p. 299).

To George Reavey
2 December 1935

Dear Reavey,

Enclosed are £11 in cash. I am sorry to have delayed so long, it was unavoidable. And as you have not yet put my MS in print, I am sending herewith a revised version of the poem "Argument with Justice." Will you substitute for the first one I sent you this one – which is very different? I hope it will not upset your arrangements to make this change. I have marked the correct version "B".

I see, of course, how much better it would be to have a title for my book but I have[ ]not been able to think of one. I intend to find something as soon as possible but I don't want to hold up the printing.

Please send me Beckett's book – (6/- copy)[.] Have sent a money order for the amount.

I could use about ten more forms for his book.

As regards my forms, red would suit me but use whichever suits you best.[1]

Yours sincerely,
Denis Devlin.

Autograph letter signed. 2 leaves, 2 sides. George Reavey Papers, Container 49.5, HRC, UTx.

---

1. In a letter of 22 November 1935, Reavey had asked Devlin whether red or green would suit him for the colour of the 'bulletin' which would advertise his poems and solicit subscriptions (George Reavey Papers, Container 49.5, HRC, UTx).

To George Reavey

8 December 1935   39 Upper Mount Street, Dublin

Dear Reavey,

I had already sent the £11 when your letter from London reached me – mine must have reached Paris just after you left. I enclosed also a second version of my poem "Argument with Justice" which I should like you to substitute for the first one sent originally with the MS. As you said the poems had not gone into print yet, I [thought] this change would be less inconvenient than rewriting it on the proofs.

I sent a money order for a Beckett (signed) edition. I have distributed the forms. His name was mentioned yesterday in the 'Irish Times' as being about to bring out a book of poems, so I suppose the forms are having some effect.[1]

I am trying to invent a title for my book; in the meantime I "say the word", and you can go ahead with the printing.

Yours

Denis Devlin

P.S. I am a bit nervous about the illustration – can you give me any idea of what it will be like?[2]

D.D.

Autograph letter signed. 1 leaf, 2 sides. The inserted 'thought' in the first paragraph fills a gap mistakenly left at the turn of the page. George Reavey Papers, Container 49.5, HRC, UTx.

---

1. In the 'Irishman's Diary' section of *The Irish Times* (7 Dec 1935, p. 6), the columnist 'Quidnunc' gave the following round-up of recent poetic activity in Ireland: 'From the poets – Frank O'Connor has a book of verse, Sam Beckett another; Mr. Yeats will give us his selection of modern poets, which, by all accounts, promises to be a highly individualistic book.'

2. The Europa Poets series was designed with artistic collaboration in mind: in promotional notices, Reavey described the series as 'limited editions in collaboration

with modern artists and engravers'. In his letter of 22 November 1935, Reavey proposed the publication of twenty special-edition volumes of Devlin's poems, 'with an engraving by a man called Buckland Wright who has a reputation and has illustrated various books including a Rimbaud' (George Reavey Papers, Container 49.5, HRC, UTx). John Buckland Wright (1897–1954), an illustrator and engraver from New Zealand, was in Paris in the 1930s and had helped the painter Stanley William Hayter to found the influential Atelier 17 studio for printmakers. The letters provide no further record of a conversation between Reavey and Devlin about the engraving for *Intercessions*, but his reservations clearly remained, and there was no illustration in the special editions. Brian Coffey was more enthusiastic, and the special editions of *Third Person* (1938) were illustrated with a Hayter engraving. Reavey included a Buckland Wright engraving in the special copies of his *Quixotic Perquisitions* (1939), the eighth volume of the Europa Poets series. For more information on this collaboration, see Sandra O'Connell, 'The Europa Press and Atelier 17 Paris: "Limited Editions in Collaboration with Modern Artists and Engravers"', in Selena Daly and Monica Insinga (eds), *The European Avant-Garde: Text and image* (Newcastle upon Tyne: Cambridge Scholars Publishing, 2012), pp. 98–115.

To George Reavey

18 January 1936   39 Upper Mount Street, Dublin

Dear Reavey,

I have succeeded in deciding on a title for my book – it is "Intercessions". As in the case of the others, I should like it not followed by Poems.

May I expect the proofs soon?

Yours etc.

<u>Denis Devlin</u>

Beckett's book looks very well, I think. I have heard a complaint from a Mrs Salkeld here that she sent for it (through Combridge's) but has not got it yet.[1] I am convinced that many more could be sold – especially of mine & Coffey's – if a Dublin bookseller displayed them.

D.

Autograph letter signed. 1 leaf, 2 sides. George Reavey Papers, Container 49.5, HRC, UTx.

---

1. Blanaid Salkeld (1880–1959), Indian-born Irish poet, dramatist, actress and reviewer. Salkeld's *Hello, Eternity!* (1933) received measured praise in Beckett's 'Recent Irish Poetry' (1934).

To Thomas MacGreevy

18 February 1936   39 Upper Mount St, Dublin

My dear Tom,

I wish to give you my most deep and sincere sympathies on ac-count of your loss by your mother's death.[1] I know that you loved her more than anyone else and you must feel very alone now. If I could do anything to soften your grief, I should willingly. Please do not hurt at my late letter – I heard the news by chance.

If you thought you might like to pass some time in Dublin, my family would be delighted to have you stay with us. It is a large active family but not inconvenient. In any case, do come and see me if you are passing through Dublin.

Yours very affectionately,
Denis.

Autograph letter signed. 1 leaf, 2 sides. *Address*: Envelope originally addressed to Thomas McGreevy, Esq., Tarbert, Co. Kerry for forwarding. Overwritten with 71 High Road, Chiswick, London, then Cheyne Gdns, Chelsea, London, SW3. Thomas MacGreevy Papers, 8112/1–16, TCD.

---

1. MacGreevy's mother had died earlier in February.

To George Reavey
4 March 1936   39 Upper Mount Street, Dublin

Dear Reavey,

I am interested to hear that you are opening a branch in London, I'm sure it will be more convenient for you. And Paris seems to be no longer the capital of the English literary world, anyhow. Do you intend broadening the "Europa"? I mean publish novels, etc. Is Stanley Nott a young publisher?[1]

I am quite disappointed that my book must be delayed further. To have to wait for months and months is very painful. Do you really think it will sell better by coming after the Eluard?[2] I doubt if it will sell much outside Dublin (where it definitely will sell) considering the present English fashions in poetry. As regards details for your partner, there are not many. I published a book of poems some years ago with Brian Coffey, have appeared since in the Dublin Magazine, the Irish Times & the old Bookman, have read in an Irish Poets series from the Dublin Radio. Also in translation in one of those small reviews in Paris.[3] Did you receive a letter from me with the title of my book? It is "Intercessions."

Will you send me a copy of Signes d'Adieu?[4] I enclose P.O. 2/6.

Yours sincerely,

Denis Devlin.

Autograph letter signed. 1 leaf, 2 sides. George Reavey Papers, Container 49.5, HRC, UTx.

---

1. Charles Stanley Nott (1887–1978), London-based publisher and author, was collaborating with Reavey on *Thorns of Thunder*, the first English-language edition of Paul Eluard translations, and subsequent Europa volumes.

2. Reavey planned to release *ToT*, which contained translations from David Gascoyne, Eugène Jolas and Man Ray as well as Devlin, Beckett, Coffey and Reavey, to coincide with the International Surrealist Exhibition in London in June 1936. This objective

caused a further delay to the publication of *Intercessions*: see DD to Thomas Mac-Greevy, 15 March 1936.

3. Gaston Bonheur's translation of Devlin's 'Passarelle' appeared in the May 1933 issue of *14 rue du Dragon*, a little magazine from the Cahiers d'Art publishing house in Paris.

4. See DD to George Reavey, 25 March 1935, n. 1.

To Thomas MacGreevy

15 March 1936   39 Upper Mount Street, Dublin

Dear Tom,

I am sure it must indeed be hard to reconcile yourself to the loss of your mother who seems to me to have been very sweet, and it is good for you that you have reasons in the faith to help you to accept it. The incident of your both thinking at the same time of McCarthy's lines is indeed remarkable but I don't feel inclined to disagree with the implication of it as similar parallelisms have occurred between me and someone I love.[1] You are relatively peaceful, at least there is a peace to which you can adjust yourself, whereas I – but let me not rant – am always 'tending towards', I am a caterpillar or an egg.

Some points: I know Pádraic [*for* Padraic] Fallon.[2] He is an agricultural poet and terrifyingly boring and his poem you praise in the Dublin Magazine I thought dreadful. Where on earth do you see any ressemblance [*sic*] between me and AE[?][3] I have never taken the slightest interest in him. At College I read something of his in an Anthology and I saw at once that he was not a poet and that he was a shoddy thinker[.] Then I met him somewhere last year and was so repelled that I could not talk to him nor even look at him. I have seldom met such pretentiousness futilily [*for* futilely] joined to such poor brains. De grâce alors, monsieur?[4] Because I love colour and sound, you imply. But I must. I say poems that way because there is no other way of saying what my poems are. I who am so scrupulous about every single word[,] who examine for months whether I have put the verse in all its original impression, it is hard to be called a dauber. You have a fallacy with your 'saying things simply' unless you mean saying them integrally. If we take a line of mine which you might describe as rich:

> "Gentle, when I am sleeping, breathe O
> summer twilight
> The fireflies of your gentle thoughts ..."[5]

I find there is no simplifying possible there. If you say 'Leave out fireflies' and if I did the meaning would be quite different, you must see, for the thoughts might then be soft like evening breezes whereas I mean them to be bright too[.] Unless I wrote 'bright' thoughts which the muse forfend. This of course is analysis after the act. And by the way I don't like your instrument[,] the design and the colouring. I admit that I get carried away often when I write but <u>never</u> without the company of my brain. But that awful Methodist illuminé hot-gospeller AE!

It is fair to say concerning Eliot in the University that Joyce's name was cheered also, that Yeats applauded too and that Eliot was the first to dare to talk about Joyce in that place.[6] However I did not like Eliot very much. He is nice of course but I can quite see him writing some of the weak stuff he has written.

My book is in a very bad way, Reavey is behaving disgracefully. It was to be out last November! Reavey left me without any information whatever for months, then wrote about a fortnight ago saying he had transferred his business to London and that he would not publish me till about the Summer. It makes me mad. Sam advised me to take the affair from him but I can't afford to lose the £20 I have paid him – he would certainly not give that back. He wants first to publish his book of translations of Eluard in time for the surréaliste exhibition in May next. Brian was to edit this Eluard, give some translations himself and Sam and I were to give the rest. In his letter to me, Reavey mentioned that Herbert Read was to do an introduction[,] Picasso an engraving. I demurred at Read, then I found R[eavey] had not told Br[ian] and Sam about Read. Anyhow Br[ian] & Sam refuse to appear with Read and I too.[7] That won't stop Reavey, of course; he'll translate them himself. I don't care a damn about that but I am bitterly disappointed that my book should be delayed again & again. There is nothing I can do. Even if I took it back and were prepared to spend more money with another and much better publisher I should spend further months in negotiating it. Brian wrote me with the romantic proposal that he & Sam & I should go to London & force R. to publish me at once. Isn't that just like Brian? I suppose you would advise me to let it go ahead with R.? It seems the only thing to do –

Mrs. McCarvill read some of you at a meeting of the Christian Art Academy recently.[8]

Yours

Denis.

Autograph letter signed. 5 leaves, 10 sides. *Dating*: Devlin dates the letter '15th March Street'; postmark shows '16 March 1936'. *Address*: Envelope addressed to Thomas McGreevy, Esq., 15 Cheyne Gardens, London, SW3. Thomas MacGreevy Papers, 8112/1–16, TCD.

---

1. The reference may be to the American lyricist Joseph McCarthy (1885–1943), whose 'Ireland Must Be Heaven, for My Mother Came from There' was a hit in Britain and Ireland during the First World War. MacGreevy shared with his mother a love of music and popular song, as we see in the childhood poem 'Homage to Marcel Proust'.

2. Padraic Fallon (1905–74), Irish poet, playwright, and civil servant, whose literary acquaintances included Patrick Kavanagh and Seumas O'Sullivan, editor of *The Dublin Magazine*.

3. AE, pen name for George Russell (1867–1935), Irish writer, artist and mystic, prominent figure in the Irish Revival. Russell was a long-standing friend of W.B. Yeats, and he became a patron to younger poets and artists, including Padraic Fallon.

4. de grâce alors, monsieur? (Fr.): for pity's sake, sir?

5. These lines are from 'Communication from the Eiffel Tower'. The published text reads: 'Gentle when I am sleeping breathe girl O summer twilight/The fireflies of your gentle thoughts through my gnarled thorntree nerves' (*CPDD*, pp. 70–1).

6. In January 1936 Eliot paid his first visit to Dublin, on the invitation of the Reverend Roland Burke Savage, SJ, then a student at UCD. He addressed the inaugural meeting of UCD's English Literary Society on 23 January and gave a lecture the following night, later published as 'Tradition and the Practice of Poetry', *The Southern Review*, vol. 21, no. 4, Autumn 1985, pp. 873–88. Eliot's presentation to the English Literary Society was a response to Rev. Burke Savage's principal address, on the subject of 'Literature at the Irish Crossroads'. In his response Eliot spoke of Yeats, Joyce and the strong tradition of a Catholic literature in Ireland.

7. Samuel Beckett's letters confirm that he had strong objections to Herbert Read's invitation to write the preface to the *Thorns of Thunder* anthology (*LSB*, vol. I, pp. 320–1, 325–7, 366–7). Eluard had suggested him as a critic with a wide audience in England, and it was perhaps Read's English establishment credentials that irked Coffey, Devlin and Beckett. Their objection might also stem from solidarity to

MacGreevy, and an earlier offence MacGreevy had taken to Read's literary criticism. In an essay on 'The Modern Novel' in *Reason and Romanticism: Essays in literary criticism* (London: Faber & Gwyer, 1926), Read had claimed that Joyce's *Ulysses* lacked 'a sense of intellectual progress' and was 'an art deficient in aspiration' (p. 221). MacGreevy repudiated this interpretation (which he dismissed as 'stupid') in a letter to *The Irish Statesman*, arguing that Read was failing to appreciate the role of Stephen Dedalus as the artistic and moral foil to Bloom, in his vision and purpose (Thomas MacGreevy, 'Reason and Romanticism', *The Irish Statesman*, 25 December 1926, pp. 879–80). Read was then editor of *The Burlington Magazine*, a fine-art magazine in a similar tradition to *The Connoisseur*, for which MacGreevy worked as assistant editor in the 1920s, and MacGreevy's reaction may have been a symptom of a general frustration with the London art scene – a frustration evident in the introduction to his 1945 essay on Jack Yeats, *Jack B. Yeats: An appreciation and an interpretation* (Dublin: Victor Waddington, 1945).

8. Eileen MacCarvill (?–1984), lecturer in the UCD English department with a keen interest in Irish art.

To George Reavey

19 April 1936   Hotel Eden Au Lac, Zürich

Dear Reavey,

As I have been abroad for the last month, correspondence has been awkward.[1] Perhaps these Eluard translations (enclosed) may arrive late but I send them in haste anyhow[.][2]

If you are writing, better continue writing to my Dublin address as I am uncertain of my movements.

Yours sincerely,

Denis Devlin

Autograph letter signed. 1 leaf (folded), 2 sides. *Header*: Hotel Eden Au Lac, Zürich. *Address*: George Reavey, Esq., 30 Red Lion Square, London, WC1, England. George Reavey Papers, Container 49.5, HRC, UTx.

---

1. Éamon de Valera was in Zürich from March to May 1936 for specialist treatment at the University Eye Clinic, under Alfred Vogt. An article in the *Irish Independent* on 11 May 1936 indicates that Devlin had accompanied de Valera on his trip.

2. The enclosures have not been found. Devlin contributed five Eluard translations to *ToT*: 'She of Always, All of Her', 'Nakedness of Truth', 'Girls in Love', 'One for All' and 'They Are Alike'.

To George Reavey

[May 1936]   39 Upper Mount Street, Dublin

Dear Reavey,

My answering letter late as usual. Sorry. Just back from Zürich.

I like some of your changes and not others. In **They are alike**

I meet you and I stop

I am young you must remember goes.[1] In **One for all** I like your suggestion for the last stanza, but not **Adorned with my desires.** [S]ouhaité surely does not mean desire, but 'wish' almost in the sense of 'will'.[2]

In **They are alike.** I think **for you to replace it** is necessary to the rhythm.[3] I would accept the other changes.

I hope you will send me a copy of the book when it appears. And could you let me know when the surrealiste exhibition is likely to take place? I might manage a weekend. Of course I have no objections to the publication of She of Always. What review is it?[4]

When do you propose to publish my book after the Eluard? I can quite see that the latter will help its sale. At the same time an excess of business method does not seem necessary in the case of a book of poems. I hope it will sell well but I find it hard to believe. Do get it out soon. People here think I am hoaxing.

Thanks for sending on the request from Jolas.

Yours sincerely,

Denis Devlin

Typed letter signed. Handwritten corrections. 1 leaf, 1 side. Text from the translations, and the poem titles up to line 8 are typed in red ink (bold grey here). *Dating*: Devlin dates the letter 'Wednesday'. It was written shortly after his return from Zürich in May 1936 (see DD to George Reavey, 19 April 1936, n. 1), and pre-dates the postcard of 3 June in which Devlin responds to an invitation regarding a possible trip to London for the International Surrealist Exhibition. George Reavey Papers, Container 49.5, HRC, UTx.

---

1. In the published text, these lines read: 'I meet you I stop/I am young you must remember' (*ToT*, p. 47).

2. The final text gives 'Adorned with that which I have wished' (*ToT*, p. 45), from Eluard's 'Parées de ce que j'ai souhaité' (*OC*, vol. I, p. 398).

3. In *ToT* the first stanza of 'They Are Alike' closes with the line: 'The subtle dress which invents you/For you to replace it' (*ToT*, p. 47) from Eluard's 'La robe habile que t'invente/Pour que tu la remplaces' (*OC*, vol. I, p. 381).

4. A publication of 'She of Always, All of Her' prior to *ToT* has not been found.

* * * * *

To George Reavey

3 June 1936   39 Upper Mount Street, Dublin

Dear Reavey,

Thanks very much for inviting me but I would not put you about & besides if I can get across I must stay with or near some people I know.

Could you send me back my MS? I have made a lot of changes & it wld. save messing up the proofs later. Charge postage to me as I don't know how much it would be & P.O.s are a nuisance now I'm in a hurry[.]

Yours

Denis Devlin

Autograph postcard signed. Prepaid Irish postal stationery postcard. *Address*: George Reavey, Esq., European Literary Bureau, 30 Red Lion Square, London, WC1. George Reavey Papers, Container 49.5, HRC, UTx.

To George Reavey

23 June 1936   39 Upper Mount Street, Dublin

Dear Reavey,

I am sending four Breton translations[:] 'Plutôt la vie' [,] 'L'Aigrette' [,] 'Allotropie' and 'La Sphinx Vertebral'[.] They are from Le
Revolver.[1] I hope they reach you in time.

I brought home a bunch of those 'Left' reviews.[2] Their poetry is
much of a muchness, isn't it? I don't imagine the Editor of 'Contemp.
Prose & [P]oetry' will want to take mine which of course are not surrealist anyhow.[3]

I hope the exhibition continues to be a success. I have sent out
the prospectuses. It occurs to me that as you already, I think, send
[*for* sent] some to Ireland, I should let you know of the people I
send them to. I will make out a list of people likely to buy in Dublin
which you might use in future if you wished. Indeed I should prefer
not to distribute the prospectuses for my own book myself. There was
another (stupid) article in the 'Irish Times' last Saturday on the exhibition.[4] Shall send you cuttings if I can get them now.

> Yours
>
> Denis Devlin

Autograph letter signed. 1 leaf, 2 sides. George Reavey Papers, Container
49.5, HRC, UTx.

---

1. 'Plutôt la vie' and 'L'Aigrette' are poems from André Breton's *Clair de terre*
(1923); 'Allotropie' and 'Le Sphinx Vertébral' are from *Le revolver à cheveux blancs*
(1932); Devlin's versions of these poems – 'Rather Life', 'The Plume', 'Allotropy'
and 'The Vertebrate Sphinx' – were published in *Contemporary Poetry and Prose*, vols
4–5, Aug–Sept 1936, pp. 82–5, evidently at Reavey's instigation.

2. Presumably Devlin did manage to attend the International Surrealist Exhibition,
which opened on 11 June 1936. In the mid-1930s English intellectual culture was
dominated by what Stephen Spender described as an 'orthodoxy of the left'. *The
Left Review* and *The European Quarterly* were established in 1934; *Poetry and the
People* followed in 1938. If these publications were not all explicitly aligned with

communism, they shared an interest in social and political issues on a domestic and international level – working-class conditions, the Spanish Civil War, the rise of fascism. W.H. Auden, Stephen Spender, Cecil Day Lewis, Herbert Read and Sylvia Townsend Warner were all contributors.

3. The editor of the short-lived *Contemporary Poetry and Prose*, which did accept Devlin's Breton translations, was the young communist poet Roger Roughton. The first issue of the magazine was a 'surrealist double number' to coincide with the International Surrealist Exhibition; a Picasso number followed, and a 'Declaration on Spain' that was signed by the English Surrealist Group.

4. *The Irish Times* ran an article headed 'More about Surrealism: The London exhibition', lampooning the absence of aesthetic standards on display. The author, 'M.C.', notes that '[i]rreverent visitors […] have attached kippers and other ornaments to the pictures (where they remained, because nobody could be quite sure that they were not a part of the original design)' (20 June 1936, p. 7).

* * * * *

To George Reavey

10 July 1936   39 Upper Mount Street, Dublin

Dear Reavey,

I am waiting for my MS and I should like to have it as soon as you can possibly send it. I have a little free time now at night, I want to use it; if you delay I shall find myself near September and in the devil of a flurry as I shall be going to Geneva then, and besides I want to go on holidays before that. So please do send it at once. I am pestered by people here asking me when the book is coming out – I hope that means they are going to buy it!

I passed through London recently twice but had no time to call. I hope the exhibition has continued to be successful.

                            Yours –

                            Denis <u>Devlin</u>

Autograph letter signed. 1 leaf (folded), 3 sides. George Reavey Papers, Container 49.5, HRC, UTx.

To George Reavey

23 July 1936   39 Upper Mount Street, Dublin

Dear Reavey,

When are you sending me my MS.? I wait it anxiously day by day – I have already explained my difficulty about time. I find it hard to understand the delay – unless the MS has got lost. And in any case since I have seen that magazine 'Contemporary Prose & Poetry' I am not particularly anxious to be published in it.

I got the autographed Eluard thanks[1] – I had something accepted by Transition.[2]

I hope you will send me the poems at once – I shall not keep them long.

Yours sincerely,
Denis Devlin

Autograph letter signed. 1 leaf (folded), 2 sides. George Reavey Papers, Container 49.5, HRC, UTx.

---

1. 600 copies of the first edition of *TofT* were published. Copy no. 1 contained an original drawing by Picasso and an Eluard MS. Nos. 2–51 were signed by Eluard.

2. See DD to Ruth de Verry, 13 October 1936.

To George Reavey

7 September 1936   39 Upper Mount Street, Dublin

Dear Reavey,

    Sorry was not able to answer your card: I have been abroad for the last 3 wks.[1] Will you be in Dublin during next fortnight? I shld. like to have seen you.

                Yours

                   Denis Devlin

Autograph postcard signed. Prepaid Irish postal stationery postcard. *Address*: George Reavey, Esq., "Stramore", Chichester Park, Belfast. Marked "Please forward". George Reavey Papers, Container 49.5, HRC, UTx.

---

1. It is likely that this trip was for pleasure rather than departmental business, taken before Devlin headed to Geneva for the League of Nations Assembly. According to an article in *The Irish Press*, Devlin and the Irish delegation left for Geneva on Friday, 18 September.

To Ruth de Verry, transition magazine

13 October 1936   39 Upper Mount Street, Dublin

Dear Mr. de Verry,[1]

I wish to acknowledge, with very many thanks, receipt of a copy of the Fall issue of Transition containing my poem.[2] Your letter of August the 14th last also arrived.

I think you must have been misinformed regarding my job – I am not Professor of English.[3] I did lecture at the University for some time, but I left it & am now in our diplomatic service.

I mention it simply in order to avoid embarrassment to the real Professor, and I don't wish you to rectify it or any thing of the sort.

           Yours very truly.

           Denis Devlin.

Autograph letter signed. 1 leaf (folded), 2 sides. Papers of the magazine *Transition*, MS Am 2068, Series II, Folder 80, HU.

---

1. Ruth de Verry (dates unknown) was secretary to James Johnson Sweeney (1900–86), who, along with Eugène and Maria Jolas in Paris, was a partner editor of *transition* magazine. Sweeney was based in New York, and worked at the Museum of Modern Art. De Verry despatched a large portion of the magazine's correspondence. Devlin has mistaken her gender, and possibly taken her for an editor.

2. Devlin's 'You Don't Know a Good Thing When You See It' was published in *transition*, no. 25, Fall 1936, p. 9. It was later published under the title 'Celibate Recusant' in *Lough Derg*.

3. The entry for Devlin in the contributor biographies to this issue states: 'an Irish poet living in Dublin, published a joint volume of poems in 1930 with Brian Coffey, and in 1935 was made Professor of English at the National University.'

To George Reavey

14 October 1936   39 Upper Mount Street, Dublin

Dear Reavey,

I wish to acknowledge receipt of your cheque for <u>two guineas</u> for the Breton translations & to thank you very much. I shall let you see any others I may do from time to time.

I quite understand why publication should be delayed since your merger, and of course I do realise it will have had many advantages – in particular I am glad to have been able to make some corrections.[1] However, I hope you & Nott will decide to bring me out soon. My poems are not very fashionable for the English market now (I don't mean to carp & suggest that the fashionable type is inferior, nothing of that sort) but I think they shld. sell pretty well in Dublin.

By the way Transition published a poem of mine in last number and as you introduced me to them, you are due the usual percentage aren't you? That is if they pay me. In the mean time, when you write me next, you might let me know all about your terms.

I have made first inquiries regarding your relative; I shall go on to more definite ones & let you know quite soon what definite chances there may be.[2] His qualifications seem impressive.

> Yours v.
>
> Denis Devlin

Autograph letter signed. 1 leaf (folded), 4 sides. George Reavey Papers, Container 49.5, HRC, UTx.

---

1. Although there was no formal merger between Reavey's Europa Press and Stanley Nott's publishing house (Stanley Nott, Ltd.), an arrangement was made for Nott to take on some of the printing and marketing for the Europa Poets series, to relieve pressure on Reavey. In a letter of 4 February 1937, Reavey informs Devlin that an excess of work with the European Literary Bureau meant that *Intercessions* may be coming out with Stanley Nott. This eventuality did not arise, and the arrangement between the two fell away – see DD to George Reavey, 7 June 1937, n. 1.

2. The relative on whose behalf Reavey has asked Devlin to make inquiries in the department has not been identified.

To George Reavey

9 November 1936   39 Upper Mount Street, Dublin

Dear Reavey,

Enclosed is MS. Please forgive delay – caused by examination I had to sit for & read for all spare time. Note that the attached "Argument with Justice" is the correct one – I have marked it with a blue x. The text, I fear, is in a dreadful mess.

I shall write in a few days about your relative. I have got in touch with people but not decisive news yet – but I think there may be some hope.

Yours

Denis Devlin

P.S. Title: "Intercessions"

Autograph letter signed. 2 leaves, 2 sides. George Reavey Papers, Container 49.5, HRC, UTx.

To Thomas MacGreevy

28 November 1936   39 Upper Mount Street, Dublin

My dear Tom,

Brian passed on to me your remark about my unpregnant silences and I realise that it is indeed a long time since I have written. My silence anyhow is sterile. I am wondering how, with such strong bones and muscles, I am so lazy, I am sure there is some physical cause for my lack of energy.

I learn you are in the country and writing.[1] I hope you are getting fun from it. Is it a novel? Otherwise how do you feel now? Rebellious as ever: Brian told me how you punctured Yeats's old Swami.[2] It must have been a luridly comic scene but you might have given yourself the chance to get into the LordAlmighty anthology.[3] It's a pity they made Yeats its editor as it will make & break loyalties for years to come which is very unfair to people who have to make money. I am thinking here of myself in perhaps the near future: my job is now odious to me. But my respectful objection – you know best your own intentions – to your anti-cant action is not there only because you are spoiling your chances of material success. I think that the object of satire especially is publication. You don't have to nourish yourself.

Reavey is at last somewhat definite about my book. I dislike intensely its coming out in a private edition as suggesting preciosity – however it is too late now to change. I was thinking of sending you a copy of the MS and asking you to be so good as to read it through and give me your opinions. Would you? I am very sick & doubtful of them now. I am extremely painstaking & conscientious in my writing and yet I feel I need the conversation of other poets more than most.

When I have plenty to say and want to write you I cannot, I am in the office, I must put it off till Sunday and then as now I am quite dried up.

Autograph letter unsigned. 1 leaf, 2 sides. *Header:* Department of External Affairs, Dublin (Roinn Gnóthaí Coigríche, Baile Átha Cliath). *Dating:* Devlin dates the letter '28.11.36' and writes above the header: 'First part of letter sent 4/12. Dislocation due to difference of locality'. Thomas MacGreevy Papers, 8112/1–16, TCD.

---

1. MacGreevy had temporarily moved from London to Toppesfield in the Essex countryside, where he had the loan of a cottage.

2. Yeats formed a close relationship with the Hindu poet and philosopher Shri Purohit Swami after Swami's arrival in Britain in 1931. In 1935 they travelled to Majorca together to work on translations of the Upanishads, published as *The Ten Principal Upanishads* (1937). A further record of MacGreevy's encounter with Swami has not been found.

3. Yeats edited *The Oxford Book of Modern Verse* in 1936. MacGreevy's 'Aodh Ruadh Ó Domhnaill' and 'Homage to Jack Yeats' were in fact included in this anthology.

To George Reavey

8 December 1936   39 Upper Mount Street, Dublin

Dear Reavey,

Have made two "contacts" which may be useful. Please send your relative's name[,] address etc. & any other qualifications he may have if you have them handy.

Yours v.s.

Denis D.

Autograph postcard signed. Prepaid Irish postal stationery postcard. Devlin's address written beneath signature. *Address*: George Reavey, Esq., European Literary Bureau, 30 Red Lion Square, London, WC1. George Reavey Papers, Container 49.5, HRC, UTx.

To Thomas MacGreevy

22 January 1937   39 Upper Mount Street, Dublin

My dear Tom,

It was very nice of you to have come to see me last Thursday at such an inconvenient hour. I hope I did not give an impression of too much officialdom – I don't care to cultivate an elaborate carelessness as some people do who are dissatisfied with civil service jobs but at the same time I don't want to look too official. Thanks for the book. The preface is shocking. There is not much in the contents either though I agree with you about C. Ewart Milne, and I think Thomas O'Brien & Patrick Rowe, also new to me, should be marked good.[1]

I have been in bed with 'flu for the last few days. Half Dublin is affected and in bed but a doctor told my sister that this is pure imagination & laziness on its part as the real 'flu has not got here, and that half-Dublin has only got a bad cold.

I am sending you the poem "Bacchanal" which you promised to read; and will you see how the interjection sounds? And what do you think of the other alterations? And could you send it back in a few days as I promised to send Reavey a good complete text for next week and I don't want to hold it up & this is the only copy of Bacchanal I possess and it's too long to type again. I intend to omit "Colonial Expansion"[,] "The Word" and "By the Boat Train".[2] I think they quarrel with the general tone. What do you think? I am also inclined to omit "Moments" I & II and "Actress Attracting".[3] What do you think of "Argument with Justice"? Please send it back too.

"The Statue & The Perturbed Burghers" is a present to you. Would you prefer "piano" to "spinet" in the 3rd last line? I might, but I hate the word piano. I am including this piece.

In "Arg. With Justice" I don't like "Rimbaud" now. I thought of putting Chartres instead – ?[4]

This ['The Statue and The Perturbed Burghers'] is not a dedication to you hence the carbon copy. I have a prejudice, which I can't explain to myself, against dedications. In any case, I won't dedicate for years ahead.

In "Death Her Beasts, Ignoble Beasts" Brian thinks the last line a bit weak in expression – the rest of the poem wld. seem to demand something more solid. Do you think so?

I can say & feel now that years have passed since … 10 years have passed since my awakened life began. I met the foulest Protestants the other night with Brian who provoked one of them very amusingly, saying to him as the climax of [a] piece of abusive repartee "You are a classified geological specimen!" Everyone was relieved and laughed – I have had for the month or two past the most unusual feelings of delight for no reason, or rather a great variety of feelings, without any object, always closed by delight. I think I have dissuaded my conscience entirely of Justification, a great relief.

– This is all blather – it's 1.30 a.m.

I have been asked to meet John Drinkwater and have refused – or rather declined – the man can't be interesting.[5] But I'm going to undo the refusal as my hostess attracts me. That sounds flatfooted but the civil service has impaired my potentialities of appropriate expression – I feel expurged.

For the nth time, I have shirked "Tristram Shandy".[6] Is it really worth reading? I liked "Pitié pour les Femmes" [by] de Montherlant.[7] Are you going to translate any of that trilogy[?][8] I felt like the questionable hero, I actually blushed at some revelation of his character. Have you read Milton's tract on Divorce?[9] To morrow I must go to the office again … my [?9] days illness has been heavenly to me[.]

Please send my Bacchanal back soon & Argument with Justice; in sheer nervousness I am sending an envelope stamped for return so that you wouldn't have to miss a mail through being far from a post office.

> Yours
>
> Denis

– I think you said Paddy cld. live in in Trinity for £10 a year! Surely not? He is quite sick now poor fellow. D.[10]

How is it about your play?[11]

Autograph letter signed. 2 leaves, 4 sides. *Header*: Department of External Affairs, Dublin (ROINN GNÓTHAÍ COIGRÍCHE, BAILE ÁTHA CLIATH). Final postscript written above greeting on recto side of first page. Thomas MacGreevy Papers, 8112/1–16, TCD.

---

1. The book is *Good-bye Twilight: Songs of the struggle in Ireland* (London: Lawrence & Wishart, 1936), an anthology of Irish war poetry edited and introduced by Leslie Daiken, with woodcuts from Harry Kernoff. In Daiken's polemical introduction he describes the two main tendencies in contemporary Irish poetry – escapism and traditionalism – as responses to the 'betrayal of the national aspiration by the Treaty of 1921'. MacGreevy, Devlin, Coffey and Beckett, placed in the former camp, are described as part of a 'cultured studentry' which has 'fostered pessimism'. Their work is not included in this anthology. Patrick Kavanagh is one of the bigger names to make an appearance, praised in the introduction as a 'traditionalist' who has been 'rescued from village obscurity' ('Introduction', pp. xii–xvi).

2. 'Colonial Expansion' has not been identified in the NLI drafts. 'The Word' is an alternative title for 'Statement' (or 'Statement of an Irishman'), which was unpublished before Roger Little's *Translations into English from French, German and Italian Poetry* (1992) – the MSS in the NLI show that Devlin translated the poem into French. 'By the Boat Train', which had the alternative title 'Easy Remorse', has not been published.

3. 'Moments I: Girl Whirling' has not been published. 'Moments: II' was omitted from *Intercessions* and included in *Lough Derg and Other Poems* (1946) under the title 'Boys Bathing'. 'Actress Attracting' was also omitted from *Intercessions*, published as 'Poet and Comic Muse' in *Lough Derg*.

4. In the published version of 'Argument with Justice', Chartres is invoked alongside the prophet Isaiah (an icon represented in stained glass and stone in Chartres Cathedral) and the allegorical figures Mercy and Charity (*CPDD*, p. 88).

5. John Drinkwater (1882–1937), English poet and playwright, best known for his historical drama. Drinkwater died two months after this letter was sent.

6. Irish novelist Laurence Sterne (1713–68) published *The Life and Opinions of Tristram Shandy, Gentleman* in nine volumes between 1759 and 1767.

7. Henry de Montherlant's *Pitié pour les femmes* (1936) is the second in a tetralogy of novels opening with *Les jeunes filles* (1936).

8. MacGreevy did in fact translate the first two volumes of de Montherlant's tetralogy, in a single volume edition, *Pity for Women* (London: Routledge, 1937).

9. English poet and polemicist John Milton (1608–74), associated with radical Protestantism and the English Civil War, published four controversial pamphlets on divorce between 1643 and 1645: *The Doctrine and Discipline of Divorce*, *The Judgement of Martin Bucer*, *Tetrachordon*, and *Colasterion*.

10. Patrick Devlin was Denis' only brother.

11. See DD to Thomas MacGreevy, 15 February 1937, n. 13.

To George Reavey

30 January 1937   39 Upper Mount Street, Dublin

Dear George,

I send enclosed the MS. It ha[s] been held up because I have been waiting to get back from Tom my only copy of Bacchanal whic[h] I sent him for an opinion on the advisability of retaining or not the expression Blast the Shites! He has not yet sent it back, althou[gh] I enjoined on him to do so at once, and I sent him a telegram yesterday. So rather than hold the matter up any longer, I am sending this[.] Could you take "Bacchanal" out of the MS. you have already and put it into this one? And could you do the same for one called "In the Last Resort" of which I unfortunately have no other copy?

I wonder if you would also make the following changes in "Bacchanal"[.] (It's a very irregular and annoying thing to ask a publisher, I know, but it's Tom's fault. Please forgive it[.])

In line I (*for* 1) write 'scissors' instead of 'sunglasses'

In the last line of the 3rd. stanza, write 'Blast the Skites'
                    instead of 'Blast the Shites'

In the 5th. line from the end write 'seminal' for abundant'

I am very sorry to trouble you in this way and I hope it will be alright. I shall send on Bacchanal if it should come from Tom in the next two days, say.

Best wishes.

Yours,

Denis.

I have taken out 5 small poems from the book as planned originally, and added 1.[1] I think it will give the book a greater consistency. Do you think it is allright as at present?

I shall send you the List of Names on Monday.   D.

Typed letter signed. Postscript handwritten. 1 leaf, 1 side. George Reavey Papers, Container 49.5, HRC, UTx.

---

1. For omitted poems see DD to Thomas MacGreevy, 22 January 1937. 'Argument with Justice' is possibly the inclusion.

* * * * *

To George Reavey
[30 Jan–3 Feb 1937]

Dear George,
        Herewith definitive text of 'Bacchanal'. Sorry so late[.]
                Yrs
                        Denis

Autograph letter signed. 1 leaf, 1 side. *Header*: Department of External Affairs, Dublin (ROINN GNÓTHAÍ COIGRÍCHE, BAILE ÁTHA CLIATH). *Dating*: The final text of 'Bacchanal' follows the despatch of the MS on 30 January; Reavey acknowledges receipt of the text in a letter dated 4 February 1937. George Reavey Papers, Container 49.5, HRC, UTx.

To Seán Murphy, Assistant Secretary, Department of External Affairs
8 February 1937

Assistant Secretary.

I beg to submit a detailed account for porterage in connection with the recent journey of the President to Zurich.[1]

As you are aware, a good deal of official luggage was necessary on this journey owing to the fact that the President had to deal with official matters of various kinds both on the outward and return journeys.

I consider, in view of the fact that the President had to have considerable luggage and extra services because he was engaged on official work during the period of his absence, that the estimated cost of expenditure on official luggage should be borne by the State.

Further, the President spent three nights in London on official business, and subsistence allowance should be granted to him in respect of the nights spent in London. The usual subsistence of £2: 2: 0, per night was entirely inadequate on this, as on previous occasions, and perhaps Finance sanction might be sought for a special rate of subsistence in the circumstances.

The total expenditure on gratuities was £9: 16: 5., the greater portion of which would appear to be a reasonable charge against public funds.

Denis Devlin.

Typed letter signed. 1 leaf, 1 side. *Header*: LEATÁN MIONTUAIRISCE, paper for taking minutes. Department of Foreign Affairs Papers, DFA/46/42, National Archives of Ireland, Dublin.

----

1. See Chronology, and DD to Ria Mooney, [?22 March 1937], n. 2.

To Thomas MacGreevy
15 February 1937

My dear Tom,

Thanks very much for your letter about my poems. I'm sorry you were so rushed. It must have been a great relief to get the translations finished; that work gets very tiring, I know.[1]

Two of your suggestions are grand & I'm accepting them – 'clavichord' which is a lovely word, and the dropping of the line about fluff which will make the little picture more vivid.[2] I would admit now that much of my poetry has too much qualification. It's disheartening but it would be silly to try to change it radically now. Luckily I can remain in [the] same emotional atmosphere for years so that the changes I have been making are safe enough organically. I know too that the cause has been my anxiety to avoid intellectualisation and at the same time to make myself understood; and where the judicious deformation of a generality, then compounded with an image (this is common and I can't see how it is not consciously mechanical in most poets) would have made my meaning clear, distrusting it ([?abl.] absolute) because of its surrender to ambiguity, I have been explaining an image by yet another.

Your opinion about the publication of Bacchanal is very just.[3] It seems absurd asking for advice and then not taking it but I feel I should never respect myself if I did not publish it. I'm not risking my job lightly especially as I have other responsibilities besides myself, but I must publish it. It should not be forgiven me because it is a poem of course but it is part of my 'transcendental actuality' (Do you like that?). I have hopes too that a subscribed & limited edition will not get into their hands, and even if it does the wrong & comfortable situating of poetry as not relevant may save me. A jesuitical compromise but I can allow it to myself.

Can you recommend a good book on Petrarch?[4] [O]r perhaps on platonic love as the Italians understood it. Ronsard & du Bellay are not so much help: you can see that Ronsard's mistresses were flesh

& blood and they must have been very charming; and du Bellay is too smoky.[5] The English, Sidney & Spenser, have the Puritan split, the meaning for the soul not connected with the parts of the body and surely Petrarch must be more interesting?[6] One cannot accept the theory of platonic love as stated quite understandably in the principles. What I want to do is quite different; I have no intention of avoiding the common beliefs of today: didn't Proust justify the tired man of business who had come to accept the facing of reality (bilge!) of the courageous man of culture.[7] Still they represent the minimum of belief & the lost generation was right enough in feeling that that was necessary to discover. Eluard does not satisfy me and in any case it is too pathetic for any more words. Yeats's love poems are thin & mechanical. Smartness suits me ill and I wish I weren't so serious and without the equipment for seriousness. What I dream of is a marvellous book careful & fresh with all the incidents of natural love with no make-believe and yet with one woman, not ideal nor hortatory nor a symbol of divine qualities, but yet unique. I believe in that. Do you think I deceive myself? I should hate to do that but I cannot rid myself of my conviction. Perhaps I am thinking of the Christian woman. It is there and it must be emphasised & praised.[8] I desperately need time for reflection and reading, I want to avoid telescoping and thus gnomic poems. For instance, people look blank at 2 or 3 things I have recently written and I think the scarcity of free time is partly responsible for their being so concentrated. And what use repeating that part of Mallarmé?

I have been having a repeating dream, a type I didn't notice myself having before. Three or four nights ago it was: O'Connell St. cleared for a ceremony at dusk or twilight: nervous yellow light in sheets. Then seeming as if gliding in a very wide space although the street did not look any bigger, lines of horsemen – the Irish Jumping Military Team in fact – came on parade. Each line composed of about 12 men close together[,] each line widely separated from the other, they galloped at amazing speed, they would suddenly stop and curvet and prance and rear, they moved as one man with the most perfect beauty and regularity. The leader too. At the end the leader reared up and three quarters backward slowly filling me with delight, and tremendously, he & his horse great till the group was a colossus ... The second dream was similar. I was in New York at an Irish gathering, deal table and drinks. An angry States-I.R.A. discussion arose. It went on for a while, I offered no comment though they wanted me to. Finally, a delapidated [*for* dilapidated] I.R.A. man attacked me with bitter words and I angrily said to the tableful that this controversy was out-of-date in Ireland, we were thinking of other things. The I[.]R[.]A[.] got slowly interested and began to talk Irish, I realised to impress the foreigners. I talked Irish with him willingly enough feeling I might as well if it pleased him. He took my arm and we walked out ... and into O'Connell Street. A carnival of the Nice type was in rehearsal and when we got half-way up the street, it began[.] It had all the usual richness and variety of colour that I like but again what was interesting was the perfection[,] cleanness and beauty of every movement. There was dancing and parading – no wonder that was drilled. But besides the ragged things a crowd does laughing and short-running even talking was organised into groups and measured movement.

Analysis of the 2nd dream is easy & does not interest me much: The day before I had been saying my weariness with Frank O'Connor and his school of short stories about the 'movement' ... All-including and symmetrical.[9]

Mother has, very tentatively once or twice, expressed some doubts about Paddy's going to Trinity. She doesn't mind au fond.[10] But the other evening while talking about [it] she laughed quietly and said "Well, I hope it isn't really like Sam Beckett's book. It's a frightful book" she said continuing to laugh.[11] I reassured her with heavy arguments. Her expression made me see that she had admired the book but it was amusing her <u>inclining</u> to hope that Trinity was not altogether like the book.

I hope you are content & going to be comfortable in your new way of living and new rooms.[12] Has anything further happened regarding the Russian play?[13] I am being painted by a girl. I fence now and like it very much.

Isn't everybody very 'honourable' in the Casement affair?[14]

Yours affectionately

Denis.

Autograph letter signed. 6 leaves, 12 sides. Thomas MacGreevy Papers, 8112/1–16, TCD.

---

1. Devlin refers either to MacGreevy's Henry de Montherlant translations (see DD to Thomas MacGreevy, 22 January 1937, n. 7), or *Forbidden Journey: From Peking to Kashmir*, published by Heinemann in 1937, from Swiss travel-writer Ella Maillart's *Oasis interdites: de Pékin au Cachemire*.

2. For the publication of *Intercessions*, Devlin in fact stuck with the original 'spinet' in the final stanza of 'The Statue and the Perturbed Burghers'.

3. 'Bacchanal', drafted under the title 'News of Revolution', is one of a few early Devlin poems that register the political temperature of the age.

4. Francesco Petrarca (1303–74), known as Petrarch, Italian Renaissance poet renowned for his innovative sonnet sequence, *Canzoniere*.

5. Pierre de Ronsard (1524–85) and Joachim du Bellay (1522–60) were members of a group of French Renaissance poets known as 'La Pléiade' ('The Host'), who studied under the classical scholar Jean Daurat, and argued in defence of the French vernacular as a language for poetry. Du Bellay's *L'Olive* (1549) and de Ronsard's *Les amours de Cassandre* (1552) were sonnet sequences that followed Petrarch's *Canzoniere* in exploring the notion of platonic love, but de Ronsard's sonnets were noted for their sensuality.

6. English Renaissance poets Sir Philip Sidney (1554–86) and Edmund Spenser (155[2/3]–99), who forged a sonnet tradition in English after Petrarch.

7. Marcel Proust (1871–1922), French novelist who exerted a great influence on modernist fiction. Devlin perhaps refers to the fate of Proust's character Charles Swann in *À la recherche du temps perdu* (1913–37).

8. In this march through love poetry in the French and English literary traditions Devlin is rehearsing concerns seen across his career, with the form appropriate for expressing 'natural love', and with the representation of woman both real and absolute. In his introduction to *The Heavenly Foreigner* (1967) Brian Coffey points us to another model Devlin was looking to in the 1930s: Maurice Scève (*c.* 1501–64), French poet of the Lyonnese school, whose theory of spiritual love derived from

Petrarch and Plato. For the fullest treatment of Devlin's engagement with Petrarchan and Scevian traditions see Alex Davis, '"Heart-Affairs Diplomat": Later poems', in *A Broken Line: Denis Devlin and Irish poetic modernism* (Dublin: UCD Press, 2000), pp. 85–125.

9. The ellipsis in this sentence is followed by a page break, and the transition to 'All-including and symmetrical' and the following paragraph about Devlin's family, is strikingly abrupt. We can make sense of the statement 'All-including and symmetrical', however, in light of Devlin's dismissive remarks about the realist response to the conflict in Ireland, exemplified by Frank O'Connor's *Guests of the Nation* (1931) and the work of Sean O'Faolain.

10. au fond (Fr.): fundamentally/at heart.

11. Beckett's short-story collection *More Pricks than Kicks* (1934), following the antics of the student Belacqua. The collection features many Trinity landmarks and detailed descriptions of the surrounding Dublin streets.

12. By December 1936 MacGreevy had returned to London and was living in Harrington Road, South Kensington rather than with Hester Dowden in nearby Chelsea.

13. The play has not been identified, and was probably never completed or performed. Devlin asks after a play in his previous letter, DD to Thomas MacGreevy, 22 January 1937. In a letter of 25 March 1937, Beckett congratulates MacGreevy on news of a play, and asks whether he should be paid a retainer between acceptance and performance (*LSB*, vol. I, p. 469). There are abandoned fragments of plays among MacGreevy's papers in TCD, some original works, some translations, though not from Russian.

14. Roger Casement (1864–1916), an Irish-born British diplomat who had been honoured with a knighthood for a report exposing human rights abuses in Peru, before devoting himself to the Irish nationalist cause. He was tried and executed for procuring German arms to assist with the Easter Rising. In the 1930s Casement's life and death were still of intense interest to the Irish public, and the campaign for the repatriation of Casement's remains (finally granted in 1965) was escalating. The British government had released pages of inflammatory diaries exposing Casement's homosexuality before the execution. In subsequent years a number of biographers voiced suspicions over the veracity of those diaries. Dr William Maloney published *The Forged Casement Diaries* in Dublin in 1936, the book W.B. Yeats responds to in his poem 'Roger Casement'.

To Niall Montgomery
17 February 1937

Dear Niall,

Could you pick out some of your translations, short, sonnets, not more than 20 lines & bring to me in the Office to-morrow (Thursday)? The review is giving one page next month & taken the G. de Nerval & a small Rimbaud but I said about your sonnets.[1] I think the most conventional wld. be best. Come in the morning before one o'clock, or if you can only come during lunchtime, leave them with the Porters for me. And could you bring the "Fleurs du Mal"?

>   Yrs
>
>   Denis

Autograph letter signed. 1 leaf, 1 side. Niall Montgomery Papers (MS 50,118), MS 50,118/26/23, National Library of Ireland, Dublin.

---

1. Devlin and Niall Montgomery had been collaborating on translations of French poetry into Irish since Devlin's return to Dublin from Paris, and the NLI archive contains close to fifty translations that are connected to this project. 'Na Leannáin' is from Gerard de Nerval's 'Les Cydalises', 'Tórramh' is from Arthur Rimbaud's 'Veillées'. These translations into Irish were published in the March 1937 issue of *Ireland Today*, vol. II, no. 3, p. 44, followed by 'La Beauté', a sonnet from Baudelaire's *Les fleurs du mal* (drafted under the Irish title 'An Áille') and 'Brise Marine' from Mallarmé (drafted under the title 'Leoithne Gaoithe Muirí') in *Ireland Today*, vol. II, no. 5, May 1937, pp. 52–3, under the pseudonym D. O'Dobhailein. Holograph MSS in Devlin's hand led J.C.C. Mays to infer, in his notes to *CPDD*, that rather than dividing the translation work between them (as one MS shows they planned to), Devlin completed the translation work and Montgomery revised them. This letter suggests that the labour of translation was, in fact, divided.

To George Reavey

[February 1937]

Dear George,

Here is the list of names & addresses to which prospectuses could be sent.[1] I don't know all of them.

Thanks for mentioning me to Wollman – I had a letter from him this morning.[2]

If there are too many names on the list, I think those ticked off in ink are the most likely[.]

Best wishes

Denis

Autograph letter signed. 1 leaf, 1 side. *Header*: Department of External Affairs, Dublin (Roinn Gnóthaí Coigríche, Baile Átha Cliath). *Dating*: In DD to George Reavey, 30 January 1937, the letter accompanying the *Intercessions* MS, Devlin promises the list of names on Monday (1 February). The sequence of letters to Reavey suggests that this is Devlin's earliest response to Reavey's letter of 4 February 1937, in which he mentions having passed Devlin's name on to Wollman. George Reavey Papers, Container 49.5, HRC, UTx.

1. List has not been found. See DD to George Reavey, 23 June 1936.

2. In a letter dated 4 February 1937, Reavey writes that he has passed on Devlin's details to a M. Wollman, who is editing an anthology of recent poetry (George Reavey Papers, Container 49.5, HRC, UTx). Maurice Wollman (dates unknown) was senior English master at Barking Abbey School, according to a brief publisher's biography. He edited three poetry anthologies in the 1930s: *Modern Poetry, 1922–1935: An anthology* (London: Macmillan, 1934), *Poems of Twenty Years: An anthology, 1918–1938* (London: Macmillan, 1938), and *Selections from Modern Poets: An anthology, 1918–1938* (London: Macmillan, 1939) – a more concise and slightly altered version of the previous anthology. No selections from Reavey, Beckett or Devlin were chosen for the Macmillan anthologies.

To George Reavey

15 March 1937   39 Upper Mount Street, Dublin

Dear George,

Anything stirring?[1] My girlfriend's getting anxious.[2] Condone colloquialisms but youth is flying; wonderful day outside after dirty weather. Patriotic wishes [on] our national fête.[3] I have just been painted: feeling cocky.

                    Yrs.
                        Denis.

Autograph postcard signed. Prepaid Irish postal stationery postcard. *Address*: George Reavey, Esq., 35 Red Lion Square, London, WC1. George Reavey Papers, Container 49.5, HRC, UTx.

---

1. Reavey had written to Devlin on 8 March 1937, enclosing a specimen page of the book, and informing him that the MS was now in the printer's hands (George Reavey Papers, Container 49.5, HRC, UTx). That letter had perhaps not been received at the time of writing this postcard.

2. See DD to Ria Mooney, [?22 March 1937], pp. 71–2.

3. Celebrations for St Patrick's Day, 17 March, were already under way in parts of Ireland and internationally. On the day itself, a national holiday in Ireland, a military parade was held on College Green.

To Thomas MacGreevy

19 March 1937   39 Upper Mount Steet, Dublin

My dear Tom,

I write briefly to enquire of your health and state, and to wonder whether I should execute a half-formed intention, which by then would have been complete, of visiting London for a few days at Eastertime. Some repose and leisure would be usefully wasted by me. In addition, I might have a progressive conference with my agent & publisher and arrange for the passage of the printing of my book from the 21st safely to the 22nd letter of the first line in the first poem. What mysterious and wearying tardiness. Or perhaps I shall weep all over George's offices.

Please write and let me know that you are not unwell.

In brevity & post haste,

Yours

Denis.

I am bored in immense prospection before the edition of Gogarty's book. All Dublin is ginger & [?*for* in] self-satisfaction to receive the two-term epigrams [of] that unbearable obvious Dublin wit.[1]

Autograph letter signed. 1 leaf, 2 sides. Thomas MacGreevy Papers, 8112/1–16, TCD.

---

1. Oliver St John Gogarty (1878–1957), Irish poet, surgeon and politician, is recognised as the inspiration for Buck Mulligan in Joyce's *Ulysses*. *As I Was Going Down Sackville Street: A phantasy in fact* (1937) was Gogarty's first substantial prose work, pitched between a memoir and a novel.

To Ria Mooney

[?22 March 1937]   39 Upper Mount Street, Dublin

Dearest Ria –

I needn't tell you of my disgust at not being able to come.[1] It was the Office. I had a row. You see I owed them a large (for me) sum of money but it had been understood, on my plea, that they would waive their claim to it till my holidays were over.[2] On Friday night & Saturday morning I had a slight row and then in pure spite, on Saturday morning, they presented me with a claim for it to be paid. Luckily I hadn't my check-book then so I couldn't pay. You can imagine how furious I was and I showed it. It meant of course that I couldn't go to Paris because I simply have got a certain sum and no more for Paris. I should have to start thinking of borrowing etc. I was so angry and dejected and thought that I could not now afford to use any money – that sounds mean but I don't intend it so – that I couldn't come down. I hope and feel that you will be disappointed like me but I hope you weren't annoyed. However now stupid & inadequate my explanation reads please darling read more into it than I've written. I wish you hadn't gone to that cursed village, to which one cannot get nor come from.[3] And sweetest I implore you not to turn to Ctn. C. Esq. for temporary amusement.[4]

Things, by the way, are clearing up about Paris now. I am arranging with the Office by devious ways. They are comical, more 'temperamental' than actresses! I'm sure you'll think. It was not "Bags" anyhow. He was nice. I'll tell you about it. My love & inmost thoughts to you. Are you having any luck in the show?

Yours

Denis

Autograph letter signed. 1 leaf, 2 sides. *Dating*: Devlin dates this letter 'Monday', but the incident in the department, related again in the following letter to MacGreevy, would place this on Monday 22 March. Ria Mooney Papers (MS 49,603), MS 49,603/10, National Library of Ireland, Dublin.

---

1. In late March 1937 Mooney was between Abbey commissions – she played Rosie Redmond in O'Casey's *The Plough and the Stars* in the first week of March, and Kit De Lury in Lennox Robinson's *Killycreggs in Twilight* from 19–24 April (this production was staged in a double bill with Lady Gregory's *Dervorgilla*, in which Devlin's sister Moya played the title role). She was launching the Abbey Experimental Theatre at this time, which opened at the Peacock Theatre on 5 April 1937 with *Alarm Among the Clerks*, the debut play from Devlin's UCD friend Mervyn Wall.

2. The money Devlin owed the department might relate to expense claims for his trips to Zürich and Geneva, about which there is a folder of correspondence in the National Archives. See Department of Foreign Affairs Papers, DFA/46/42, NAI.

3. The village is possibly Annamoe, County Wicklow. Lilian Roberts Finlay, a novelist who graduated from the Abbey School of Theatre, wrote of the parties Ria Mooney hosted for younger actresses at a cottage in Annamoe, in her autobiographical novel *Always in My Mind* (London: Collins, 1988). This detail is corroborated in the findings of research student Ciara O'Dowd, author of the *Chasing Aideen: Encounters with women in Irish theatre history* blog, who identifies this cottage as a Mooney family holiday home. See https://chasingaideen.com/2016/04/14/79-rias-sunset-wealth-in-wicklow/ [accessed 28 June 2017].

4. 'Ctn. C', who has not been identified, is mentioned as a potential love rival in two of Devlin's letters to Mooney. He is presumably a fellow actor (see DD to Ria Mooney, [26 May/2 June 1937]).

To Thomas MacGreevy

23 March 1937   39 Upper Mount Street, Dublin

Dear Tom,

It's disastrous but I can't come. I'm absolutely & completely broke, haven't a sou[.] I have to give up my whole month's pay for a debt to the Dept. I'm very disappointed. Isn't it appalling not to be able even to make some money since I have to waste my time in this pigsty!

I hope you haven't already cancelled your holiday; I did say <u>might</u> didn't I? I do hope so. I've fallen in love again – it's the only thing you can do without money.

Yours in black melancholy
Denis

Autograph lettercard signed. Prepaid Irish postal stationery lettercard. *Address*: Thomas McGreevy, Esq., 49 Harrington Road, London, SW7. Thomas MacGreevy Papers, 8112/1–16, TCD.

To George Reavey

24 March 1937   39 Upper Mount Street, Dublin

Dear George,

I had hoped to be able to come to London for a few days during Easter but I can't now manage it to my great disappointment.

I have been published in "Transition"[,] "The Dublin Magazine"[,] "Ireland To-Day"[,] and if you think it useful to mention it, the Eluards & Bretons in "Contemporary Prose and Poetry." I was concerned when a student in Paris with a Left Bank review of post-surrealist tendency and was published therein (in translation of my work).[1] The fact that I am in the Foreign Office is not to go in, please. Nott has already put it in notices in the Dublin papers confound him![2] I find it hard to write the actual words which would be suitable for a blurb (not that I object to blurbs) but I offer you with some diffidence the following remarks which you may be able to transpose a little:

These poems are intended to show the hunger for faith as a de [*for* un-] differentiating emotion between men and acceptance of it as a vessel for holding again the antique virtues. Of these it is clear that their contents will be different, but that is the concern of ethics & of moral poets, and it is prayed that they become immanent: our least possible conviction of God, through momentary sensation, is evidence enough (Est Proest [*for* Prodest]); the virtues (Argument with Justice) should move in us and not be merely the complement of evil.[3] To make the 2 irreconcilables, transcendance [*for* transcendence] and movement, go on fire not in a muddy unity but as companions. The poems are metaphysical and their mode is a sort of sensorialism, near animism, and so not <u>referring</u> to their realisation in ethics. [The] frozen mallarmean lake [is t]he logical counterpart of the modern dialectical movement in practical ethics & politics.

That is vague & pompous but it's the best I can do. Technically: the most important phrases in a development of thought with the conjunctions dear to administrative prose omitted: the whole governed by rhetoric. And I like the French poets best. I like passion & brilliance and dislike satire and acedia.

Will you send me the proofs?

By the way, I'm afraid the result of my enquiries regarding that cotton-mills affair has been disappointing. There seems to be nothing open. I shall keep trying of course. The trouble is, the positions are filled already and there are so few available. It's a great pity.

In the blurb please don't mention
{politics; "pattern"; materialism[}]
(dialestic [*for* dialectic] is allright)

    With best wishes,
        Yrs
           Denis.

Autograph letter signed. 3 leaves, 6 sides. There are substantial crossings-out in this letter, which make the sense of some sentences difficult to determine: 'the frozen mallarmean lake', for example, is a relic of an abandoned sentence, which proceeds into 'The logical counterpart …'. George Reavey Papers, Container 49.5, HRC, UTx.

---

1. The review is *14 rue du Dragon* – see DD to George Reavey, 4 March 1936, n. 3.
2. These notices have not been found.
3. 'Est Prodest' and 'Argument with Justice' are poems from *Intercessions*.

To George Reavey
[11] May 1937

Dear George,

I got my father to speak to a Senator Douglas who is important in the linen trade re your friend. Senator Douglas did not hold out any hopes for the present but said he would keep the thing in mind. It might be as well for your friend to write to him, simply to have him remember. In the meantime, I shall forward the references etc. My father's name (Mr. Liam Devlin) could be mentioned in reference.[1] Address: Senator James G. Douglas, Director, Greenmount & Boyne Linen Co. Ltd., Greenmount, Harold's Cross, Dublin.

I like the specimen page you sent me.[2] Are the proofs coming soon?

Yours

Denis.

Autograph lettercard signed. Prepaid Irish postal stationery lettercard. *Dating*: Devlin's initial dating, '15.5.1937' is corrected in a different ink to '11.5.37'. Postmark reads 11 May 1937. *Address*: George Reavey, Esq., 30 Red Lion Square, London, WC1. George Reavey Papers, Container 49.5, HRC, UTx.

---

1. Devlin's father Liam Devlin (1875–1964) ran a successful confectionery and manufacturing business, Liam Devlin and Sons, and was director of both the Irish Sugar Company and the Castleguard Textile Company.

2. See DD to George Reavey, 15 March 1937, n. 1.

To Ria Mooney

[?26 May/2 June 1937]   39 Upper Mount Street, Dublin

I present, dear Ria, a most ill-favoured countenance, having had some teeth extracted Monday; my jowl is swollen[,] puffed out most outrageous to an effect that brings me near to an Asiatick for aspect: bethink you of the Turques who have it like a white dumpling or other of our rustique puddings on either side of a shapeless mouth, so am I. I have been obliged to remain abed during today.

I have just stopped to look at your letter telling me when my train leaves. The last letter tells me when it arrives so that's good enough, is it not? It will be good to see you. It was nice of the Fannings to ask me.[1] It's hot in my room. So you are having trouble with Ctn. C. I suppose he must be bewildered: it must be irritating to act love with someone dressed so well for it. I cannot be jealous of your American friend now that you have said I might. Only ignorance makes me jealous. I have only been deeply jealous once, and it was purely physical. The weather was stifling, everything went up in a blaze and then puff! It was all over and all concerned were defeated in their intentions, including me. It's another reason why I don't let temperament rule me – because I should always lose.

And how is plumblossom? I can imagine you so brown and healthy and bewitching. My love be with you.

au revoir

Denis.

Poem is herewith[2]

A Loving Argument

My temperate south
What summer have you lit in me?
Holding by choice your body rare.
Give as your mouth

Does, liberal kisses open there
Of all shades like the anemone.

It will be all one
When we tire but now, ageing suspended,
Loving can stroke day into night.
What have you done
Sweet, to my heart? Love starting light,
Like travel reversed, heavy, must end it.

Let's join and be
A unit charging June's breath.
Love's favourites are few
Let him have me
And you, all lovely you, all of you
Nothing will use us after death.

Denis Devlin   April 1937

Autograph letter signed. 2 leaves, 3 sides (including poem). *Dating*: Devlin dates the letter 'Wednesday', but the mention of Jim Fanning would put this at the end of May or the beginning of June 1937, when Mooney was in Birr for the production of *The Light of Ulster*. Ria Mooney Papers, MS 49,603/10, NLI.

---

1. Jim Fanning (dates unknown) was the founder of the Birr Little Theatre in Birr, County Offaly. It ran an ambitious programme for a small midlands theatre, and at the end of its third season, in June 1937, staged the premiere of Dublin playwright David Sears' *The Light of Ulster*. Mooney was brought over from the Abbey to guest star as Fand, along with set and costume designers from the Abbey and the Gate.

2. There is no published version of this poem, nor are there any drafts in the NLI archive.

To George Reavey
7 June 1937

Dear George,

Brian has been telling me of his conversation with you. I was very sorry about the Nott affair; I hope it did not hit you too hard.[1]

What Brian told you about my anxiety to have the book out as soon as possible is quite the case. I shall be sent abroad within the next two or three months and be certainly away from home for many years. So I would like very very much to have my poems in my friends' hands before I go, to have them spread round Dublin[,] which I know, of course, and to test my employers as well. I'm sure you will feel how much pleasure and excitement I should have lost if it appeared when I should be no longer in Dublin. Waiting for it is producing a kind of atrophy in me which is very trying. I hope I shall have the proofs this week.

I shall be passing through London in the next month or so and shall come round to see you. – Did you get my note about the cotton-mills affair?[2]

Best wishes,

Yrs ever

<u>Denis</u>

Autograph letter signed. 1 leaf, 2 sides. *Header:* Department of External Affairs, Dublin (Roinn Gnóthaí Coigríche, Baile Átha Cliath). George Reavey Papers, Container 49.5, HRC, UTx.

---

1. Stanley Nott's publishing house, Stanley Nott, Ltd., folded in the summer of 1937.
2. See DD to George Reavey, [11] May 1937.

To Niall Montgomery
[11 June 1937]

Dear Niall –

I'm sorry, stupid of me, I forgot I had arranged for something else on Monday. Could you come Tuesday? I'll be at home anyhow so don't bother to reply. Hope you don't mind.

Yrs.

Denis.

Autograph lettercard signed. Prepaid Irish postal stationery lettercard. *Dating*: postmark. *Address*: Niall Montgomery, Esq., Wellington Lodge, Booterstown, Blackrock, Co. Dublin. Niall Montgomery Papers, MS 50,118/26/23, NLI.

To Thomas MacGreevy
[28 June/July 1937]

Dear Tom,

Excuse this hurried note. I wrote to the H[igh] C[ommissioner] a few days after I came back but found out afterwards that he was on holiday.[1] This morning I received a nice reply saying that he was getting in touch with you & that it would be a great personal satisfaction to him if he could be of help.[2] Are you well? I am (really) writing soon[.]

Yrs Ever

Denis.

Autograph lettercard signed. Prepaid Irish postal stationery lettercard. *Dating:* Card is undated, but the postmark, partially obscured, reads either 28 June or 28 July 1937. It may have been written after Devlin's return from Birr. *Address:* Thomas McGreevy, Esq., 49 Harrington Road, London, SW7. Thomas MacGreevy Papers, 8112/1–16, TCD.

---

1. John Whelan Dulanty (1883–1955) was high commissioner for the Irish Free State in the United Kingdom from 1930 to 1949. Following the Republic of Ireland Act in 1948, and the Ireland Act of the following year, Dulanty briefly became the first Irish ambassador to the court of St James.

2. In 1937 MacGreevy was earning money from translation work, art criticism and lectures at the National Gallery in London. Beckett's letters reveal that this was a difficult year for MacGreevy – he had teeth pulled in March (Beckett asks after the operation with concern in a letter of 25 March (*LSB*, vol. I, p. 468, n. 471)), and on 22 December Beckett wrote to MacGreevy that he was thinking of approaching Henri Laugier (French scientist and occupational therapist, later assistant secretary general for social affairs at the UN) about the possibility of arranging a government subvention for foreigners in France who would promote awareness of French cultural affairs abroad (*LSB*, vol. I, pp. 572–5). MacGreevy's friends were trying to help and support him at this stage, and Devlin may have been investigating the possibility of financial assistance from the Irish embassy in London.

To George Reavey
15 August 1937

Dear George,

   Any news of my intercessions? – I hope you both had a good time abroad.[1]

                Yrs,

                      Denis.

Autograph postcard signed. Prepaid Irish postal stationery postcard. *Dating*: postmark. *Address*: George Reavey, Esq., 30 Red Lion Square, London, WC1. George Reavey Papers, Container 49.5, HRC, UTx.

---

1. Reavey was in Florence – see DD to George Reavey, 27 August 1937 – with his wife Gwynedd, probably on their honeymoon. Devlin and Coffey had sent Reavey a telegram of congratulations on 17 July (George Reavey Papers, Container 49.5, HRC, UTx).

To George Reavey

27 August 1937   39 Upper Mount Street, Dublin

Dear George,

It's good news that the book is coming out soon.[1] I think that the fewness of forms is not to be worried about; they should come in as soon as a notice has appeared in the Dublin papers.[2] I have no other adresses [*for* addresses] so far more than the list I sent which was a full typewritten page, I think, and I have enough forms here.[3] Do you intend making any arrangements with Combridge as I suggested?[4] Perhaps you might do so when the effectiveness of the forms has worn out as Combridges are likely to want to make some profit on sales.

As regards the twenty-five signed copies, I'm afraid you'll have to send them to me for signature. I shall not be in London for a while, in any case I have'nt [*for* haven't] the least idea when. The Department has told us nothing about when we'll be sent abroad.

I do hope more forms come in. It will be very surprising if they don't as I've heard plenty of talk about them and promises to buy.

Did you have a charming holiday? I envied you so much being in Florence which I have never seen. Please give my best wishes to Gwynedd.

> Yours,
> > Denis.

Typed letter signed. Handwritten corrections. 1 leaf, 1 side. George Reavey Papers, Container 49.5, HRC, UTx.

---

1. On 31 August 1937, four days after this letter, Devlin sent Reavey a telegram stating: 'DELIGHTED BOOK BEAUTIFULLY DONE = DENIS' (George Reavey Papers, Container 49.5, HRC, UTx).

2. Subscription forms.

3. See DD to George Reavey, [February 1937], n. 1.

4. See DD to George Reavey, 22 October 1935, n. 2.

To George Reavey
10 September 1937

Dear George,
    I have received, signed & passed on copies 9 & 10 for Mr Ernest Keegan[1]; the same for 8 Mr. Nial [*for* Niall] Montgomery & for 6 & 7, my father & sister.[2] I got the A and nos 2 to 5 for myself for which I thank you. I will not, as you advise, give out such copies for the present. I also returned your B signed & dedicated.[3] I am looking forward to seeing the ordinary copies. Will it be possible to have Tom's review in "Ireland To-day" October number?[4] That will depend on how soon you can send it to them, and it wld. be good for sales.
    I love the pattern of the cover.
          Yrs
              Denis.
I note your change of address as from the 21st.

Autograph letter signed. 1 leaf, 2 sides. *Header*: 39 Upper Mount Street, Dublin. George Reavey Papers, Container 49.5, HRC, UTx.

---

1. Ernest Keegan (dates unknown) was a Dublin-based solicitor and a sometime translator. The circumstances of his friendship with Devlin are unknown.

2. Devlin had seven sisters. He seems to have been closest to Moya Devlin at this stage of his life.

3. In the Europa Press print runs, copies A and B were reserved for author and publisher.

4. MacGreevy's review of *Intercessions*, 'New Dublin Poetry', appeared in *Ireland Today*, vol. II, no. 10, October 1937, pp. 81–2.

To George Reavey
[Early October 1937]

Dear George,

You must forgive me for not writing you for so long: I am really being worked very hard in the Department, all my colleagues are absent and I have their work, that my free moments are scarce. However, things will improve in a day or so, I hope.

I am hearing nice things about my book; the make-up is making a very favourable impression[.]

The following are some addresses of booksellers[1]: –

Fred. Hanna, Nassau Street.
The Three Candles Press, Fleet St.
D.F. Fitzgerald, 17 Up. O'Connell St.
Eason & Son, Lr. O'Connell St.
James Duffy & Son, Westmoreland St.
Hodges, Figgis & Co., Nassau St.

Am sending back 4 signed copies to day[.]

    Yrs

      Denis Devlin.

Autograph letter signed. 1 leaf, 2 sides. *Header:* 39 Upper Mount Street, Dublin. *Dating:* Devlin does not date this letter, but marking in a different hand (presumably Reavey's) indicates that it was received on 7 October 1937. George Reavey Papers, Container 49.5, HRC, UTx.

---

1. In a letter dated 29 September 1937, Reavey sends Devlin a list of publications that had been sent review copies, sends four copies for signing, and asks Devlin to send him a more complete list of likely booksellers in Dublin (George Reavey Papers, Container 49.5, HRC, UTx).

To George Reavey
15 October 1937

Dear George,

Sweeney's remarks are overwhelming and of course I'm thrilled – a lot of it is American excitement though.[1]

The bookshops are trying. I shall talk to two of them I know. I will refund you for the 'Independent' ad. I gave one of my copies to the 'Irish Press' which has promised to review so you owe me one.[2] Could you send it as I want to give it to a friend[?] Also Austin Clarke has promised to review from Dublin Radio which should get a review copy.[3] As his talk is coming off soon, he asked could you send it direct and soon to him at

> Bridge House
>
> Templeogue/Co. Dublin

Ernie O'Malley talked a lot about the format, he couldn't understand its being done so well at the price. On such occasions of course I always drop a remark about your Agency & Translation.

> Yrs,
>
> Denis.

Autograph letter signed. 1 leaf, 2 sides. *Header*: 39 Upper Mount Street, Dublin. George Reavey Papers, Container 49.5, HRC, UTx.

---

1. James Johnson Sweeney, co-editor of *transition* – see DD to Ruth de Verry, *transition* magazine, 13 October 1936, n. 1. If Sweeney's praise for *Intercessions* was published, it has not been found. Eugene Jolas commissioned Beckett to review the volume for *transition*; the response, 'Denis Devlin', was submitted in October or November 1937 (see *LSB*, vol. I, p. 561), and published in the April–May 1938 issue.

2. A review of *Intercessions* from poet and freelance journalist M.J. MacManus (1888–1951), entitled 'Denis Devlin's Poems', appeared in *The Irish Press*, Tuesday, 19 October, p. 7.

3. Clarke's radio feature on *Intercessions* has not been found. He had recently returned from London with his partner Nora Walker, was reviewing for *The Irish Times*, and had begun a long-standing broadcasting role at Radio Éireann. This included a show, 'Irish Poets of Today' in a similar format to Devlin's earlier poetry review show – Clarke made Devlin the subject of this show once again on 20 August 1951.

To Ria Mooney
8 November 1937

My dear Ria,

I got your letter more than a week ago and of course I have been thinking of writing to you but that's not the same thing as writing actually which I am doing now. I may have been tentatively regarding the various points of approach from which one might consider the writing of a letter!

I am very shocked and sorry that you should have been so ill and from what a curious unexpected cause.[1] It was foolish of you to dye your hair and I'm sure you will look much more distinguished and lovely in silver – or silverblack? It will be quite an adventure for you to appear in Dublin so changed, people will think you had a serious mental shock in America. Poor darling, you must have been miserable in that big can of a hotel and lonely too. Will the colour of your hair seriously affect your acting? I wonder where you are now. In Milwaukee perhaps which I hear is a very elegant city. This is a very beautiful day, cold and crisp[,] sunny, not like the rest of the weather now which is appalling. I shall quote some news[:]

I am learning Italian[,] reading much German[,] sleeping a lot. I have taken some unprecedented walks in the Canal Zone round about Clondalkin etc[.] which were nice, full of the most depressing pubs and mature expansive nature.[2]

Brian has returned to Paris to continue his philosophy. He has a French Govt Scholarship, was very sad at leaving and disinclined. Moya is in a nursing home having had her tonsils out, they were very bad. She had quite a little success in the Far Off Hills, playing the prude sister.[3] The Abbey seems to be doing very well in audiences – people are saying the "home company" (that is what it is being called!) has more life and freshness than the American. So you had better all come back. O'Gorman was very fine in "The Invincibles."[4] Mervyn has bought some new tankards, pipes, picture frames and shaving mugs and is upset about how many combinations of plots there can be – 33 or 34. He is making a strategic study of the possibility of hanging a meat safe outside the window, safe from the exploitations of cats and unfavourable rains. "Winterset" and your friend Burgess Meredith did not impress me much though I went with a prejudice in their favour.[5] Perhaps Meredith's popularity is due to his representing a type now very evident – the détraqué, the misfit, the unemployed etc. His eyes are uncertain and defiant, covering a wide underground life like a rodent's. I forget his mouths [*for* mouth] but my sisters liked it. His forehead is appealing, I suppose women like it. But a lot of life seems to escape him, he did not seem to have the least idea what some of his lines meant – the speeches to God for example. I grant that they were bad in themselves. The play itself is nothing, mechanic and compromising. The best thing was the timing of the camera: that was really a person. Some good images but in general the pro Hitler German film has done much better.[6]

– This is days later. I must really send the letter such as it is; I continually hope for improvement on it.

My love and I hope very much you are not ill any longer.

Denis.

Love from Moya & Maureen

Autograph letter signed. 5 leaves, 10 sides. *Header*: 39 Upper Mount Street, Dublin. Text from 'This is days later' onwards written in a darker ink. Ria Mooney Papers, MS 49,603/10, NLI.

---

1. Mooney was on an American tour with the Abbey from October 1937 to May 1938. Mooney makes no mention of this illness in her memoir 'Players and the Painted Stage', printed in *George Spelvin's Theatre Book*, vol. 1, no. 2, Summer 1978, pp. 3–120, but in an unpublished doctoral thesis, Ciara O'Dowd finds evidence in F.R. Higgins' letters home from the Abbey tour in America of an undiagnosed illness that struck Mooney on her arrival in New York, and left her listless and incapable of work. See 'The On and Off-Stage Roles of Abbey Theatre Actresses of the 1930s' (submitted May 2016), p. 231, published online by NUI Galway: https://aran.library.nuigalway.ie/handle/10379/5789 [accessed 28 July 2017].

2. Clondalkin is a town in the west Dublin suburbs.

3. *The Far Off Hills* (1928) is a three-act comedy by Lennox Robinson.

4. *The Invincibles*, by Hugh Hunt and Frank O'Connor, was first produced at the Abbey Theatre on 18 October 1937, with William O'Gorman in the role of Joe Brady.

5. *Winterset* (1936) is an American film adaptation of a play by Maxwell Anderson, based on the Sacco and Vanzetti robbery trial in Massachusetts. Burgess Meredith, a former student of Mooney's, starred as Mio Romagna in what was his breakthrough film role.

6. The pro-Hitler film has not been identified.

To George Reavey

12 November 1937

Dear George,

    I happened to be at Combridge's, Grafton St, and to mention the book which is not displayed. The manager got very indignant and said he had written to yo[u] 4 times and got no reply. He had ordered 12 copies, 6 of which were bespoken by customers, who are naturally annoyed at the delay. And Combridge would be able to sell more, I was informed, at Christmas. You might look up your correspondence.

    – I have returned 19 & 20 to you[.]

           Yrs

                Denis.

Autograph letter signed. 1 leaf, 2 sides. *Header:* 39 Upper Mount Street, Dublin. George Reavey Papers, Container 49.5, HRC, UTx.

To Thomas MacGreevy
5 December 1937

My dear Tom (contd. Friday)[1]

What on earth does the Apocalypse mean? I don't like it much, those composite jewelled beasts seem to me more anxious than fetching, except for a few moments['] surprise[.][2] {Vallombrosa has just appeared in an official document being 'dealt with' by my colleague opposite. This is the Office[.]}[3] Can you suggest an exegesis[?] It seems rather primaire[,] not much better than Blake's Phrophetic [*for* Prophetic] Books which I have been reading.[4] Aren't they twaddle? I can't see why there should be so much fuss about their obscurity. They are just het up ideas of quite a general kind. He could have made a straightforward Dryden argument in couplets instead of which he presents what are opinions in an ignorant cloud & braids them with those absurd Orcs & Enitharmons.[5] The 'terrible' imagination certainly makes me laugh really anyhow.

Who is Glass, an English Surrealist painter[?][6] He is here and I was to meet him but missed doing so.

I have thought of a journalese job which you could do well. Do you know "Lancelot's" weekly column in the Temps called ["]Défense de la Langue Française"?[7] The same thing for English (you could call yourself Guinevere and put your picture beside it!) would seem to be very pleasant, say in the "Manchester Guardian"[?]

Do you think my degrees, academic experience, wld. get me a job in London? Or my office training another kind of job? It's a stupid question I know. And I know you would advise against it but I am (secretly) determined to leave this.

Brian seems really to have lost some of his old gaiety. Otherwise he is more tolerant and so learned. We would be able to renew our ancient friendship of unblushingly serious, and what must have seemed to you at the time jejune, mental earnestness. He said quite distinctly at Reddin's on Sunday night where my sister was acting to an old lady who questioned him about the big man with the crimson necktie:

"That is Mr. Higgins, the songster!"[8]

Isn't it grand to have Voltaire rehabilitated?[9]

Do you remember a Claudel poem on Judith which I admired? I have tried to get it in Paris[.] It was in 'Mesures'[.][10] Could you give me the month or number of the issue?

Re your last letter: I still like inversion. And the lines you liked but thought pantheistic were not in the least meant to be so, so I stuck a vocative girl in the middle.

Brian & Sam have both been praising your satires to me.[11] I saw one or two[,] have you more? I should like to hear from you.

Bien vôtre

Denis

Autograph letter signed. 5 leaves, 5 sides. Thomas MacGreevy Papers, 8112/1-16, TCD.

----

1. If there was an earlier instalment to this letter, it has not been preserved in MacGreevy's archive.

2. Devlin presumably refers to the Book of Revelation in the New Testament, and John's account of the four beasts of the Apocalypse.

3. Vallombrosa is a town in Tuscany, famous for its Benedictine abbey, and its place in Book I of John Milton's *Paradise Lost* ('Thick as autumnal leaves that strew the brooks/In Vallombrosa', *Milton: Paradise Lost*, 2nd ed., ed. Alastair Fowler (Harlow: Pearson Longman, 1997)); Devlin is eager to share the allusion with MacGreevy.

4. English poet and artist William Blake (1757–1827) wrote a series of long, interconnected poetic works in which he established a personal mythology. These works, including *The Book of Urizen* (1794), *Vala, or the Four Zoas* (begun 1797), *Milton* (1804–10) and concluding with *Jerusalem: The emanation of the giant Albion* (1804–20), have been described as the Prophetic Books, and were renewed in the public consciousness by W.B. Yeats and Edwin Ellis's 1893 edition.

5. John Dryden (1631–1700), English Restoration poet and dramatist. Orc and Enitharmon are symbolic characters in Blake's *Vala, or the Four Zoas*.

6. Glass has not been identified.

7. Abel Hermant (1862–1950), French novelist and essayist, published a series of articles in *Le Temps* under the name 'Lancelot', in which he defended the purity of the French language.

8. F.R. Higgins (see DD to Thomas MacGreevy, 26 [April] 1934, n. 2). Devlin may be referring to the Gate Theatre as 'Reddin's' – the Reddin family in Dublin were associated with the Gate Theatre, and its predecessor, the Irish Theatre in Hardwicke Street. Gerard Norman Reddin (1894–1942), a solicitor, was one of the original directors of the Gate; his twin brother John Kenneth Reddin (1894–1967) was a playwright who wrote under the pseudonym Kenneth Sarr.

9. In 1937 the Classiques Larousse Series published Voltaire's *Lettres choisies* and *Oeuvres critiques et poétiques: extraits*. This was also the year in which Tobias Smollett's translation of *Candide: And other tales* was revised and reissued by London's J.M. Dent & Sons.

10. Paul Claudel's 'Judith' appeared in the first (1935) issue of the French journal *Mesures*, edited by the American expatriate and patron of the arts, Henry Church, a friend of MacGreevy's.

11. It is unclear which of MacGreevy's works Devlin refers to. MacGreevy was moving away from poetry in the late 1930s, focusing on reviews, translation work and art criticism. Some of his unpublished poems from the late 1920s and early 1930s, such as 'La Calunnia e un Venticello', are aiming at a subdued form of satire – see Susan Schreibman, 'The Unpublished Poems of Thomas MacGreevy: An exploration', in *Modernism and Ireland: The poetry of the 1930s*, ed. Patricia Coughlan and Alex Davis (Cork: Cork University Press, 1995), pp. 129–49.

To Ria Mooney
[?22 January–21 February 1938]

[First page of letter missing]

[…]

As for myself, I have been living a very frivolous life without work – except 2 recent poems which are rather poor. I haven't been to the theatre for ages so I cannot tell you what O'Faolain['s] play was like – Mervyn found it bad though.[1]

I think of you often and often. You come to my mind very vividly in odd places such as the Fun Palace bus-stop![2] What will your movements be and when is the company returning? I am guessing this: you intend to stay in America. Is that so? I should love to see you again, especially to go to New York and see you there; your charm and lovingness are very real to me. I have not, as you ask, <u>ceased</u> to love you; I think my sentiment is unchanged. But you know its nature. I suppose I sound subtle or roundabout. But it looks rather likely that I shall be sent away in perhaps two months so I may not see you.[3] It would be good if the company did happen to be coming back and you happened to decide to come back and I could see you. Not that it would mean much since I have to go anyhow. And this place is so dreary and spiritless, like an old man with weak eyes.

Please write and tell me that you are well and amused and busy with your chattering, attractive goings and comings.

> My love
> Denis

Autograph letter signed. 3 leaves, 5 sides (surviving). *Dating*: This letter was written during Mooney's American tour with the Abbey (Oct 1937–21 May 1938), and the mention of O'Faolain's play, which premiered in late December 1937, places it in early 1938. Reports in the *Irish Independent* and the *Irish Press* indicate that Devlin was in London

19–22 January, and again from 21 February, as part of the Irish delegation for the Anglo-Irish Trade Agreement talks. Ria Mooney Papers, MS
49,603/10, NLI.

----

1. Sean O'Faolain's *She Had To Do Something* premiered at the Abbey on 27 December 1937.

2. The Fun Palace was an amusement arcade on Burgh Quay, Dublin.

3. Devlin was appointed secretary to the Irish legation in Rome in May 1938; he
missed Mooney's return.

To Shiela Devlin
25 June 1938   [Teach] Ósda an Baile

                                       An Chathair Giorruí

A Shighle a Chroidhe –

    Is duairc dobrónach atá me sa nóiméad so ón teas agus ós na spaghettiouchtána go bh[fuil] mo sháith agam dióbh [*for* dóibh] agus conas ba mhaith liom anois bheith im shuidhe go ciúin sásta ós comhair cupán té agus ham-and-eggs nó cheese sandwich agus buidéal stout, agus conas taoi? Ba dheas uait an litir úd i dteangain ár sínnsear agus ambaiste ba dheas an péire bhéarsaí a d[he]inis suas ann, agus ba [?chéolaihar] agus an é a bhe[a]dh ionnat-sa ná file sa bhláthóig, póit bhuddáltá, mar adeir na Sasanaigh.

    Cad a déarfaidh me dhuit fá'n Iodáil agus fá'n Róimh? Sár-áit is-eadh an beirt ac[u]. Beirt eile anois agus ar aghaidh leis an spórt. Bíonn spórt mór agam ag dul treasna [*for* trasna] an tsráid annso i gcoinne na lampaí, na soluis traffic. Tá na gárdaí annso an dheas agus culaith éadaigh bána ortha, cótaí bána agus glovaí bána. Bím-se i lán-lár na coirnéala im aonar agus na scataí gluaisteáin agus rothar mór-thímpeall orm agus na gárdaí ag scréachaigh. Ní leigtear dos na gluaisteáin buabháin a bheith aca – horns dtuigeann tú? – toisc go ndeinidís an iomad clampair fad ó [*for* fadó], agus mar sin bíonn do saoghal in do lámhaibh agat.

    Rud atá uaim, 'sé photographanna de'n chlaina go léir. Ba mhaith liom ceann leis féin de gach doinne agaibh agus an bhéacfaidh tú chuige?

    Maidir le spórt agus rinnce níl mórán le fáil annso ach anois tá cuirmeacha céoil [*for* ceoil] le cosnú agus ra[gh]aid[h] mé ann agus opera à la belle étoile imeasc sean-bhallaí agus sean chlochanna an forum.[1] Tá culaith éadaigh nua agam[,] lán-bhán.

        Tá súil agam go bheicfead sibh sa b[h]Frainnc

        Má tá an t'airgead agaibh sa bhainnc,

        Mór an truagh má tá sibh briste

        Prátaí á n-itheadh agaibh i n-ionad chiste.

i.e.   Fuaireas litir ó Áine á rádh go dtéigheann sibh go Trouville[.]²

         Mo siare 7rl

            Denis

[*Postscript*]

      O tá an róisín dubh fá scamall anocht

      Oró agus hei di danoi danoi

Autograph letter signed. 2 leaves, 4 sides. Postscript appears at top of 4ᵗʰ side, separated from the rest of the text by a bold underlining. Private collection, Caren Farrell.

[*Translation*]

                      Hotel de la Ville

                      [?Short] City

Dear Shiela,

I am sorrowfully afflicted at the moment by the heat and the spaghetti-excess which is my diet – and how I would like to be sitting quietly and happily before a cup of tea and ham-and-eggs or a cheese sandwich and bottled stout [–] and how are you? It was nice to get that letter in the language of our ancestors, and indeed that couple of verses you included in it. What you are looking for is poetic flowering – a budding poet, as the English said.

What am I to say to you about Italy and Rome? Excellent places the two of them. Another couple here now, so on with the fun. I have great fun crossing the street here against the lamps, the traffic lights. The guards here are very smart with their white uniforms, white coats and white gloves. I find myself in the midst of it at the corner[,] all alone[,] surrounded by groups of cars and bikes and screeching police. The cars are not allowed to have hooters – horns do you understand? – as they were judged to make too much noise in the past, and so you take your life in your hands.

One thing I want is photographs of the whole family. I'd like one individually of each of you [–] will you see to that?

As for fun and dancing there is little to be had here. But now there are music concerts coming up that I will go to and the *belle étoile* opera within the old walls and stones of the Forum. I have a new suit[,] all-white.

> I hope that I'll see you all in France
> If you have money in the bank,
> What a pity if you're broke
> And eating spuds instead of cake.

i.e.   I got a letter from Anne saying that you go to Trouville[.]

             My regards etc.,

                Denis

[*Postscript*]

      O the dark rose is under a cloud tonight

      Oro and hei di danoi danoi

---

1. The Teatro di Marcello, an ancient open-air theatre, overlooks the ruins and temples of the Roman Forum. It was restored as part of Mussolini's architectural renovation in the 1920s.

2. Trouville is a coastal resort in Normandy.

To George Reavey

29 June 1938   Albergo Excelsior, Rome

Dear George,

The rumours are well founded – I am in Rome. I am not settled down yet, however, but looking around for somewhere to sit. I have not seen the <u>London Bulletin</u>. Is it your publication?[1] Please send me a copy, I should like to see it. I have some Eluard done recently, one of the numbers goes quite well, I shall send it on when I've made one or two changes. The description of the paper of Brian's book is most impressive: "toned hand made rag antique wove deckle edge paper"[,] how meticulously expensive![2] It is good that his book is coming out at last; the title is good, I think.[3] I am sending a cheque, I am ~~pretty~~ [( ]I met a cockeney last night[ )] sure that the National Bank cheque can be cashed in London[,] it is really an English bank – but if not let me know. I want these 2 copies for use as presents. If you have any spare copies of "Intercessions" could you let me have a few? if they cannot be sold. I enclose also 1/- in the cheque for postage. Did the exhibitions go well, <u>van Velde</u>[,] <u>Hayter</u> etc.?[4]

My very kindest regards to Gwynedd. How is her brother's shop doing?[5]

All best to yourself,
Yours ever
Denis.

Personal address for some time: –

Hotel de la Ville
via Sistina
Rome.

Autograph letter signed. 1 leaf, 2 sides. *Header*: Légation d'Irlande. Text placed in parenthesis is inserted below "pretty", explaining the deletion. Postscript with personal address written on top right-hand corner of recto side, above date. George Reavey Papers, Container 49.5, HRC, UTx.

1. *London Bulletin* (1938–40) described itself as 'the only avant-garde publication in [England] concerned with contemporary poetry and art'. It was edited by the Belgian surrealist artist and writer Edouard Léon Théodore Mesens, with assistance from Reavey and others.

2. This description was presumably on the subscription form.

3. Brian Coffey's *Third Person* was published shortly after his wedding to Bridget Baynes in October 1938.

4. Geraldus (Geer) van Velde (1898–1977), Dutch surrealist-expressionist painter, was exhibited in London at the Guggenheim Jeune in May 1938, largely as a result of Samuel Beckett's efforts. The Hayter exhibition Devlin mentions may be the Atelier 17 studio exhibition, which ran concurrently with a Julian Trevelyan exhibition at the end of the Guggenheim Jeune's second, and final, season in 1939.

5. The profession of Gwynedd (née Vernon) Reavey's brother is unknown.

To Ria Mooney
4 August 1938

Hotel de la Ville
Via Sistina, Rome

My dear Ria,

Moya has written to me about your having to have another operation on your return from New York and it has made me see [*sic*] and angry with myself for having proved so poor a friend last year.[1] There was no excuse for my not writing oftener and more personally when you were hurt by so much pain without reason and so unexpectedly, and I should not have allowed myself to be convinced by my usual lazy self-forgiveness that I find it hard to write. I did realize it when I got your letter and it was as much a guilty feeling as the fury of that letter that kept me from replying. I hope you have forgiven me and now if you have be sure that I am really shocked and sorry about your illness and agree with you, I mean I have deep affection for you inside in spite of my filthily meagre correspondence. Perhaps now that you are back in Dublin you feel more content, especially as you need not live cheek by jowl with that verminous company.

As for myself, I am rather content here on the whole. The work is comfortably inactive; the relations I hold with events and people bothe[r] me a little sometimes as fretwork would, the people have not exactly the quality of those I knew in Dublin and I have lost my pleasure in foreignness; but I "make do" (Is that an Americanism?)

Please do write and make friends again, won't you?

Love and best wishes,

Denis

P.S. I've forgotten your address so I'm sending through Moya as I don't trust the Abbey till you say I may. D.

Autograph letter signed. 1 leaf, 2 sides. *Header*: Légation d'Irlande. Header crossed out in ink, hotel address written in top right-hand corner. Ria Mooney Papers, MS 49,603/10, NLI.

---

1. Details of this operation have not been found in the Irish press, and once again Mooney refrains from mentioning it in her memoir.

To Shiela Devlin

[November 1938]

Private address:
23 Viale Liegi, Rome

My dear Sheila [*for* Shiela],

I didn't think you would have gone to Amiens after all even when the war-scare had died down.[1] I gather the life is not overwhelmingly exciting but it never is in a school. It is something that you have freedom, and if you have, all the same, fits of homesickness, I sympathise with you for I sometimes wish terribly to be in Dublin, vigorously and unreasonably telling myself that only our ways and our countryside and food are right and all others incomprehensibly hostile. Oh fine goins' on, indeed. However, even if one doesn't like a place very much, I've found that it very generously does give one some enjoyment; one suddenly realises that some things, streets or times of day or people, have worked themselves quietly into the mind and claim affection; it is some consolation.

I'm in my flat now, as you see. It is a very nice place, pleasantly furnished in old Florentine which means heavy angular chests in rough wood polished by years & years of use. There is a gate[,] a gravel little garden, a door, a hall way, a drawing room, a diningroom, a bedroom and a study. Then there is a corresponding space downstairs with kitchen maid's quarters and some empty rooms. And a garage! But no car¡ It's a most unusual size for a flat, everyone thinks I have been very lucky: the usual flat-to-let here is small and frightfully badly furnished and yet the same price as mine. The reason is that it is not really a "flat-to-let" but has been lived in by a husband & wife, who are in the Italian diplomatic service and who are going to a post in Washington. I took their maid who has been with them for 10 years. That seemed to me a good recommendation and in fact she is very good. She cooks perfectly and does everything for me, laundering & suit-pressing. I find, though, with some amusement, that living by oneself with a maid means being "tied down" almost more than living at home with the family. The only disadvantage about the place is that it has not much sunlight, it will be annoying in summer.

It is terribly cold here now. The heating is central everywhere, there are no fires and people won't start the radiators because it is not the custom to heat so early! In the meantime, one freezes so I hope the custom will be due to start soon.

I didn't know the water would be so bad that you wld. have to drink the Vin Rouge[.] Our water here is marvellous but of course we drink an odd noggin of sack.[2] You are certainly having a pretty rough time if you have to be able to translate "David Copperfield".[3] What dough. Our old enemy Addison would be easier from that point of view even though he be in truth a Bore.[4] Swift too would be easy – and amusing.[5] Have you got good dictionaries? If not, you should make the College get some.

The only way to get letters would be to circularise all your girl friends. The family is hopeless.

I shall try to get home at Christmas but of course I can't tell.

> Yours ever
> Denis.

Autograph letter signed. 2 leaves, 4 sides. *Header*: Légation d'Irlande. *Dating*: Mention of the war-scare dying down dates this letter after the Munich Agreement. It was written before Devlin had decided against returning to Ireland for Christmas (see DD to George Reavey, 5 December 1938), and in cold weather. *Address*: Mademoiselle Sheila Devlin, 1, rue de l'Oratoire, Amiens, Somme, FRANCIA. Private collection, Caren Farrell.

---

1. The letter is addressed to the rue de l'Oratoire in Amiens, the site of the Lycée Sacré-Coeur, a boarding school for girls founded by the Societas Sacratissimi Cordis Jesu (Society of the Sacred Heart of Jesus). Shiela Devlin was studying at the lycée, and tutoring, as this letter suggests. The first line of Devlin's letter refers to the Munich Agreement of September 1938, which ceded the Sudeten German territory of western Czechoslovakia to Nazi Germany, and was thought to have averted the threat of war.

2. noggin of sack: drop of wine. Noggin (Irish and Scottish English) refers to a small drinking vessel; sack (early modern English) was a general term for white wines imported from Spain and the Canaries, or an equivalent of the French 'vin sec'.

3. Charles Dickens'[s] eighth novel, first published in book form as *The Personal History of David Copperfield* (1850).

4. Joseph Addison (1672–1719), English essayist, poet and playwright, best known for his work on *The Spectator*, a daily magazine he co-founded with Richard Steele.

5. Jonathan Swift (1667–1745), Irish poet, satirist and clergyman.

To George Reavey

5 December 1938   23 Viale Liegi, Rome

Dear George,

   I am sending an Order Form for a 12/6 copy of "Quixotic Perquisitions" and cheque attached.[1] I hope it will have success – from the publicity angle as well; there shd. be some chance of that now that the Auden ramp has died down a bit – when his followers are being invited to Dublin to Trinity inaugurals it must be near the end.[2]

   I did think I should be passing through London at Christmas but now it's off and for some time ahead[.]

   I don't know of any periodicals in Rome interested in English verse; I doubt very much if such exist. To tell the truth I haven't been able to bring myself round to an interest in reviews etc. But I'll have a look around now that you mention it. Has anything come of your plans for a poetry review?

   I have been writing nothing myself – some lines. As regards translation I sometimes do an odd bit to amuse myself but so much of Breton & Eluard is being rendered now that one is almost sure to do something already done by someone else; and they are not such guys as stretch one's power[s] overmuch. I've been rolling off Hugo too on the typewriter not even bothering to rime which will show you how little are my exigencies.[3] But his Satyre is a tremendous poem; and others too, acres of them.[4]

   Is Gwynidd [*for* Gwynedd] well? Please give her my best wishes. Good luck.

               Yours ever
                    Denis.

P.S. Horror of amazements! I have a cat. It was thrown in, willy nilly, with the lease of my flat behind which all the cats of north west Rome have their nasty quartiers. My cat is a Sagliardo and the females come after him![5] How is yrs.?

Autograph letter signed. 1 leaf (folded), 3 sides. George Reavey Papers, Container 49.5, HRC, UTx.

---

1. Reavey's *Quixotic Perquisitions*, the ninth number in the Europa Poets series, was published in 1939.

2. Stephen Spender was invited to speak at the inaugural meeting of the Trinity College Dublin Philosophical Society on 27 October 1938, on the subject of 'The Totalitarian State'.

3. Victor Hugo (1802–85), French Romantic poet, novelist and dramatist.

4. 'Le Satyre' is a poem from Hugo's epic *La légende des siècles* (1859–83).

5. Possibly a reference to Sogliardo, a character from Ben Jonson's comedy *Every Man Out of His Humour* (1599), notable for his virility and his risible aspirations to become a gentleman.

To Niall Montgomery
[December 1938]

I had thought of going home about Christmas but have now decided not to. I shall mouze here. I saw Pompei [*for* Pompeii], it's very pleasant and like an orchard though there aren't apple-trees, of course, nothing but grass.[1] I saw the men doing excavations; probably the film was better, I could see nothing but rubbish and brick, not a bit of antique leg anywhere. So I gave the men a cigarette which they asked for and went away. Everyone roared out Have you read Bulwer Lytton?[2] I said No in an annoyed way but that didn't shut anyone up. The fact is I'm sick of tombs and their bull-necked consular occupiers. I tried to read the Urn Burial as a homeopathic but the syntax was too involved and I wished to God people wld. say what they mean.[3] – Prof. O'Briain [*for* Ó Briain] did turn up and I think we found each other quite agreeable, I agreeing that I knew no Irish and he agreeing that the translations were a worthy effort.[4] He's likeable, all the same.

Congratulations on getting your degree.[5] It's a rough time afterwards of course looking for a job but surely there shouldn't be much difficulty in London. Or perhaps the German Jews have got all the surplus. Best luck in yr. search anyhow.

I see by your reference to the Holy Father that you are as incorrigible a Catholic as ever!

    Yrs.

      Denis

Autograph letter signed. 1 leaf, 2 sides (surviving). This MS contains no opening greeting, date or address – it is unclear whether other leaves are missing from the archive. *Dating*: Montgomery's graduation (1938) and the Italian location show that this was written during Devlin's Rome posting. The news about Devlin's decision not to return to Britain or Ireland for Christmas (see DD to George Reavey, 5 December 1938, and DD to Brian Coffey, Christmas 1938) places this letter in or around December. Niall Montgomery Papers, MS 50,118/26/23, NLI.

1. Pompeii, Roman town near Naples, destroyed by an eruption of Mount Vesuvius in AD 79. In 1938, Amedeo Maiuri was directing the archaeological excavations at Pompeii. Maiuri had been appointed by Mussolini, who was at this time pursuing a vigorous large-scale archaeological programme.

2. English novelist Edward Bulwer-Lytton (1803–73), whose popular novel *The Last Days of Pompeii* (1834) was adapted into a number of film versions in the early twentieth century.

3. Sir Thomas Browne's *Hydriotaphia, Urn Burial* (1658) is a philosophical treatise responding to the discovery of Roman sepulchral urns in Norfolk.

4. Professor Liam Ó Briain (1888–1974), professor of romance languages at University College Galway from 1917 to 1959, who worked to promote the Irish language in culture and education. Devlin was probably showing Ó Briain the translations from French into Irish that he and Montgomery had been working on.

5. Montgomery's UCD degree was in architecture.

Cardinale di Riciliu

Rome
Christmas 1938

Dear Brian,

I have a fair to middling chance of getting in next time. Meantime, this is a prospective portrait.

Hope you are better after illness. Have had a spell myself.

All the best. Writing proximately. And thank Bridget for lovely card. Can't get away this time, perhaps yes in 2 mths.

Bernard for

Denis.

To Brian Coffey
Christmas 1938 [Rome]

Dear Brian,

I have a fair to middling chance of getting in next time. Meantime, this is a prospective portrait.[1]

Hope you are better after illness. Have had a spell myself.

All the best. Writing proximately. And thank Bridget for the lovely card. Can't get away this time, perhaps yes in 2 mths.

    Bien à toi
     Denis.

Autograph postcard signed. Recto image is a handpainted colour portrait of Cardinal Richelieu. Brian Coffey Papers, Box 30, Folder 22, UDel.

---

1. On the recto side of the postcard is a colour portrait of Cardinal Richelieu, seventeenth-century French nobleman and clergyman who became Louis XIII's chief minister (see image on previous page); Devlin is presumably making a joke about not being elected cardinal. By coincidence these were the final months of the papacy of Pius XI, who died in February 1939.

To Brian O'Nolan

1 June [1939]   23 Viale Liegi, Rome

Dear Brian,

You must think it very rude of me not to have acknowledged your gift of "At-Swim-Two-Birds" [*sic*] and it is indeed.[1] But I have been very keen on writing at length about it and so kept putting off a letter. Now I want to thank you and to apologise for my delay. It might have been better just to say it was a grand or a swell book but that seemed inadequate, although you might have preferred it, but I would like to say in what way it interested me from chapter to chapter. It wld. be dangerously near taking on the pomposity of a critic which I dislike myself so why shld. I want to do it with others? I don't know but I "feel impelled to" try; it may be no damn use whatever.

I hope the book is selling well. It wld.n't in Ireland of course but it might in Am. & Eng. I hope to reciprocate with my next if anyone takes it.

I will send on what I have to say.[2] "At-Swim-["] is a big thing.

Yrs. Ever

Denis.

P.S. Have any <u>serious</u> reviews come out?

Autograph letter signed. 1 leaf, 2 sides. *Header*: Légation d'Irlande. Header crossed out in ink, address written in top right-hand corner. Brian O'Nolan Papers (1/4/MSS 051), Box 1, Folder 2, Southern Illinois University Special Collections Research Center.

---

1. Brian O'Nolan's *At Swim-Two-Birds* was first published in March 1939 by Longman, Green & Co., under the pseudonym Flann O'Brien.

2. The follow-up letter is not preserved in the O'Nolan correspondence at Southern Illinois University. Devlin was abruptly transferred from Rome to New York in July 1939, as war was breaking out, and it is possible that he never managed to write or send his critical response to the novel.

Washington DC
and London,
1939–50

CHRONOLOGY

1939

August   DD appointed Irish consul in New York.

1940

March   DD quickly transferred to the legation in Washington
              DC after an urgent request for more staff.

April   Appointed acting secretary of the Irish legation; his
              position as secretary is soon secured.

May   DD gives a reading of his poems at the 'Y' in New
              York, organised by Norman Macleod.

1941

February   'Farewell and Good' is published in *Poetry*, vol. 57,
              no. 5.

July   DD begins discussion with publisher William M.
              Roth regarding a Celtic poetry anthology, co-edited
              with Macleod.

1942

Spring   'Lough Derg' is published in the final issue of the
              The Southern Review before it suspends publication
              during the war years.

June   Roth announces that his publishing house, the Colt
              Press, will have to cease operations because of the war.

1943

Winter   'Ank'hor Vat' is published in *The University Review*,
              vol. 10, no. 2.

1944

October   'Rains', DD's translation of Alexis Leger's 'Pluies', appears in *The Sewanee Review*, vol. 52, no. 4.

November   DD attends the International Civil Aviation Conference in Chicago.

1945

Spring   Leger's 'Neiges' and DD's 'Snows' are published as parallel texts in *The Sewanee Review*, vol. 53, no. 2.

           DD spends two months in Ireland, returns by flying-boat from Foynes.

Summer   'Twenty-four Poets', a review of a number of contemporary poetry volumes, appears in *The Sewanee Review*, vol. 53, no. 3.

1946

January   Leger's 'Poème à l'étrangère' and DD's 'Poem to a Foreign Lady' are published as parallel texts in *Briarcliff Quarterly*, vol. II, no. 8.

May   *Lough Derg and Other Poems* is published by Reynal & Hitchcock.

1947

January   DD marries Caren Randon in Washington; they honeymoon in Mexico.

February   Assigned to London as counsellor of the High Commissioner's Office; the Devlins depart.

December	DD and CD spend Christmas at the Slopes, the Devlin family home in Dún Laoghaire.

1948

Summer	Devlins vacation in Sirmione, Italy, joined by Robert Penn Warren and his wife Emma Brescia.

1949

May	DD involved in discussions at St James's Palace leading to the Treaty of London, and the establishment of the Council of Europe.
Summer	*Exile and Other Poems* is published in a bilingual edition with DD's translations, as the fifteenth number in the Bollingen Series.
	DD transferred to Department of External Affairs headquarters in Dublin, in the role of counsellor in the Political Division.
August	Attends the first international parliament of the Council of Europe in Strasbourg.

1950

March	Dublin's *Envoy* and the Italian journal *Inventario degli oggetti d'arte d'Italia* publish, respectively, a short extract and a longer version of *The Heavenly Foreigner*; the *Inventario* publication includes a parallel Italian translation by Tommaso Giglio.

To Niall Montgomery
10 January 1940

Dear Niall,

As you know, the post is haphazard and I didn't hear till well afterwards about your marriage. My congratulations to you and my best wishes to Hop on the same account.[1] I wish you both luck and fun.

I am settling down with less surprise than I had thought, due to my advancing years, no doubt. Eire doesn't cut any ice as a sensation now nor North Eire either. Finland is the baby.[2] America is worrying itself sick about the European War and all the moral values that are being destroyed. It says it is preparing itself to be the reservoir of Western civilization, so far they have buried several of the major poets well below the surface in special-process anti-dissolution steel books. That's the Universities. As for the Government, it has accepted the custody of 71 Masterpieces of the Italian Renaissance and the Domesday Book.[3] The Book of Kells is not felt to be such a Significant Landmark of Progress. They are also embalming Toscanini and making citizens out of Auden & Isherwood; though some of them are suspicious regarding the motivation behind these Limey poets' casual activation – and would you blame them?[4] But Finland is real front-page – to Finland they are giving their moral support with an open hand. The conscience of the nation has been so deeply shocked by the brutality of Russia that Senate Commissions have been able to reprove various schoolboy organisations for unAmericanism. If I go any further, it might look as if I were being amusing whereas I'm merely being coy. But there are no public lavatories in the whole bloody town.

You know, I suppose, that Carroll's <u>Kindred</u> got a hell of a slashing here and only lasted two weeks.[5] Carroll did the Dublin trick of protesting, in letters to the papers, against the poor reviews and how his message was misunderstood. As a matter of fact, I thought the play a lot better than was said, as a simple audience, I enjoyed it. But poor Carroll is tearing the skin off himself with rage. They are all trying to take up a position about <u>Finnegan's [*for* Finnegans] Wake</u> but it has them flat – me too if I had read it.[6]

I liked your card which arrived a few days ago. – I see the Sweeneys from time to time and they're very kind – Didn't everybody meet Saroyan when he was in Dublin?[7] I think you must have been in London at the time. It's very queer. He has got a very successful play running now and it seems he wrote it simply to fulfil a life-long ambition to go to Dublin. So he wrote it and the backer gave him a lump sum and off he went to Dublin. It seems he refuses to say a word about it. People are curious & they ask him [ʔan[d] be jamesy] if the lad will say a word except "Yes, I've been to Dublin" in a pleasant informative voice.

Well all the best. Remember me to Hop.
Denis.

Personal address   43 E. 50th St.,
                                     New York City

Autograph letter signed. 2 leaves, 4 sides. *Header:* Consulate General of Ireland, New York. Niall Montgomery Papers, MS 50, 118/26/23, NLI.

---

1. Niall Montgomery married Rose Anna Hopkins (known familiarly as Hop) in October 1939.

2. The Soviet Union invaded Finland in November 1939, marking the beginning of the Winter War. President Roosevelt responded quickly by extending financial aid to Finland; the League of Nations expelled the Soviet Union.

3. Devlin is being flippant here; before the USA entered the Second World War, and Americans made a significant contribution to the cultural preservation of 'The Monuments Men', there was no government-led initiative for American custody of European art. At the approach of war, the Roerich Pact, an agreement for the protection of artistic and scientific institutions, was signed in Washington in 1935. In a non-governmental move that was nonetheless political for the cultural platform it gave Mussolini, an exhibition of Italian Renaissance masterpieces 'Lent by the Royal Italian Government' was on an extended tour of American galleries including the Art Institute of Chicago and the Museum of Modern Art in New York in 1939–40.

4. Arturo Toscanini (1867–1957), Italian conductor, was a fierce critic of Mussolini and Hitler, and left Milan for New York in 1938 to lead the NBC Symphony Orchestra; Christopher Isherwood (1904–86), English novelist of the Auden Group. Auden and Isherwood entered the United States on temporary visas at the outbreak of war in 1939, becoming American citizens in 1946.

5. Paul Vincent Carroll (1900–68), Irish dramatist and screenwriter. *Kindred*, a play about the artist in wartime, premiered at the Abbey in September 1939 and came to New York in December of the same year.

6. *Finnegans Wake* (1939) was Joyce's final and much-vaunted novel which had been unfolding under the title *Work in Progress* while Devlin and Coffey were in Paris. It is notorious for its linguistic and narrative difficulty.

7. James Johnson Sweeney (see DD to Ruth de Verry, *transition* magazine, 13 October 1936, n. 1) and his wife Laura (Harden) Sweeney (1902–82). William Saroyan (1908–81), Armenian-American novelist and playwright, sold *Sunset Sonata* to Broadway actor-producer-director Eddie Dowling in 1939. *The New York Times* reported that Saroyan would be spending two or three weeks 'loafing among the Irish' (9 June 1939, p. 30).

To Amy Bonner, Poetry Magazine
23 January 1940

Dear Miss Bonner,

Thanks very much for your kind invitation to join your table at the dinner of the Poetry Society of America to be held on January 25th at the Biltmore Hotel. I am very sorry I shall not be able to come. It would indeed have been a pleasure to join you and to hear the very wise words that will be spoken.[1]

With best wishes and thanks,

Yours sincerely,

Denis Devlin

Typed letter signed. 1 leaf, 1 side. *Header:* Consulate General of Ireland, New York. Amy Bonner Papers, Box 1, Folder 5, Special Collections Research Center, University of Chicago Library.

---

1. The dinner was hosted by A.M. Sullivan (see letter dated 24 April 1940, and Correspondents' Biographies), the newly-appointed president of the Poetry Society of America. He gave an address about the deplorable lack of interest in poetry in contemporary society (*The New York Times*, 26 January 1940, p. 13).

To Norman Macleod
30 March 1940

Dear Norman,

It occurs to me that you may be getting anxious about my poems for mimeograph; I have just finished the last non-published one I wish to include and I shall send you the whole list next week.[1] I have not said how glad I am for the chance of becoming better known but I am deeply grateful to you and I'm looking forward to the reading with excitement.[2] My apparent indifference to fame – let me use the old word – has been, of course, partly a reactive defense [sic] against disappointment. But if you have no signs of being believed, your belief in yourself slips away without noticing and that was happening to me. The poem I have just finished was written five years ago en bloc and there were few changes to be made but I just let it drift until New York.[3] Fortunately, I don't depend on the continuance of the mood in which a poem was begun. Now I can polish all my raw work of the last few years; it is good for me now. I think I shall do you justice at the reading: I shall read slowly and that will overcome the disadvantages here of my different pronunciation. I shall also have to see to it that my voice carries, even in Ireland that has been a difficulty, but I shall manage.

I am to be Secretary of Legation here.

I enjoyed our night out immensely. I hope Vivienne was not too fatigued.[4] I've been thinking about our discussion about conventional forms & self-discovering, self-resolving forms, it is an old preoccupation. I've not been convinced by the <u>productions</u> of those who practise the latter. However, till another date.

Best wishes

Yours.

Denis

Autograph letter signed. 1 leaf, 2 sides. *Header:* Irish Legation, Washington, DC. Norman Macleod Papers, Yale Collection of American Literature (MSS 718), Box 7, Folder 65, Beinecke Rare Book and Manuscript Library, Yale University.

---

1. Macleod had requested poems for a contemporary poetry anthology he was editing as an extension of his work for the YMHA Poetry Center in New York, *Calendar: An anthology of 1940 poetry* (Prairie City: The Press of James Decker, 1940). A single poem of Devlin's was included, 'Little Elegy', which had previously been published in *Ireland Today*, vol. II, no. 3, March 1937, pp. 33–4. mimeograph: the process of reproducing text from a stencil with the use of a mimeograph machine.

2. Devlin gave a reading of 'Little Elegy' and other poems at the 'Y' on 6 May 1940.

3. There were no unpublished Devlin poems included in the 1940 edition of *Calendar*. Devlin may have sent along 'Love from Time to Time': J.C.C. Mays notes that a typescript of this poem in the NLI archive is marked '*Published Calendar*', although it never appeared in Macleod's *Calendar* anthologies of 1940 or 1942.

4. Macleod was at this time married to Vivienne Koch. See Correspondents' Biographies.

To George Dillon, Poetry Magazine
6 April 1940

Dear Mr. Dillon,

Mr. James Sweeney told me some time ago that you were good enough to say you liked my book Intercessions and that I might send you something with a view to possible publication in Poetry. I am therefore sending the enclosed poem Farewell and Good for your consideration.

I should have hurried much sooner to get in touch with you had I not been prevented by the unfinished state of the poetry I have by me at present and by the confusion accompanying a sudden transfer from New York to Washington. I hope you will not think I have been casual about your kind invitation.

A stamped addressed envelope is enclosed.

Yours very faithfully,

Denis Devlin.

Typed letter signed. 1 leaf, 1 side. *Header:* The Fairfax Hotel, Washington DC. *Address:* George Dillon, Esq., Editor, Poetry, 232 East Erie Street, Chicago, Illinois. *Poetry: A Magazine of Verse.* Records, 1895–1961, Box 74 Folder 1, Special Collections Research Center, University of Chicago Library.

To A.M. Sullivan, Poetry Society of America
24 April 1940

Dear Mr. Sullivan:

Many thanks for your kind invitation to the meeting of the Poetry Society to be held on Thursday, April 25 at Roosevelt House. I much regret, however, that I shall not be able to attend as I have been transferred to the Legation here at Washington.

I hope things are going well with you in the society. You seem to be putting new blood into it and even if you don't agree with Oscar Williams (I don't know whether you do or not) it seems a useful sort of thing to have people like him about.[1]

If I should come to New York sometime I shall give you a ring and I hope to see you.

Very sincerely yours,
Denis Devlin

Typed letter signed. 1 leaf, 1 side. *Header*: Irish Legation, Washington, DC. *Address*: Mr A.N. Sullivan, President, Poetry Society of America, 290 Broadway, New York City. A.M. Sullivan Papers, Correspondence Box 3, Special Collections Research Center, Syracuse University Libraries.

---

1. Oscar Williams, born Oscar Kaplan (1900–64), American poet, editor and anthologist, became a member of the Poetry Society of America in 1937. In the 1920s Williams had edited *Rhythmus*, a short-lived magazine devoted to avant-garde and experimental poetry; *Rhythmus* had promoted the work of Eugene Jolas, editor of *transition*, in which some of Devlin's early poems had appeared.

To Joseph P. Walshe, Secretary, Department of External Affairs
25 November 1940

On the invitation of the Emmett Club (Clan-na[-]Gael) Baltimore, Maryland, I attended their Annual Banquet in celebration of the Manchester Martyrs on November 23rd, 1940. Having been asked to speak I conveyed to the club greetings from Ireland and described recent social and economic developments which the independence of Ireland made it possible to achieve. Most of the speakers had supported Irish neutrality and I, therefore, felt obliged to make some reference to the subject, although, as there were newspaper representatives present, I thought it necessary not to be too direct on account of the sensitiveness of American opinion, at present getting more marked, to propaganda. I confined myself, accordingly, to generalizations on the necessity and the advantage to Europe of maintaining the independence of small countries, pointing out that these countries being without the means to practice imperialism, always tended to support peace and also that the maintenance of their cultural particularity made for the greater variety and richness of the general European culture.

Denis Devlin

Typed memo signed. 1 leaf, 1 side. *Address*: included as an enclosure in a letter from Minister Robert Brennan to The Secretary, Dept. of External Affairs, Dublin, dated 10 December 1940. Department of Foreign Affairs Papers, DFA/219/3A, NAI.

To Joseph P. Walshe, Secretary, Department of External Affairs
11 December 1940

As the Minister was suddenly called to New York, he was unable to make the usual report on the political situation.[1] I am forwarding herewith the newspaper clippings which would have accompanied the report. It will be seen that the important topic is America's entry into the war, and that most opinion and feeling is tending to urge in that direction.

> Denis Devlin
> for Minister

Typed letter signed. Handwritten annotations and filing stamp from the Department. 1 leaf, 1 side. *Header*: Irish Legation, Washington, DC. *Address*: The Secretary, Department of External Affairs, Dublin. Marked with departmental ref. no. 108/109/40. Department of Foreign Affairs Papers, DFA/219/3A, NAI.

---

1. Robert Brennan (1881–1964) was minister plenipotentiary to the USA at this time.

To the Editors, Poetry Magazine[1]
27 January 1941

Gentlemen:

I return herewith corrected proof of "Farewell and Good." I have made two changes; I hope this will not be inconvenient to the printers.[2] The words "at bay" are inserted between "world" and "bitten" in line 4; "of" is changed to "by" in the twelfth line. The second last line which must have crept in by mistake is erased. I hope I have not delayed too long in returning the proof.

Yours sincerely,
Denis Devlin

Typed letter signed. 1 leaf, 1 side. *Header:* Irish Legation, Washington, DC. *Address:* The Editors, Poetry: A Magazine of Verse, 232 East Erie Street, Chicago, Ill. *Poetry: A Magazine of Verse.* Records, 1895–1961, Box 74, Folder 1, UChi.

---

1. George Dillon's editorship of *Poetry* magazine ran from 1937 to 1949. Devlin was evidently known to the wider team at *Poetry* at this time. He is cited in the 'News Notes' section of the January 1941 issue for providing comment on a shift taking place in contemporary Irish poetry, away from agricultural themes and 'sophisticated ballad' forms, towards a poetry that is 'urban and sociological in emphasis' ('News Notes', *Poetry*, vol. 57, no. 4, January 1941, p. 282).

2. 'Farewell and Good' was published in *Poetry*, vol. 57, no. 5, February 1941, pp. 300–1.

To William M. Roth
8 August 1941

Dear Mr. Roth,

Many thanks for your letter of the 1st. July about the possibility of publishing the <u>Celtic Anthology</u>.[1] As regards copyright, there would be little difficulty, I think, as the poets were asked to send unpublished work, copyright free for this country; Mr. Macleod was given the right to use the material by the poets submitting it to him for publication in a Celtic Anthology. In the case of Dylan Thomas, I shall set about obtaining permission from NEW DIRECTIONS to include poems, previously sent by him to Macleod, which were brought out by that house in their Thomas volume.[2] The same for McGreevey [*for* Mac-Greevy] who is the only other exception.[3]

I quite agree with you that some of the poetry is bad but the material I sent was intended as a representative selection from the rather large amount of mss. on my hands; and at the time I was undecided about editorial policy. I wondered, that is, whether a publisher might not be more interested in a book made up with an eye to other values than the strictly poetic, whether, especially in the case of foreign poetry, social or merely geographical interests might not be inviting. Heresy, of course. I had much rather the book were exclusive and, helped by the point of view in your letter, I agree that only the very best should be included. Will you, therefore, kindly return to me the mss. I forwarded (for which postage forwarded) and from that and the material I have here I will make a selection on the principle of poetic quality for submission to you.

About Higgins: he was too well established, I think, for our company of unknown poets and, from my knowledge of him, I don't think he would have taken kindly to being presented as what he would have called a "modern" poet. And there may be devotional poetry in the making under the impact of war but, unfortunately in the bad state of communications, I have been rather out of touch with things for the last year or so. I don't think much is being done in Ireland though; among my own contemporaries, prose has been practised with more interest than poetry.

What are your ideas about contract terms[?]

Forgive me for taking so long in replying: I had to make sure about the copyright position by writing to Macleod.

With best wishes,

Denis Devlin

Typed letter signed. Handwritten corrections. 2 leaves, 2 sides. *Header:* Irish Legation, Washington, DC. Colt Press Records, *c.* 1941–70 (MSS 94/15), Bancroft Library, University of California, Berkeley.

---

1. This Celtic anthology (the MS for which eventually circulated under the title *Modern Celtic Poetry: An anthology*), an editorial collaboration with Norman Macleod, originated as a solo project for Macleod in the late 1930s. A letter from Macleod to James Decker in January 1940 suggests it was originally destined for the Decker Press. Macleod seems to have been particularly interested in representing poets associated with the 'New Romantic' and 'New Apocalypse' movements, which were emerging from the Celtic nations in the British Isles. Dylan Thomas (see n. 2 below) was the poet principally associated with New Romanticism; the work of the New Apocalypse poets was heralded by an anthology of that name, edited by Henry Treece and J.F. Hendry, and characterised by anti-rationalist, politically sceptical poetry reacting to the work of the Auden generation. As an early draft of Macleod's prefatory note indicates, he was particularly interested in the representation of war ('on the breadline as well as in the trenches') in these national poetries. Devlin was likely recruited to add his expertise to the Irish selections. A copy of the letter to Decker, along with the table of contents and editorial preface, are contained in the Brian Coffey Papers, Box 29, Folder 43, Special Collections, University of Delaware Library.

2. Dylan Thomas (1914–53), Welsh poet. Thomas was introduced to American audiences in a *New Directions in Prose and Poetry* anthology of 1938, from James Laughlin's recently founded New Directions press. The following year Laughlin published *The World I Breathe* from New Directions, which gathered selected poems from Thomas' British volumes and a clutch of stories.

3. MacGreevy's *Poems* (1934) was published by London's Heinemann, and reprinted by Viking Press in New York. He had largely moved away from poetry by the late 1930s, his attention turned to critical prose. The poems Devlin hoped to include were 'Nocturne', 'Homage to Marcel Proust' and 'Nocturne of the Self-Evident Presence'.

To Joseph P. Walshe, Secretary, Department of External Affairs
2 October 1941

I beg to state that the Consul at Boston reports that he was invited to give a talk at a luncheon meeting of the Kiwanis Club of Somerville, Mass. on the 25th of September last, on the subject of Ireland's Neutrality.[1]

The Kiwanis Clubs are an important benevolent association, many of them are unsympathetic to our position; however, none expressed any feeling after the talk except that they did not envy us "the spot" on which we have been placed by circumstances outside of our control.

Denis Devlin

for Minister

Typed letter signed. Handwritten corrections; stamped by the department. 1 leaf, 1 side. *Header:* Irish Legation, Washington, DC. *Address:* Secretary, Department of External Affairs, Dublin. Marked with departmental ref. no. 36-5/41. Department of Foreign Affairs Papers, DFA/219/3A, NAI.

---

1. Brendan O'Riordan (dates unknown) had been consul in Boston since 1939, after a period as consul in New York. In 1955 he was appointed Irish representative to the Council of Europe. The Kiwanis Club is a charitable organisation founded in Detroit in 1915, dedicated to improving community services for under-privileged children.

To William M. Roth
11 October 1941

Dear Mr. Roth,

I am sending you the manuscript now, the final choice. I hope it will look more attractive to you. The <u>Preface</u> enclosed is merely tentative and I shall be glad to alter it if you wish – it is perhaps too long.[1] The contract terms you mention seem pretty fair and we accept them. Sales, by the way, in this case, may be better than average as I may succeed in interesting our Consuls in various cities in the book; a word of recommendation here & there from them would be helpful.

I shall send you the biblio biographical notes on the authors next week. I've had to revise what was there & do some research.

I hope I've not delayed too long in sending back the MS. The work was slowed down when I went on holiday. It seems to me now to have the makings of an interesting book.

    [W]ith best wishes.

     Denis Devlin

Autograph letter signed. 1 leaf, 2 sides. *Header*: Irish Legation, Washington, DC. Colt Press Records (MSS 94/15), UCB.

---

1. If Devlin redrafted Macleod's preface, the later version has not been found.

To William M. Roth
2 December 1941

Dear Mr. Roth,

I am wondering if you have received the MSS for the Celtic Anthology, which I despatched to you by registered mail on the 11th October. If not, would you kindly let me know so that I can take the matter up with the Post Office.

I'm glad to see, from its advertisements, that the Colt Press is making itself known[.][1]

With best wishes,

Denis Devlin

Autograph letter signed. 1 leaf, 1 side. *Header*: Irish Legation, Washington, DC. Colt Press Records (MSS 94/15), UCB.

---

1. A recent Colt Press volume, *The Epicure in Imperial Russia* (1941) by Marie Alexandre Markevitch, had received publicity in Edward Larocque Tinker's 'New Editions, Fine & Otherwise' column for *The New York Times* (23 November 1941).

To William M. Roth
22 December 1941

Dear Mr. Roth,

Thanks for your note of December 9th. I shall be glad, of course, to wait until after the New Year for further discussion of plans regarding the book.

With best wishes,

Denis Devlin

Typed letter signed. 1 leaf, 1 side. *Header*: Irish Legation, Washington, DC. Colt Press Records (MSS 94/15), UCB.

* * * * *

To William M. Roth
6 February 1942

Dear Mr. Roth,

I am very sorry that you find it impossible to proceed with the publication of the anthology. I had counted on it and, indeed, the course of our correspondence implied, I think, that you had decided to go ahead with the book.

Naturally I understand that your firm, a new one, should have been faced with difficult problems, especially with the outbreak of war. I hope things will pick up.

I have considered your offer to keep the MS. with a view to eventual publication. There is, however, a possibility of publication elsewhere and I'd therefore like you to return it to me as soon as possible.

With best wishes,

Denis Devlin

Typed letter signed. 1 leaf, 1 side. *Header*: Irish Legation, Washington, DC. Colt Press Records (MSS 94/15), UCB.

To John Palmer, The Southern Review
19 March 1942

Dear Mr. Palmer,

I am extremely sorry to learn that The Southern Review will have to cease publication.[1] Its place can't be taken by any other magazine and its loss will be a great blow to your readers as it must be to yourselves.

I don't know whether, in the circumstances, you intend to publish my Lough Derg in the final issue; but if you do, and if there is still time, could you substitute for the copy I gave you, the enclosed version? I have inkmarked it B for your convenience.

Very sincerely yours,

Denis Devlin

Typed letter signed. 1 leaf, 1 side. *Header*: Irish Legation, Washington, DC. *The Southern Review* Records, Yale Collection of American Literature (MS 694), Series 1, Box II, Beinecke Rare Book and Manuscript Library, Yale University.

---

1. *The Southern Review* suspended publication in 1942, in the wake of America's entry into the war, not resuming until 1965. John Palmer, managing editor 1940–2, served in the US Navy.

To William M. Roth
19 March 1942

Dear Mr. Roth,

I'm afraid you can't have had much time to prepare your memorandum that night. But it was good fun.[1] I hope you were able to finish it later. It's an exciting publishing scheme.

Miss Steloff is really very interested in the anthology: [s]he thinks she can push it and is strongly of the opinion that summer publication would be advisable.[2] Naturally I agree with her! She emphasised that the sale of poetry has nothing to do with the seasons. And you would have it off your hands for the strenuous autumn publishing.

I am making the changes we agreed on. I think they will definitely improve the book.

I'm looking forward to hearing from you on all this.

With best wishes,

Denis Devlin

Typed letter signed. Some punctuation marks inserted by hand. 1 leaf, 1 side. *Header*: Irish Legation, Washington, DC. Colt Press Records, UCB.

---

1. In a letter from Norman Macleod to Roth, dated 26 February 1942, we see that Roth changed his mind about cancelling publication weeks after Devlin's letter of 6 February, possibly as a result of a conversation with Macleod. Macleod's letter also indicates that Roth was planning a trip to Washington and a meeting with Devlin in person. See Colt Press Records, *c.* 1941–70 (MSS 94/15), Bancroft Library, UCB.

2. Frances Steloff (born Stelov) (1887–1989), founder of the Gotham Book Mart in New York City, which became a hub for avant-garde literary artists. Devlin and Macleod were both urging Roth to publish quickly, perhaps mindful of the effects of the war on the publishing industry.

To William M. Roth
8 April 1942

Dear Roth,

I am enclosing a contract in one copy signed and initialed [*sic*] where necessary.

I am very happy to hear that you will try to get the Anthology out during the summer. I shall send the manuscript very soon; I am waiting the publisher's permission to include MacNeice and Rodgers.[1] I have seen White here; he showed quite some interest in the book.[2]

I hope you are keeping well.

With best wishes,

Denis Devlin

Typed letter signed. 1 leaf, 1 side. *Header*: Irish Legation, Washington, DC. Colt Press Records (MSS 94/15), UCB.

---

1. Louis MacNeice (1907–63), Belfast-born poet, playwright and critic associated with the Auden Group in the 1930s, and W.R. Rodgers (see Correspondents' Biographies). Both were working in radio broadcasting in the 1940s.

2. White has not been identified.

To William M. Roth
16 April 1942

Dear Roth,

I asked permission of the publishers of MacNeice (Random House) and Rodgers (Harcourt, Brace) to include them in the anthology. Random want $10 per poem and Harcourt sent me a contract form to be filled out. I know you, as the publisher, did not envisage paying out fees for copyright stuff and I don't feel inclined to either. So I think we shall have to leave MacNeice & Rodgers out – a pity from the publicity point of view. I am asking Macleod if he thinks we should pay the fees & get the poems. In the meantime, in case we decide to do so, I am sending you the Harcourt forms; they are only applications which need not be followed up. As for Higgins, I am including poems which have not been published here.

Would you, then, complete the forms and lodge them with Harcourt? I shall send you Random's forms later, if necessary.

Yours,

Denis Devlin

The typing is mine, unfortunately.

Typed letter signed. Corrections and postscript handwritten. 1 leaf, 1 side. *Header*: Irish Legation, Washington, DC. Colt Press Records (MSS 94/15), UCB.

To John Palmer, The Southern Review
22 April 1942

Dear Mr. Palmer:

The following are some facts about myself, from which you might make the biographical note for <u>Notes on Contributors</u>:

Formerly instructor in English Poetry at University College, Dublin. At present, Secretary of the Irish Legation in Washington. Book of poems, <u>Intercessions</u>, published London, Europa Press, 1937. Have appeared in various reviews, Dublin Magazine, Transition, The New Republic, and Poetry. Translations from Paul Eluard in the English edition of his poems, <u>Thorns of Thunder</u>, 1938. Editing, with Norman Macleod, <u>Modern Celtic Anthology</u>, to be published this summer by the Colt Press, San Francisco.

> With best wishes,
> Very sincerely yours,
> Denis Devlin

If the type is not already set up, I should be much obliged if you would inscribe the poem as follows: <u>To Adrienne Koch</u>.[1] I hope my requests for changes have not been too much of a nuisance to you.

Typed letter signed. 1 leaf, 1 side. *Header*: Irish Legation, Washington, DC. *The Southern Review* Records, Series 1, Box II, Beinecke, YU.

---

1. Adrienne Koch (1913–71), renowned historian and Jefferson scholar, was completing her philosophy doctorate at Columbia Graduate School at this time. It is likely she was introduced to Devlin by her sister Vivienne Koch and brother-in-law Norman Macleod, and a close relationship developed – the NLI drafts show that Devlin is thinking of Koch during the composition of other early American poems.

To William M. Roth
23 April 1942

Dear Bill Roth,

I agree that it would be of great advantage to include Rodgers & MacNeice. I had an agreeable letter about the latter from Saxe Cummings [*for* Commins] of Random House, so I shall write to him and ask him to send the contract forms direct to you.[1] It will be good if yo[u] can get the poems for a small fee.

The MacNeice poems I want are from Poems 1925-40, Random House; they are, Dublin (p.260), The Expert (p.280) and Cradle Song (p.322).[2]

I shall seem vacillating but, on thinking it over, I am again doubtful of the wisdom of including Higgins.[3] It would defeat the purpose of the Irish section, which is to show what has been done since the days of the Celtic Twilight school; and we should be questioned about the absence of Austin Clarke, Padraic Colum and James Stephens, as well as others closely associated with him in style and outlook.[4] I think our book is happily homogenous without them. Besides, they have all copyright and the fees would amount to more than we should like to pay when there's no pressing reason for it.

I shall [send] you a list of possible subscribers in a few days.

       Yours,

           Denis Devlin

           ↓

        (one n)[5]

Typed letter signed. Some over-typing to cover mistakes. 1 leaf, 1 side. *Header*: Irish Legation, Washington, DC. Colt Press Records (MSS 94/15), UCB.

---

1. Saxe Commins (?1892–1958), editor in chief at Random House, who had worked with Eugene O'Neill and William Faulkner. Devlin's mistake with the surname was

not uncommon. The Saxe Commins Papers at Princeton do not contain a record of Devlin's correspondence with Random House.

2. All of these poems are from *Plant and Phantom* (London: Faber, 1940). 'Dublin' is the opening poem in 'The Coming of War' (later 'The Closing Album') sequence; 'The Expert' was part of the 'Novelettes' sequence, although it was omitted after *Poems 1925–1940* (New York: Random House, 1940); 'Cradle Song' later took the title 'Cradle Song for Eleanor' – the volume was dedicated to MacNeice's lover Eleanor Clark (see Correspondents' Biographies).

3. See DD to William M. Roth, 8 August 1941, and DD to William M. Roth, 16 April 1942.

4. Padraic Colum (1881–1972), Irish playwright and poet, had emigrated to America in 1914 and achieved great success as the author of children's books. For Clarke and Stephens see Correspondents' Biographies and DD to Thomas MacGreevy, 10 November 1933, n. 2.

5. In Roth's publishing memoir he notes that both Devlin and Macleod had cause to complain about the persistent misspelling of their names – we see Devlin campaigning on Macleod's behalf in the letter below, dated 22 May 1942. Devlin's first name is, on one occasion, misspelt in this memoir. See *The Colt Springs High: A publishing memoir of the Colt Press, 1939–1942* (San Francisco: The Book Club of California, 2004), p. 185.

To William M. Roth
8 May 1942

Dear Bill Roth,

We might as well go ahead with our plan & have Rodgers & MacNeice, though I think their publishers have a nerve. I agree to what you propose, namely, to include <u>The Raider</u> & <u>Life's Circumnavigators</u> of Rodgers, half the fee of 15 dollars being paid by each of us.[1] And if Random insist on their terms for MacNeice, I think we should cut out one poem there also; i.e. <u>Cradle Song</u>, retaining <u>Dublin</u> & <u>The Expert</u> for 20 dollars[.] That's 10 dollars each.

I hope to goodness priorities are'nt [*sic*] going to catch me in poetry too. It's becoming a nightmare with me at my office.

By the way, what about the advance? Will you send it to me: you must have received the contract, duly signed?

All the best,

Denis Devlin

Typed letter signed. Handwritten corrections. 1 leaf, 1 side. *Header*: Irish Legation, Washington, DC. Colt Press Records (MSS 94/15), UCB.

---

1. 'The Raider' and 'Life's Circumnavigators' are poems from Rodgers' *Awake: And other poems* (London: Secker & Warburg, 1941), which was renamed *Awake! And other wartime poems* on its American publication by Harcourt, Brace & Company in 1942.

To William M. Roth
22 May 1942

My dear Bill Roth,

I am sending you herewith the script of the anthology with prefatory note and table of contents. I have adopted some of your suggestions, as you will see, and added one or two poems to the Irish section which improve it, I think. The poems of Denzell [*for* Denzil] Dunnett and G.S. Fraser (Scots section) were missing from t[he] script, as returned by you; perhaps they are among your files.[1] I have omitted Dunnett anyhow, but, if you have the poems, you might insert Early Spring by Fraser; if not, take his name off the table of contents.[2]

What's the position now about MacNeice and Rodgers? We should have them in; I have typed out those I want and include th[e]m here.

I also send a list of names from Norman Macleod – by t[he] way, note the spelling of his name.

> With all best wishes,
> Yours,
> Denis Devlin

Typed letter signed. One handwritten amendment, lots of faded type and incomplete words towards the right margin. 1 leaf, 1 side. *Header:* Irish Legation, Washington, DC. Colt Press Records (MSS 94/15), UCB.

---

1. Denzil Dunnett (1917–2016), Scottish poet and diplomat born in India, who had published in various magazines and edited a literary journal as an undergraduate at Corpus Christi, Oxford. He joined the Royal Artillery in 1939. George Sutherland Fraser (1915–80), Glasgow-born poet and critic associated with the New Apocalypse group. He published his first volume of poems, *The Fatal Landscape* (1941), while serving in the Royal Army Service Corps in Cairo.

2. On the original table of contents, one poem by Dunnett, 'Fantasy', is included (this poem has not been identified), and three from Fraser: 'Early Spring', 'The Fatal Landscape' and 'Meditation of a Patriot', from *The Fatal Landscape and Other Poems* (London: Poetry London, 1944).

To William M. Roth
15 June 1942

Dear Bill Roth,

I quite understand your difficulties about the book though, of course, it is a pity that it will not come out in summer. I'm sorry your last few books lost money: may that not be an ominous portent for ours!

I'm sending you the third MacNeice poem, The Expert.

I don't suppose it matters very much if you don't find the Fraser and Dunnet [*for* Dunnett] poems; they were'nt [*sic*] very good anyhow.

This shocking typing is by myself.

All best wishes,

Denis Devlin

Typed letter signed. Drawings and notes in lower left-hand corner in a hand other than Devlin's, probably Roth's. 1 leaf, 1 side. *Header:* Irish Legation, Washington, DC. Colt Press Records (MSS 94/15), UCB.

* * * * *

To William M. Roth
20 June 1942

Dear Bill Roth,

I am very upset to hear that the firm has to stop. Indeed, though the news that the book will not appear is a severe blow, I can truly say that I am more affected by the general loss of the Press's going; I have seen one or two of your books, fine jobs. Without being sentimental, I am sure that books is one of the few reliefs in the foul shrieking of the war. And your press meant more to you than the anthology to me, so you have my full sympathy.

I do, of course, want you to try and get Laughl[i]n interested in the book.[1] Will you send on the MS to him? I shall take it that you will and write to him myself in a week or so. It would be good if he would accept it. I notice from British magazines that some of our Celts are already making a name for themselves: Vernon Watkins, Henry Treece, Ruthven Todd.[2] What happens about the copyright for MacNeice & Rodgers? If you have paid the fees, will they carry over to the next publisher?

Well, hard luck and best of luck. If you come to Washington, as almost everyone does nowadays, be sure and look me up; I shall be very glad to see you[.]

[A]ll the best,

Denis Devlin

Typed letter signed. Overtyped corrections. 1 leaf, 1 side. *Header:* Irish Legation, Washington, DC. Colt Press Records (MSS 94/15), UCB.

---

1. James Laughlin (1914–97), American poet and publisher, founder of New Directions. Roth had written to Laughlin on 10 June 1942, recommending the Celtic anthology along with other manuscripts ready for the printers. New Directions (Am 2077), Series 1, Folder 1470, Houghton Library, Harvard University.

2. Vernon Watkins (1906–67), Welsh poet, translator and painter. After Watkins' first volume of poetry, *Ballad of the Mari Lwyd* (1941), was published by Faber with the endorsement of T.S. Eliot, his poems appeared in *The Welsh Review*, *Horizon* and *The Listener*. Henry Treece (1911–66), British poet and teacher of Welsh-Irish extraction, later the author of historical novels aimed at adults and children. Treece associated himself with Scottish and Welsh movements and writers, co-founding the New Apocalypse group with Scottish poet J.F. Hendry (see DD to William M. Roth, 8 August 1941, n. 2), and producing the first critical study of Dylan Thomas' work in 1949. Ruthven Todd (1914–78), Scottish poet, novelist, biographer, and editor of William Blake's works. Todd's biography of Alexandre Dumas, *The Laughing Mulatto*, was published in 1940, and his poems were appearing in anthologies of New Apocalypse writing as well as English literary journals and reviews such as *New Verse* and *Twentieth Century Verse*.

To James Laughlin, New Directions
24 August 1942

Dear Mr. Laughlin,

I understand from Mr William Roth of the <u>Colt Press</u>, San Francisco, that you expressed interest in an anthology of modern Celtic verse which I compiled and that he forwarded the script to you for consideration.

I wonder if you have been able to look through the collection and to decide whether you would be interested in taking it up for publication[?]

> Yours sincerely,
> Denis Devlin

Autograph letter signed. 1 leaf, 1 side. *Header*: Irish Legation, Washington, DC. New Directions Corp. Records, Series 1, Folder 438, HU.

To James Laughlin
3 September 1942

Dear Mr. Laughlin,

We have permission to publish in the case of all the poets represented in the anthology except two, MacNeice and Rodgers. In the latter instances, the American publishers have agreed to allow publication on payment of fees and Roth[,] on breaking the contract with us[,] undertook to meet part of this expense.

The position with regard to the others is that Norman Macleod, who collected their stuff some four years ago, asked them to submit unpublished, copyright-free poems, which they did. There would seem to be no difficulty here. There are, however, two borderline cases: Dylan Thomas and Thomas McGreevy [*for* MacGreevy]. Some of the poems in the book were later issued in your D. Thomas book, but Thomas had previously given them to us as free. I had intended to write to you on this point, once I was sure that our book was coming out. Would your permission be necessary in this case? Much the same holds for McGreevy, who came out here with the Viking Press; and if the anthology is to be brough[t] out, I shall write them in the matter.[1]

I'm glad you find the book interesting. It is very kind of you to consider it.

Yours very faithfully,

Denis Devlin

Typed letter signed. 1 leaf, 1 side. *Header:* Irish Legation, Washington, DC. New Directions Corp. Papers (Am 2077), Series 1, Folder 438, HU.

---

1. See DD to William M. Roth, 8 August 1941, n. 3.

To Clarence Decker, University Review[1]
27 October 1943

Dear Mr. Decker,

Thank you very much indeed for the news that you have accepted my poem "Ank'hor Vat" for publication in the University Review.[2] I am deeply gratified.

As for autobiographical details: I was born in Scotland and educated in Ireland and France – am in our Foreign service and have served in various posts abroad – book of verse "Intercessions" published in London in 1937 – since I came here in 1939, have appeared in Southern Review, New Republic and Poetry (Chicago).

Again, with many thanks,

Yours sincerely,

Denis Devlin

Autograph letter signed. 1 leaf, 1 side. *Header*: Irish Legation, Washington, DC. David Ray Papers 1936–2008, Box 47, Folder 23, Special Collections Research Center, University of Chicago Library.

---

1. *The University Review*, founded in 1934, became *The University of Kansas City Review* in 1944, and was again re-branded as *New Letters*, its current title, in 1971.

2. Devlin's 'Ank'hor Vat' appeared in *The University Review*, vol. 10, no. 2, Winter 1943, p. 117, alongside poems from Norman Macleod. The editorial correspondence in the University of Chicago archive shows that Macleod sent the poem to the journal on Devlin's behalf (David Ray Papers 1936–2008, Box 47, Folder 23, UChi).

To Alexis Leger
3 August 1944

Dear Léger [*for* Leger],

Forgive me for not replying sooner to your letter – I have been out of town for a few days. I think you could publish *Neiges* with advantage in the North Carolina <u>Quarterly Review</u>: it is young, of course, but quite respectable from what I have seen of it.[1] As for the translation, I would undertake that with great pleasure, should you wish me to; you know I should look on such a commission as an honour. I should, nevertheless, have found it difficult to ask Tate for the manuscript, unless you had done so too, as I understood that he had already given it to Cummings.[2] However, I learned yesterday from Miss Clarke [*for* Clark] that you handed her the poem for transmission to me; and I shall set to work on it with gusto when it comes to hand.[3]

    With kindest wishes,
        Yrs.
           Denis Devlin

Autograph letter signed. 1 leaf, 2 sides. *Header:* Irish Legation, Washington, DC. Correspondance particuliere de Saint-John Perse (Alexis Leger) et Dorothy Leger, Les Collections Patrimoniales, Fondation Saint-John Perse, Aix-en-Provence.

---

1. *The Quarterly Review of Literature* was founded by the poets Theodore Weiss and Warren Pendleton Carrier in 1943, while they were teaching at the University of North Carolina, Chapel Hill. *Neiges* had first appeared in the Buenos Aires-based journal *Les Lettres françaises*, July 1944, pp. 6–10.

2. e.e. cummings (1894–1962), American poet and occasional translator. Cummings was a friend of Leger's, and his poem 'being to timelessness as it's to time' was dedicated to him and intended for a special 1950 tribute number of *Cahiers de la Pléiade* (the poem arrived too late for inclusion). See St-John Perse, *Letters*, trans. and ed. by Arthur J. Knodel (Princeton: Princeton University Press, 2014), pp. 615–16. It is not known whether he was ever given the translation commission for *Neiges*.

3. 'Miss Clarke' is a misspelling of Eleanor Clark (see Correspondents' Biographies), a mutual Washington friend and occasional translator; her translation of Leger's 'Berceuse' was published with the French text in *Partisan Review*, vol. XIII, no. 4, 1946, p. 442. Devlin's translation, 'Snows' was published alongside the French text in Tate's *Sewanee Review*, vol. 53, no. 2, Spring 1945, pp. 186–97.

To Allen Tate
10 August 1944

Dear Allan [*for* Allen],

Impediments, ending now with the illness of my colleague, which will keep me in the office for some time, are piling up on me and I shall have to put off my visit till September. I hope that will not inconvenience you. My Minister, you see, is away too and I have also one of those brews stewing, in the office, which never comes to a head because there are too many cooks, merry damn to them!

I had a letter from Léger [*for* Leger] asking me if I knew anything about <u>Neiges</u> and if you had given it to E.E. Cummings. The Chapel Hill <u>Quarterly</u> had approached MacLeish for something of his (L.'s). He would like me to translate it. A few days later Eleanor Clarke [*for* Clark] phoned saying that she had the MS from Leger for me – although L. had implied in his letter that he had no copy of the poem by him. It's all rather odd & roundabout and Leger is away, so I can't clear it up with him. I'd do the translation if it weren't bespoken but wouldn't dream of interfering otherwise, of course. What's the position thereabout?

I'm looking forward to <u>SR</u>.[1]

Yours,

Denis

Autograph letter signed. 1 leaf, 2 sides. *Header*: Irish Legation, Washington, DC. Allen Tate Papers (C0106), Box 25, Folder 27, Manuscript Division, Department of Rare Books and Special Collections, Princeton University Library.

---

1. The anticipated issue of *The Sewanee Review*, vol. 52, no. 4, Oct–Dec 1944 contained 'Rains', Devlin's translation of Leger's 'Pluies', pp. 483–92.

To Allen Tate
15 September 1944

Dear Allan [*for* Allen],

I'm afraid I shan't be able to come after all: I hope this will not have inconvenienced you in any way and that you and Caroline will not too much blame my discourtesy.[1] It amounts to that, really, for when the day of my deliverance approached, at the end of August, I was so damp & so null from the heat-wave that I couldn't resist the temptation to go to the seaside. It's an annual pilgrimage with me anyhow; I always manage it no matter where I am. Then I thought I might get down to Tennesee [*for* Tennessee] at the end of this month; now, I find myself tied here in view of the Int[ernational] Aviation Conf[erence] in November.[2] I'm sorry for what I'm missing.

I wonder if you are writing anything these days? I've done some small pieces, singularly bad – Léger [*for* Leger] has been away from Washington for the last 6 weeks so I've not settled about the appearance of <u>Nuages</u> [*for* Neiges]; however, I'm going ahead with the translation.

Warren tells me you are coming up in October. I look forward to seeing you then. Reading the <u>Paradiso</u>; full of delight.[3]

     With all best wishes.

        Yours

          Denis Devlin

Autograph letter signed. 1 leaf, 2 sides. *Header:* Irish Legation, Washington, DC. Allen Tate Papers, Box 25, Folder 27, PU.

---

1. Tate and his wife, the novelist Caroline Gordon (1895–1981), were at this time based in Sewanee, Tennessee. Tate became managing editor of *The Sewanee Review* in 1944, after having served as an advisory editor.

2. See DD to Allen Tate, 12 November 1944, n. 1.

3. Dante Alighieri's *Paradiso*, the third book of his epic poem *Divina Commedia* (completed *c.* 1320).

To Allen Tate

12 November 1944   Rm 642A

Stevens Hotel, Chicago

Dear Allan [*for* Allen],

I am marooned here at the Aviation Conference and I'm very disappointed as it's probable that I shan't be back in time to see you on your visit to Washington – unless you are staying longer than the 2 or 3 days you foresaw! It looks at present as if we shall not finish here until the 23rd or 24th.[1]

The Conference is one of the most interesting I've attended but I'm so loaded with work that I've not even read a poem for weeks. I'm sure you must have something new which I cld. have seen in Washington but for this ill-timed excursion.[2] It's a damn shame, really.

Enjoy your stay in what I think of in Chicago as my home town. Though I rather like Chicago.

Yours

Denis

Autograph letter signed. 2 leaves, 2 sides. *Header:* International Civil Aviation Conference. Allen Tate Papers, Box 25, Folder 27, PU.

---

1. The International Civil Aviation Conference in Chicago took place from 1 November to 7 December 1944. Representatives of fifty-four Allied and neutral nations met to discuss the principles for international cooperation with regard to the safety and efficiency of post-war global air travel; the resulting agreement, the Chicago Convention, anticipated the emergence of the United Nations, establishing the International Civil Aviation Organization which became the UN agency responsible for regulating air travel.

2. Tate's *The Winter Sea* was to be published the following month by the Cummington Press.

To Joseph Hergesheimer
13 February 1945

Dear Mr Hergesheimer,

Thanks very much for such a good time at your dinner party last week[.] I enjoyed it all, the good talk, the good cheer, even your mysterious allusions to Planck & Venetian Blinds[.][1]

I look forward to seeing you again sometime here.

Yours very sincerely,

Denis Devlin

Autograph letter signed. 1 leaf, 1 side. *Header*: University Club, Washington. Joseph Hergesheimer Collection (MS 1921), Container 32.5, Harry Ransom Center, University of Texas at Austin.

---

1. Max Planck (1858–1947), German theoretical physicist who won the Nobel Prize in 1918 for his contribution to quantum theory.

To Allen Tate
28 February 1945

Dear Allen,

Thank you very kindly for your present of a copy of <u>The Winter Sea</u> and for inscribing it; I shall cherish it.[1] You should be pleased and satisfied; it's a fine collection. I like <u>Seasons</u> the best still, it becomes richer with growth and those parts I couldn't quite understand at first now fall necessarily into the course of the poem.[2] I notice the reviewers, though they praise it, are being rather wary of tackling it head on and I won't try to yet, or in a letter, but I should think it will be recognised as one of the major poems since the last war. My next favourites are the sonnets, which are powerful and sombre, and then the <u>Proconsuls</u>.[3] I haven't been able so far to place the final satirical poems in my mind justly.[4] May the book receive the esteem of the best!

The proofs of <u>Neiges</u> arrived today; I shall return them with all despatch. This winter has been dirty and disagreeable and its breaking up will be welcome. Woe to the conquered!

All best wishes,
Denis

Autograph letter signed. 1 leaf, 2 sides. *Header*: University Club, Washington DC. Allen Tate Papers, Box 25, Folder 27, PU.

---

1. *The Winter Sea* was published in a limited edition of 330 in December 1944 by the Cummington Press, a fine hand-printing outfit run by Harry Duncan in Massachusetts. The small print run and expense of the volume meant that it was very gradually taken up by reviewers the following year; Cleanth Brooks' review appeared in *Poetry*, vol. 66, no. 6, September 1945, pp. 324–9.

2. 'Seasons of the Soul', a poem dedicated to the memory of John Peale Bishop. First published in *The Kenyon Review*, vol. 6, no. 1, Winter 1944, pp. 1–9, it is the opening poem in *The Winter Sea*.

3. 'More Sonnets at Christmas', a sequence Tate was later to dedicate to Devlin's memory; 'Ode to Our Young Proconsuls of the Air', dedicated to St-John Perse.

4. The volume closes with 'Eclogue of the Liberal and the Poet' and 'False Nightmare'.

To Allen Tate
8 March 1945

Dear Allen,

Rains is a beautifully done job, the design and printing.[1] There is nothing but good words for it from all sides. You may want to know the numbers of the copies taken: by Léger [*for* Leger], I, II, 1, 2, 8 and 9; by me III, VII, 3, 12, 18 and 34.

I am amusing myself more than necessary but I have a mountaineous [*sic*] aversion to turning to higher pursuits after the brutal futilities of my days in the Legation. Consequently, I am behind with my translations and have not started to write the review of poetry yet.[2] And my holiday is looming ahead. So won't you let me know for which issue of the Sewanee you want my review and what is the deadline. The books have been reviewed threadbare by now, you will have noticed[,] and I'm appalled when I think of the only solemn generalities which seem to be within my reach on the subject. Jarrell's notice in the last Partisan is good.[3]

All best wishes,
Denis

Autograph letter signed. 1 leaf, 2 sides. *Header*: Irish Legation, Washington, DC. Allen Tate Papers, Box 25, Folder 27, PU.

---

1. Following the publication of Devlin's translation of 'Rains' in *The Sewanee Review*, January 1944, Tate issued a pamphlet version of Leger's original poem accompanied by the Devlin translation in 1945.

2. The review was 'Twenty-four Poets', treating a number of recent poetry volumes, including Robert Lowell's *Land of Unlikeliness* (1944) and Auden's *For the Time Being: A Christmas oratorio* (1944). It appeared in *The Sewanee Review*, vol. 53, no. 3, Summer 1945, pp. 457–66.

3. Randall Jarrell (1914–65), American poet and critic. Jarrell published 'Poetry in Peace and War', an omnibus review of recent poetry volumes, including those of Lowell, Marianne Moore and William Carlos Williams, in *Partisan Review*, vol. XXII, no. 1, Winter 1945, pp. 124–5.

To Norman Macleod
24 March 1945

Dear Norman,

I must wish you and Vivienne well this fine Spring. I'm going home on leave at the end of next week and shall be there for two months. I'm flying. So be good in the mean time and we must meet when I come back.

Your Briarcliff Quarterly continues to be most interesting, viewed from the basis on which it's run – I mean student management, editorship, etc.[1] You will have the last <u>Sewanee</u> with Vivienne's review, which is first-rate, my congratulations.[2] There's a bad misprint in <u>Snows</u> (English version) – "liberation" shld. read "libration".[3]

I mean to write poetry when I go home. I'm crowded with work these days, but secondary stuff; and with pleasure – Spring always complicates my affairs.

Best wishes

Denis

Autograph letter signed. 1 leaf, 2 sides. *Header*: Irish Legation, Washington, DC. Norman Macleod Papers, Box 7, Folder 65, Beinecke, YU.

---

1. The *Briarcliff Quarterly* began as the *Maryland Quarterly*, a journal which ran for three issues under Macleod's editorial direction, from the English department of the University of Maryland. When Macleod moved to Briarcliff Community College in New York in 1945, it became the *Briarcliff Quarterly*. In addition to high-profile contributors like Weldon Kees and William Carlos Williams, the journal represented the work of students.

2. Vivienne Koch's 'Accentuate the Positive', a review of Van Wyck Brooks' *The World of Washington Irving*, was published in the Spring 1945 issue of *The Sewanee Review*, which also contained the parallel text of 'Snows'/'Neiges'.

3. Devlin's translation of 'rompant soudain l'immense libration' should have read: 'suddenly breaking asunder the vast libration' (*CPDD*, p. 256). libration: state of balance, the oscillating motion of a balance beam upon a pivot.

To Allen Tate
11 September 1945

Dear Allan [*for* Allen],

I'm looking forward to seeing you when you come up. Thanks very much for your invitation; I assure you I shall take you up on it for the first leave I can take after my long spell in Ireland.

I see Léger [*for* Leger] has brought out his four poems in B[uenos] A[ires].[1] I've not seen him recently[.]

V's review was the only intelligent one so far of <u>Seasons</u> that I've seen.[2]

> All the best
>> Yrs
>>> Denis

Autograph letter signed. 1 leaf, 2 sides. *Header:* Irish Legation, Washington, DC. Allen Tate Papers, Box 25, Folder 27, PU.

---

1. *Quatre Poèmes: 1941–1944*, collecting 'Exil', 'Pluies', 'Neiges' and 'Poème à l'étrangère', and introduced by Archibald MacLeish, was brought out by Roger Caillois' Buenos Aires-based *Editions des lettres françaises* in February 1945.

2. If the 'V' Devlin refers to is Vivienne Koch, it is not clear which review he is referring to. Four years later, Koch published an influential essay on 'The Poetry of Allen Tate', *The Kenyon Review*, vol. XI, no. 3, Summer 1949, pp. 355–78, the final section of which is devoted to *The Winter Sea*. Perhaps a version of this essay was circulating long before its publication.

To Alexis Leger
5 November 1945

Dear Mr. Léger [*for* Leger],
    Enclosed is a draft of the translation of <u>Poème à L'Etrangère</u>.[1] Would you, as in previous cases, look through it with a view to our discussing meanings and amendments? I shall get in touch with you to arrange a meeting.
        Best wishes,
                Yours very sincerely,
                    Denis Devlin

Autograph letter signed. 1 leaf, 1 side. *Header*: Irish Legation, Washington, DC. Les Collections Patrimoniales, FSJP.

---

1. Devlin's translation of Leger's 'Poème à l'étrangère', 'Poem to a Foreign Lady', was first published alongside the French text in *Briarcliff Quarterly*, vol. II, no. 8, January 1946, pp. 214–21 (217–21).

To Niall Montgomery
24 March 1946

Dear Niall,

A friend of mine, Frank Taylor of Reynal and Hitchcock, New York, is go[i]ng to Europe on a publisher's tour to see what he can get in the way of MSS. for his firm.[1] He is including Dublin, on my advice, and will be there for about a week in the near future. At his request I gave him a list of names of people he should see; and included yours. I hope you will not mind. You may have something to offer him or may, in talking to him, work out a book to be written. I made the list as comprehensive as I could, which meant the inclusion of people whose writing I don't necessarily think good; but I felt I had to be impartial in the circumstances. Reynal and Hitchcock are the publishers of my book. It will be out in May and will be called: <u>Lough Derg and Other Poems</u>, in slightly archaic style, I suppose. I shall send you a copy; you may be surprised to see a few included from <u>Intercessions</u>, but I put them in on advice.[2]

I was delighted, on picking up the phone not long ago[,] to hear the voice of Ruth.[3] We met and had dinner and a talk, together with her husband, John Boland, who seems very nice.[4] Ruth was looking very pretty and sparkling and is enjoying herself and amusing John with her discovery of America. They seem very happy.

Are you writing? or is you[r] free time still taken up with M. n. gC.?[5] Colum in an article in the Saturday Review of Literature on MacDonagh's anthology says "someone called Myles na gCopaleen, which must be a misprint."[6] (I don't know whether I quote exactly). I'm glad to hear that you've set up in private practise [*sic*], though it's probably pretty tough, at first.[7]

Best wishes. Remember me kindly to Hop. And, if you can, I should like to hear from you when you've seen T.[8]

Yours,

Denis.

Typed letter signed. 1 leaf, 1 side. *Header:* Irish Legation, Washington, DC. Niall Montgomery Papers, MS 50,118/26/23, NLI.

---

1. Frank Taylor (1916–99), editor in chief at Reynal & Hitchcock. Taylor's publishing clients included Arthur Miller, Vladimir Nabokov, George Orwell and Karl Shapiro. He worked in the film industry during his long publishing career, producing *The Misfits* (1961), scripted by Miller.

2. Devlin and Taylor's correspondence over the publication of *Lough Derg* is not included in Taylor's archive at the Lilly Library, Indiana University, and the Reynal & Hitchock publishing archive has not been found. The firm was absorbed by Harcourt, Brace in 1948. A later letter (see DD to Selden Rodman, 29 June 1946) reveals that Devlin struggled to find a publisher for his poems. In William Roth's publishing memoir he notes that a selection of Devlin's poems was another project the two had discussed before the Colt Press folded, in addition to the Celtic poetry anthology. See *The Colt Springs High*, p. 185.

3. Niall Montgomery's sister, Ruth Montgomery (1916–2002).

4. Ruth Montgomery married Major John P. Boland (1907–76), a major in the US Army in Europe and a trained attorney, in Dublin in September 1945. They were among the first passengers to embark on a transatlantic flight to New York from Shannon (then Rineanna) airport in December 1945 ('Record-Making Continues at Rineanna', *The Irish Times*, 29 December 1945).

5. Montgomery collaborated on Brian O'Nolan's satirical 'Cruiskeen Lawn' column, under the shared pseudonym Myles na gCopaleen.

6. Padraic Colum's review of Donagh MacDonagh's anthology *Poems from Ireland* (Dublin: *The Irish Times*, 1944), 'The Irish Are Still Poets', appeared in *The Saturday Review of Literature*, vol. XXIX, no. 12, 23 March 1946, pp. 18–19, and was reprinted in *The Irish Times*, 4 May 1946, p. 4. The line reads: '[T]here [is] a contrasting lightness and gracefulness that [is] also in the direct translations [from Irish Gaelic] made by the poet whose pseudonym, Myles na gCopaleen, looks like a misprint.'

7. Montgomery set up his private architecture practice in Merrion Square, Dublin, in 1946.

8. If 'T' is not Frank Taylor, Devlin possibly refers to Thomas MacGreevy, a mutual friend. MacGreevy had moved back to Dublin in 1941 and was earning a precarious living as an art critic. In 1946 he moved into the house of his recently widowed sister in Fitzwilliam Place.

To Mervyn Wall
24 May 1946

Dear Mervyn,

Of course I am pleased and very grateful that you should think of dedicating your book to me; and I gladly agree.[1] I prefer your ③ suggestion[:] namely my full name, Christian and sur.

I shld. commiserate with you on your exile from Dublin but if it has wrung a book out of you, it won't have been so bad. The book may be a success, I mean may make a lot of money; and make it possible for you to leave your job[.][2] I'm glad you've found a publisher – and so easily and am looking forward to Fursey.

My own book is out at long last – so long after its proper time, which would have been about two years ago, that most of the excitement has evaporated. I have sent you a copy. All the same I'm pleased with it and about it and am deliberately fending off all my criticisms & scruples so as to enjoy the feeling.

I don't know whether it was Longman's man or not who was looking for you.[3] I gave your name to Taylor of Reynal & Hitchcock (my publishers.) It's a pity you'll miss him.[4] However your Mavis sounds all right.[5] I'll probably be seeing you within the next year!

All best wishes
Denis

Autograph letter signed. 1 leaf, 2 sides. *Header*: Irish Legation, Washington, DC. Mervyn Wall Collection, HRC, UTx

---

1. Wall dedicated his first novel, *The Unfortunate Fursey* (London: Pilot Press, 1946), to Devlin. The novel follows the adventures of Fursey, a medieval Irish laybrother plagued by the devil.

2. Wall had been working for the Irish civil service since 1934; he left in 1948 to join the features department at Radio Éireann.

3. Longmans, Green & Co., the contemporary imprint of the London-based Longman publishing company, headed by Mark Longman.

4. See DD to Niall Montgomery, 24 March 1946, n. 1.

5. Possibly the New York-based literary agent Mavis McIntosh (1903–86).

To Selden Rodman
29 June 1946

Dear Selden,

I am deeply grateful to you for your generous letter about my book. I suppose it must seem, looking back, as if I had been secretive while you were in Washington but that was not really the case. I had the poems finished about three-quarters and started sending the manuscript around about two years ago; and the more rejections it got the less inclined I felt to work on the poems or talk about them. I really finished them during the six months before publication, which was on May 26th last. It has not been reviewed anywhere yet so far as I know.[1] I would indeed like you to review it.

The list of poems you liked was interesting since "Bacchanal" was written about twelve years ago and "Vestiges" about two months ago. I am glad you like "Ank'hor Vat". The rhythm of the last line is meant to be different from the general; it is meant to be read legato.[2]

I hope I may be in New York some time soon. If so I shall let you know.

Again, many thanks.

Yours,

Denis Devlin

Typed letter signed. 1 leaf, 1 side. *Header:* Irish Legation, Washington, DC. Selden Rodman Papers, Collection No. 4259, American Heritage Center, University of Wyoming.

---

1. *Lough Derg and Other Poems* received its first reviews in July 1946, beginning with Marguerite Young's 'New Volumes of Verse in Review' in *The New York Times Book Review* on 21 July, p. 7. Reviews appeared in subsequent months in *Nation* (Arthur Mizener, review of Henry Treece, *Collected Poems*, and Denis Devlin, *Lough Derg and Other Poems*, vol. 163, no. 3, 10 August 1946, pp. 160–1), *Irish Independent* (T.O'H, 'Verse on Lough Derg But Not So Happy', Monday, 23 September 1946, p. 6), *Poetry* (Inez Boulton, 'Celtic Nova', vol. 69, no. 1, October 1946, pp. 169–71), and *The Sewanee Review* (Vivienne Koch, 'Poetry Chronicle', vol. 54, no. 4, Oct–Dec 1946, pp. 699–716).

2. The final couplet of the poem reads: 'Let us lie down before him/His look will flow like oil over us' (*CPDD*, p. 160).

To Selden Rodman
8 July 1946

Dear Selden,

Lough Derg is [a] small lake in the wildest parts of Northwestern Ireland, in Donegal, with an island which has been a place of pilgrimage for the last thousand years. The atmosphere is severe, undecorative and narrow. With this as starting point, the poem goes into a meditation on religion and anti-religion, through the great religion systems, as they appear to one predisposed to the sacred: to whom both opposites seem to have failed. I feel I can't go any further at this point. I don't know, without whittling definition to too fine a point, whether poetry is a vehicle for conveying judgements of this kind; I think not, in fact[,] but I am not for detachment either. Bacchanal is meant to be a general celebration of revolution in its first few months, when it glorifies our view of ourselves; but there again the leaders have some doubt. This is all very inadequate and I have'nt [*sic*] thought out for rational statement the themes that run through these poems, and the others; so I know you will not pin me down to what I say here.

Information is different! Francois of Touraine is an accidental arbitrator; but his country and the view he urges are connected and are opposed to the befogged religiousity [*sic*] of the two islanders.[1] A "bosthoon" is a sort of village innocent.[2] I think Jansenism was pretty well stamped out by Louis XIV but as an attitude it persists still in some of the ingrown pious provinces of France, as you can see from Mauriac, for example.[3] In Ireland I mean it to describe the same thing: a sort of Catholic puritanism, a restricted, contracted puritanism, at that. The Dante reference in Lough Derg is more than symbolic, though it'[s] enough for it to be so.[4] There's a legend that Dante came to the place during his travels and had a vision of Inferno through a burning hole in the ground.

It will be fun seeing your review. I must show you some newspaper reviews I've had.

All best wishes,
Denis.

Typed letter signed. 2 leaves, 2 sides. *Header:* Irish Legation, Washington, DC. Selden Rodman Papers, AHC, UWy.

---

1. In 'Encounter', 'François from Touraine' is positioned between 'the Englishman' and the 'Celt' (the poem's speaker) in a dramatised debate about poets and saints (*CPDD*, p. 136).

2. A 'bosthoon' appears in the opening line of the short poem 'Handy Andy' (*CPDD*, p. 156).

3. Jansenism: a theological movement emerging in the seventeenth century from the doctrine of Cornelius Jansen, bishop of Ypres, concerned with the problem of reconciling divine grace and the natural human will. Jansenism is invoked as part of the landscape of faith and deprivation in 'Lough Derg', and again in 'Jansenist Journey' (*CPDD*, p. 132, pp. 145–6). François Mauriac (1885–1970), French novelist, poet and critic. A devout Catholic whose stern and puritanical upbringing infused his fiction, Mauriac had criticised the Catholic Church for its support of Franco during the Spanish Civil War, and was involved with the French resistance during the Second World War.

4. As '[t]he pilgrims blacken/Out of the boats to masticate their sin' in 'Lough Derg', Dante is figured 'smell[ing] among the stones and bracken/The door to Hell' (*CPDD*, pp. 133–4).

To Selden Rodman
[?19] July 1946

Dear Selden,

Am returning the review herewith.[1] It's a quite direct insight, I think, even to the 'qualification'.[2] It is fortunate for me to have the first review by a poet and favourable; since the 'average reader' has no taste whatsoever, he might as well be led by you as misled by some pained elephant in the <u>N.Y. Times</u>. I like the style, for itself, of your statements, by the way[.]

Best wishes

Yrs. Denis

About my leaving: it's that I'm being tra[?nsferred] to London at the end of autumn.

> Autograph letter signed. 1 leaf, 1 side. *Header*: Irish Legation, Washington, DC. *Dating*: Number illegible. Postscript written above letterhead. Top right-hand corner torn, obscuring some text. Selden Rodman Papers, AHC, UWy.

---

1. Rodman's review, 'Daemonic Poet', appeared in *The New Republic*, vol. 115, no. 4, July 1946, pp. 106–7.

2. Rodman suggests that *Lough Derg and Other Poems* contains both the promise, and the achievement, of a rare quality in modern verse: the coexistence of a complex individuality and an unmistakeable consistency of style. He goes on to explain that the qualification (the areas of promise) refers to parts of the more ambitious poems like 'Lough Derg' which 'are so densely elliptical that they stagger as if translated literally from some other language', in which 'the voice is still thick, not blurred by echoes of other poets [...] but too bursting with brilliant analogies to let the theme rise above its modulations' (ibid., p. 106).

To Robert Penn Warren
19 November 1946

Dear Red,

I am sending you attached, a clipping from the "Irish Times" of the 28ᵗʰ September last, with a review, rather good, of <u>At Heaven's Gate</u>.[1]

I am still here, as you see[,] and have no exact knowledge as to the time of my leaving. Perhaps you will be coming down for one of your library meetings?[2]

    With best wishes,

        Yours sincerely,

          Denis

Typed letter signed. 1 leaf, 1 side. *Header:* Irish Legation, Washington 8, DC. *Address:* Mr. Robert Penn Warren, Department of English, University of Minnesota, Minneapolis, Minnesota. Robert Penn Warren Papers, Box 21, Folder 410, Beinecke, YU.

---

1. The unattributed review of Penn Warren's novel *At Heaven's Gate* (1946) is titled 'All Hail!' (*The Irish Times*, 28 September 1946, p. 4).

2. Penn Warren had been consultant in poetry (a position later named poet laureate) at the Library of Congress in Washington from 1944 to '45.

To Shiela Devlin
[January] 1947

Dear Sheila [*for* Shiela].

a chauntynge

EPITHALAMIUM OF

blessings and rustlings

(leaves all song)

to

Y O U[1]

(on your marriage
  *(don't let this be read

out

loud

at

the

wedding

breakfast

MAY YOU BE
as
BRIGHT
as a red tanager[2] and as
BRILLIANT
as a Pacific Ocean king dancing
and as
HAPPY
as your own laughter
is the wish of
your brother
Denis.

*written in the office at 5.20 p.m.

∴ I am not  ed nor ed

Autograph letter signed. 1 leaf, 2 sides. *Header*: Irish Legation, Washington, DC. *Dating*: By wedding date. Private collection, Caren Farrell.

---

1. epithalamium: a song or poem celebrating a marriage. Shiela Devlin married Kevin Healy in late January 1947.

2. Scarlet tanagers are bright red American songbirds.

To John Frederick Nims, Poetry Magazine
11 February 1947

Dear John Nims,

Thank you very much for your letter which I have just received. I am about to leave for London and my address there will be c/o High Commissioner's office for Ireland. Regent S[treet]. London.

Now to answer your letter in detail! First of all I shall be glad to send you some of my new poems when they are ready. This won't be for a while since I am so busy now with the transfer.

Secondly about the Irish issue: I have been giving this much thought, and I don't believe that I shall be able to do it – because of lack of time.[1] However, I shall be glad to give you the names of people you might get in touch with about it. I should like to be represented in an Irish issue (to answer your question on this point).

About the London letter – at present I do not see how I would have time to do it.[2] You see I have so little time to write my own verse. However, I shall write you about this again.

Caren asks me to relay to you her thanks about your suggestion on French poetry.[3] She might have something after visiting Paris – at any rate, she will get in touch with you about this.

It was very pleasant meeting you.

Sincerely

Denis Devlin

Dictated letter, written and signed in Caren's hand. 1 leaf (folded), 2 sides. Pencil markings on top verso side in a hand other than Caren's, possibly that of Nims. *Poetry: A Magazine of Verse*. Records, 1895–1961, Box 74, Folder 1, UChi.

---

1. *Poetry* occasionally grouped its contributors on thematic or national lines; the issue that followed shortly after Devlin's letter purported to be an 'English number'; it was more properly a British number with a strong Celtic showing, including Vernon

Watkins and Dannie Abse from Wales, and W.S. Graham from Scotland. An Irish number was not published in this period of Nims' associate editorship (1942–9).

2. These reports from abroad were a periodic feature of the journal. A 'Letter from Ireland' by Patrick Kavanagh was published in *Poetry* in 1949, commenting on the current state of poetry and poetry publishing (and summarily observing that '[n]o books of creative interest have been published by an Irish writer recently' (*Poetry*, vol. 74, no. 5, August 1949, pp. 286–91, at p. 289)). A few years later, John Montague's 'Letter from Dublin' began with an appreciation of Patrick Kavanagh (*Poetry*, vol. 90, no. 5, August 1957, pp. 310–15).

3. Caren Devlin (née Randon) (?1922–64) and Denis married on 9 January 1947. Caren wrote and translated poetry, and practised sculpture.

To Allen Tate
11 February 1947

Dear Allan [*for* Allen],

I am leaving from New York on the 20th of this month for England, aboard the Queen Elisabeth [*sic*].[1] The news of my transfer came just after my return from Mexico a few days ago.

I would love to see you and your wife before leaving. Caren and I shall be up in N.Y. from the 17th until the 20th, and hope to see you then.

What is happening to the Irish anthology? I see it announced here and there. Would it be possible to get the contract matter before my departure?[2]

[L]ooking forward to next week;

as always

your devoted

Denis

[*Postscript*]
Dear Allen,

Since Caren wrote this for me, our reservations have become shaky and we may have to fly straight through from Washington.

I shall phone you at yr. office; that's best.

As ever

Denis

Dictated letter, written and signed in Caren's hand. Postscript in Devlin's hand. 1 leaf, 2 sides. Pencil marks (Tate's?) underlining paragraph at bottom of recto side, regarding the Irish anthology. Allen Tate Papers, Box 25, Folder 27, PU.

---

1. The RMS *Queen Elizabeth*, a luxury ocean liner operated by Cunard White Star Line, providing a service between New York and Southampton.

2. Devlin's 'Encounter' and 'The Statue and the Perturbed Burghers' appeared in *1000 Years of Irish Poetry*, edited and introduced by Kathleen Hoagland (New York: The Devin-Adair Company), published in February 1947. Devlin is among the poets Hoagland acknowledges for his advice and assistance in putting together the twentieth-century section.

To Brian Coffey
25 March 1947

My dear Brian,

Might we come down next week-end, i.e. Saturday the 29th, to see you? and if so would you book a room for us at the Inn?[1] It will be splendid to see you again; we shall have a lot to talk about. The American offer sounds interesting.[2] We must see what I can remember about salaries. Unless I get word from you that it's inconvenient, then, we shall come down on Saturday.

Theoretically I like being back but I haven't got into it yet. And this office is damn busy. And after having defended the English for five years, I suddenly don't know what to make of them. For one thing their poetic criticism is childish. But let's wish ourselves and them good fortune[.]

Looking forward to seeing you[,]

Denis

Autograph letter signed. 1 leaf, 2 sides. *Header*: High Commissioner for Ireland, 33-7 Regent Street, London, SW1. ÉIRE, printed under the embassy's harp logo, is over-written with 'IRELAND' in Devlin's hand. Brian Coffey Papers, Box 8, Folder 66, UDel.

---

1. Coffey was teaching in Spinkhill, Sheffield at this time, probably at Mount St Mary's College.

2. Coffey's doctorate in philosophy at L'Institut Catholique de Paris, which had been disrupted by the war, was finished in 1947. Soon afterwards he was offered a job as assistant professor of philosophy at St Louis University, Missouri; the Coffeys relocated there.

To Kimon Friar

29 July 1947

25 Cheyne Place
Chelsea
London, SW3

Dear Mr. Friar,

Thank you very much for your letter concerning the anthology of contemporary poetry which you are bringing out.[1]

I am very sorry to have delayed my reply to you for so long. I have been out of town. I am very pleased to hear that my poem 'Lough Derg' is to be included in your anthology.

I am enclosing some biographical material which might be helpful to you, but can unfortunately not provide you with a 'Note on the Poetry' for the appendix, due to lack of time.

As concerns my poem itself, perhaps you will allow me just to add a few words about it in this letter.

The title 'Lough Derg' is the name of a place of pilgrimage in Ireland.

The items you ask me about in your letter can be found in any dictionary, and I would appreciate the descriptions below as remaining anonymous:

Clan Jansen: the clan of the Jansenists[2]
Orphic egg: origin of life in the religion of Orphisism
    [*for* Orphism].[3]
Academy: the Academy of Plato
Tragic Choir: the chorus in tragedy[4]
Merovingnian: Medieval French dynasty[5]
Bruno: Giordano Bruno, the philosopher
Watt [*sic*] Tyler: English agrarian rebel.[6]

Thanking you very much,
    I am sincerely yours,
        Denis Devlin

[*Enclosure*]

Biographical Material

Denis Devlin

<u>Born</u>: Greenock, Scotland, April 15ᵗʰ, 1908

<u>Education</u>: Belvedere College, Dublin;

University College, Dublin; Munich University; Paris University (Sorbonne)

<u>Taught</u>: English literature in University College, Dublin (1935-36)

In <u>Irish Foreign Service</u>: 1936 Dublin; then Posts at Geneva,Rome, London, New York, Washington. At present Counsel[l]or in the London office.

<u>Published</u>: 'Poems' (with Brian Coffey) in Dublin, 1932; 'Intercessions' in London, 1937; 'Lough Derg and other poems', in New York, 1946.

Also (in book form) translations of Paul Eluard's Poems, in 'Thorns of Thunder', London, 1937; translations of St. J. Perse's 'Rains' and 'Snows', published both by the Sewanee Review in 1945.

My poems have also appeared in anthologies. ([B]ut not 'Lough Derg' yet[.])

Dictated letter, written and signed in Caren's hand. Enclosed biographical note also in Caren's hand. 3 leaves, 5 sides (including biographical material). Kimon Friar Papers (C0713), Box 137, Folder 12, Department of Special Collections, Princeton University Library.

---

1. Friar edited various poetry anthologies, including *Modern Poetry, American and British: An anthology* (New York: Appleton-Century Crofts, 1951), with John Malcolm Brinnin. Devlin did not appear in this volume. Friar's papers suggest

that around this time he was working on the Borzoi Book of Contemporary Verse (1944–6); I have not found any evidence of that anthology's publication.

2. See DD to Selden Rodman, 8 July 1946, n. 3.

3. Orphism: a set of beliefs and ritual practices dating from the sixth century BC, supposed to have been based on the teachings of Orpheus, Greek mythological poet and musican.

4. The Academy was founded by Plato in Athens in *c*. 387 BC. These references appear in the sixth stanza of 'Lough Derg': 'Close priests allegorized the Orphic egg's/ Brood, and from the Academy, tolerant wranglers/Could hear the contemplatives of the Tragic Choir/Drain off man's sanguine, pastoral death-desire' (*CPDD*, p. 133).

5. The Merovingian dynasty (*c*. AD 500–750) was the first dynasty of Frankish kings. 'Part by this race when monks in convents of coracles/For the Merovingian centuries left their land,/Belled, fragrant;' (*CPDD*, p. 134).

6. Giordarno Bruno (1548–1600), Italian philosopher and cosmological theorist who was tried for heresy and burned at the stake. Wat Tyler (?–1381), leader of the 1381 Peasants' Revolt. Tyler was killed during negotiations with King Richard II. The lines read: 'I who, in my books,/Have angered at the stake with Bruno and, by the rope/ Watt Tyler swung from, leagued with shifty looks/To fuse the next rebellion with the desperate/Serfs in the sane need to eat and get;' (*CPDD*, p. 134).

* * * * *

To Kimon Friar

28 September 1947

25 Cheyne Place
Chelsea
London, SW3

Dear Mr. Friar,

I hope you did get my previous letter with the information wanted. So many letters get lost in the mail these days that I am never sure whether one does reach its destiny or not.

Sincerely yours

Denis Devlin

Dictated letter, in Caren's hand. 1 leaf, 1 side. Kimon Friar Papers, Box 137, Folder 12, PU.

To Alexis Leger

14 November 1947   *address privée*: 25 Cheyne Place
                                                            Chelsea
                                                            London, SW3

Cher ami,

Il y a si longtemps que je ne vous ai pas écrit: les devoirs professionnels m'occupant ces jours[-]ci à un tel point et j'ai peu de temps libre. Cela n'empêche que je ne me rappelle souvent à votre souvenir à travers vos poèmes dont le travail de traduction m'est une inspiration continuelle; et je pense avec nostalgie à nos sympathiques entretiens de Washington qui m'apparaît, de cette grande Ville de Londres dégringolante et brumeuse, une vraie ville-lumière. Elle est devenue pour moi une ville d'hier pleine de charme irréele [*for* irréel], bien que je s[a]che que les ennuis et les petites charges de la vie quotidienne y pèsent autant qu'ici. Il est agréable d'entendre au moins que notre travail poétique avance et de souhaiter que vous y trouviez grande satisfaction et joie.

Je regrette que vous ayez eu à vous inquiéter à propos de la traduction. J'ai été étonné de savoir – moyennant une lettre de Mde Dawson à Caren – que la Bollingen Press ne vous avait pas fait transmettre les trois textes – i.e. <u>Pluies</u>, <u>Neiges</u>, et <u>Poème à L'Etrangère</u> [–] dont j'avais fixé la version définitive et que je leur ai envoyé à New York il y a un mois et demi.[1] Il est vrai que j'étais convenu avec Chisholm, lors de son passage à Londres en été, de préparer un poème (<u>un</u> seulement) pour le commencement du mois de Septembre; mais la réalisation en a été, hélas! différée par des exigences familiales aussi bien que par une maladie passagère.[2] Cependant, j'ai bien terminé et envoyé les trois poèmes mentionnés trois ou quatre semaines plus tard; et j'en ai annoncé à Bollingen la dépêche par deux télégrammes: il ne m'en ont pas encore accusé réception. C'est pourquoi je me demande s'il est arrivé quelqu'empêchement [*for* quelque empêchement], si le projet d'édition a été abandonné, et dans cette crainte j'ai différé de confier à Bollingen le texte d'<u>Exil</u>. En y réfléchissant, pourtant, je crois que le mieux serait de vous l'envoyer; vous êtes sur place et saurez mieux que moi l'état présent du projet; si tout va bien vous seriez très aimable en confiant mon texte d'<u>Exil</u> à cette <u>Press[e]</u>.

Je ne veux pas que les éditeurs altèrent en rien mon texte; cela est une question pour vous et pour moi.

Quant au contrat, que je n'ai pas encore eu de Bollingen, je crois que je ferais bien de réserver les droits anglais afin de sortir le livre ici, chez Faber et Faber peut-être. Etes-vous d'accord? Je n'ai pas encore fait la connaissance de T.S. Eliot mais j'ai rencontré un de ses amis les plus proches qui m'a dit qu'il est entièrement remis de sa maladie; je le verrai sans doute d'ici peu et ne manquerai pas de lui faire part de vos vœux.[3]

Caren vous remercie de votre lettre si aimable. Nous sommes très bien; Londres est triste mais Caren le rend gai. Elle trouve de quoi s'amuser, prend des leçons de guitare et de cuisine française. Nous comptons passer la Noël auprès de mes parents en Irlande et ce sera une grande réunion de famille [?et] il y aura quatre sœurs avec leurs maris, un frère marié et une douzaine d'enfants petits.[4] Mon père présidera à la grande table en patriarche (sans barbe, Dieu merci!)

Je vous souhaite bon Noël aussi et tous mes vœux les plus amicaux[.]

Bien vôtre

Denis Devlin

Autograph letter signed. 3 leaves, 6 sides. *Header*: High Commissioner for Ireland, Éire, 33-37 Regent St., London, SW1. Les Collections Patrimoniales, FSJP.

[*Translation*]

> *private address:* 25 Cheyne Place
> Chelsea
> London, SW3

Dear Friend,

It's been so long since I last wrote to you: my days are so occupied with professional duties here that I have little free time. This doesn't prevent me from remembering you often through your poems, the work of translating them being a continual inspiration to me; and I think with nostalgia of our enjoyable meetings in Washington, which appears to me, in this great tumble-down and murky city of London, a true city of light. It has become for me a city of yesterday full of unreal charm, even though I know that the boredom and small duties of daily life weigh as heavily there as here. It is good to hear at least that your poetry progresses and I hope that in it you find great satisfaction and joy.

I'm sorry that you have had to worry about the translation. I was amazed to learn – through a letter from Mrs Dawson to Caren – that the Bollingen Press hasn't sent you the three texts – i.e. Rains, Snows, and Poem to a Foreign Lady [–] for which I fixed the final versions and which I sent to them in New York a month and a half ago. It's true that I had agreed with Chisholm, during his visit to London in the summer, to prepare a poem (one only) for the beginning of September; but this work has alas!, been delayed owing to family circumstances as well as a passing sickness. However, I did indeed finish the three poems mentioned, and sent them three or four weeks later; and I announced their dispatch to Bollingen in two telegrams: they have not yet acknowledged receipt. This is why I wonder whether there has been some impediment, or if the project of the edition has been abandoned, and fearing this I have deferred sending the translation of Exil to Bollingen. Thinking about it, however, I believe it would be best to send it to you: you are on the spot and you know better than I the present state of the project; if all goes well it would be very kind of you to pass on my Exile text to this Press.

I don't want the editors to alter anything in my text: this is a question for you and me.

As for the contract, which I have not yet had from Bollingen, I think I would do well to reserve the English rights in order to bring the book out here, with Faber and Faber perhaps. Do you agree? I have not yet made the acquaintance of T.S. Eliot but I have met with one of his closest friends who told me that he is entirely recovered from his illness; I will undoubtedly see him here soon, and I will not fail to pass on your greetings.

Caren thanks you for your kind letter. We are very well; London is sad but Caren makes it gay. She finds things to amuse her, taking lessons in guitar and French cooking. We plan to spend Christmas alongside my relatives in Ireland and it will be a big family reunion with four sisters and their husbands, one married brother and a dozen small children. My father will preside over the large table like a patriarch (without a beard, thank God!)

I wish you a merry Christmas also, and all my warmest regards.

Ever yours,

Denis Devlin

---

1. Possibly Carley Robinson Dawson (1909–2005), American composer, actress, author and translator, and a prominent figure in Washington society; the Bollingen Foundation (in association with Pantheon Books in New York) were publishing Leger's *Exile and Other Poems*, in a bilingual edition with Devlin's translations, as the fifteenth number in their Bollingen Series (1949).

2. Hugh Chisholm (see Correspondents' Biographies) was an assistant editor for the Bollingen Foundation in the late 1940s, with whom Devlin corresponded over the progress of the edition (see letter below dated 12 May 1948). Chisholm's translation of Leger's *Vents* (Paris: Gallimard, 1946) was published in *The Hudson Review*, vol. 4, no. 3, Autumn 1951, pp. 366–95; it was republished alongside Leger's text in a Bollingen Series edition (1953).

3. Eliot, who had translated Leger's *Anabase* in 1930, had some minor operations in the summer of 1947, and spent August and September convalescing. See Lyndall Gordon, *T.S. Eliot: An imperfect life* (London: Vintage, 1998), p. 412.

4. At this time the Devlin family had relocated to The Slopes in Dún Laoghaire, a large house in an affluent Dublin suburb. Denis and Caren stayed here during their Dublin visits, and for the brief period of Devlin's return to the department's head-quarters in Dublin (1949–50).

To Alexis Leger

2 February 1948

25 Cheyne Place
Chelsea
London, SW3

Dear Leger,

At last here is <u>Exil</u>[.] I have taken a long time but it wasn't easy to get time and I was particularly anxious to make a good job of it.

I'm writing to you immediately on many points that arose throughout the text; so do not send to the publishers until you have received my next letter, which will be in a few days.

I had a very agreeable letter from Chisholme [*for* Chisholm] a few weeks ago.

All best wishes – in haste[,]

Yours

Denis Devlin

Autograph letter signed. 1 leaf, 2 sides. Les Collections Patrimoniales, FSJP.

To Alexis Leger
14 February 1948   25 Cheyne Place
                                                      Chelsea
                                                      London, SW3

My dear Léger [*for* Leger],

I forward the notes on <u>Exil</u>; they consist of elucidations of versions differing from your suggestions and some questions: the latter very important. Will you kindly make any changes necessary, as indicated? In the prose passage, I have dropped the "it being" etc[.] for the phrases beginning "et c'est" and used "and it is" and variants: that is nearer the meaning & movement of the French.

It has been hard & lovable work; I shall never forget.

And now, I post this immediately though my letter is meagre – and I'm going to the Ireland-England Rugby to prolong the old enmity harmlessly.[1]

Yours

Denis Devlin

<u>p.1</u>.

l'ossuaire des saisons: I preferred "bone-heap" to "ossuary" both for sound and clarity. "Ossuary" wld. not sound well here and, besides being archaic, conveys nothing of the meaning, since "os" as "bone" is not present to the English ear. I did use it in <u>Pluies</u> but it sounds well there in the middle of the long sweeping verses and in that context of limitlessness.

l'esprit du dieu fumant: "ghost" here sounds better than "spirit" and one of its meanings is identical with "spirit". It does not necessarily mean only "revenant". "Smoking" is not possible because of its associations.

amiante: "Amianthine" which I formerly used is a pretty word but I could not manage it in relation to the beat of the verse. "Aesbestos" [*sic*] fits in with the beat and the sound-pattern; and the meaning is sufficiently close, I think.

---

p.2.

une science m'échoit aux sévices de l'âme: My final version may appear unduly shortened. But the essential meaning is there, I think, and all other more literal translations I could find were most unsatisfactory – clumsy.

l'exil n'est point d'hier: "exile is not of yesterday" – you passed this version in this place (in the annotated text you sent me) but compare page 11 where you changed the same phrase to "exile is not from yesterday only." Will you make the change necessary to make them conform? The latter (p.11) version seems the closer of the two.

L'Etranger [*for* L'Étranger][:]

Stranger? Or Foreigner? here and all through the poem. Foreigner has the precise meaning in English of "alien". It is not without poetic ambiance but it conveys a sense of hostility. I prefer "Stranger".

p.4.

où fume encore le goût de néant:

> the phrase gave me great trouble because of the lack of dignity of the word "nothingness" and the abruptness of "smoke". So I had to elongate the sentence as at present in order to carry these awkward words. The final effect is not bad. "Nothingness" had to be retained, for meaning: I considered others such as "void" & "naught" but they sounded affected.

p.5.

l'[é]chéance d'un mot pur[:]

> "Pure statement fallen due" – I am not sure of this. Would the following be closer: "for a chance fall of pure statement"[?] If so, wld. you amend? "statement" is much better than "word" here.

l'affleurement des signes:

> I've retained "surfacing". "Efflorescent" adds too many valueless syllables to the phrase, already loaded[.]

ainsi va toute chair <u>au</u> cilice du sel:

> Is my translation right? It is "<u>to</u> the hairshirt" and not (dressed) "<u>in</u> hairshirt"? If correction necessary, please make it.

p.6.

un pur langage sans office:

> Very difficult. The final version is nothing more than the best compromise between meaning & rhythm.

p.7.

l'élytre pourpre du destin[:]

> I took "shard" & "red" for their sound, in [?illeg.] and in the rhythm. Besides, purpureus was really our "red" wasn't it?[2]

à la mi-nuit:

> Does this mean "in the half-night" (since of colour) or "half-way through the night" (time)?

p.8.

latomie:

> no comparable English word!

cinéraires:

> Is this a) the plant or b) burial place. If a) no change. If b) the best version is "urn-burial"

p.9.

haras:

> Inadvisable to use hara which is completely unknown in English.

princes sauvages:

> "Fiery" is a literary equivalent. But I'm not sure: wld. you prefer "mettlesome" or simply "shy"[?]

p.10.

pavis

> "forecourt" not lovely in sound gives the best picture.

Autograph letter signed. 4 leaves, 8 sides, including enclosure. Letter on blue airmail paper, enclosure on headed departmental paper. *Header*: High Commissioner for Ireland, Éire, 33-37 Regent Street, London, SW1. Pencil markings in red and blue crayon, underlining passages of text and words and phrases in Devlin's suggested translations, are probably made by Leger. Les Collections Patrimoniales, FSJP.

---

1. On 14 February 1948, England were defeated by Ireland at Twickenham (10–11) in the Five Nations Championship. Ireland went on to win the tournament.

2. purpureus (La.): purple or dark red.

To Hugh Chisholm (Bollingen)

12 May 1948

25 Cheyne Place
Chelsea
London, SW3

Dear Chisholm,

I am wondering how the plans for "Exile" are proceeding – have there been further difficulties? I've been expecting to receive the contract for signature as it is possible that I may get part of the text accepted for review publication here and want, naturally, to reserve British and European rights. I am, however, hampered in following up any openings by uncertainty as to the terms of our association. You will understand, I am sure, my anxiety to be informed of the position.

My best wishes and many thanks for the kindnesses expressed in your last letter. I hope your general publication plans are beginning by now to bear good fruit.

I hope to hear from you at your early convenience.

Yours sincerely,
Denis Devlin

Typed letter signed. 1 leaf, 1 side. *Header*: High Commissioner for Ireland, 33-37 Regent Street, London, SW1. Header address crossed out and overwritten with Devlin's home address. *Address*: Hugh Chisholm, Bollingen Series, 41 Washington Square Sth., New York 12, New York. Bollingen Foundation Records, Box I:91, Library of Congress, Washington DC.

To Ernest Brooks (Bollingen)
1 June 1948

Dear Mr. Brooks,

Thank you for your letter of the 21st. May.

I agree with your suggestion and will accept the sum of $250 by way of a fixed fee, provided:

    i) all rights are reserved to me in respect of the publication of the book, or part of it, outside the United States,

    ii) a new agreement be arranged between us, should you decide to issue a second edition of the book.

No doubt these points can be embodied in the agreement. I should be grateful also if you would make out the cheque to "Edith Bennett["] and send it to her – Mrs. J.B. Bennett at 1701 Massachusetts Avenue, Washington, DC.[1] This, by th[e] way, is not against British currency regulations.

Yes, I have Mr. Leger's agreement to publication of the poems here. I shall, of course, see to it that no copyright difficulties fall on you as a result of any such publication.

        With kind regards[,]

           Yours sincerely,

             Denis Devlin

Typed letter signed. 1 leaf, 1 side. Bollingen Foundation Records, Box I:90, LoC.

---

1. Edith Randon Bennett (?–1965), Caren's mother, a singer and prominent figure in Washington society. After the death of Caren's father, Edith Randon married Air Force Reserve Officer Colonel Jess Bryan Bennett (dates unknown).

To Brian Coffey
16 July 1948

Dear Brian –

N'y pensons plus. Tu m'excuses mon exaltation – après Londres {(même qu'on se foute (ces subjonctif[s]) de l'exotisme)}[.] Je pense souvent à toi et tes aventures – tout va bien?

Denis.

[*in Caren's hand*]
Cher Brian

"Et nos amours faut-il qu'il m'en souvienne"[.]¹ I hope all is well with you, Brigitte and the children.

Caren.

Co-authored postcard signed. *Dating*: postmark, from Sirmione, Brescia. *Address*: Brian Coffey Esq., Dept. of Philosophy, St. Louis University, St Louis, Missouri, USA. Postscript in Caren's hand begun bottom left-hand corner, continuing top left-hand corner. Arrow pointing from "Et nos amours ..." to recto image of two lovers. Brian Coffey Papers, Box 30, Folder 22, UDel.

[*Translation*]

Dear Brian –

Let's think no more about it. Forgive me my exaltation – after London {(even if we couldn't care less (these subjunctives) about exoticism)}[.] I think often of you and your adventures – is all well?

Denis.

---

1. 'And our loves must I remember' – the lines are from Guillaume Apollinaire's 'Le Pont Mirabeau' (1912).

I hope all is well with you,
Brigitte and the children. Cares

Dear Brian — N'y pensons

plus. Tu m'excuses mon
exaltation — après Londres (même
qu'on se foute (au subjonctif) de
l'endroit)}. Je pense souvent
à toi et tes aventures — tout
va bien. Denis.

Oct Brian " Et nos amours
faut-il qu'il m'en souvienne " √

Brian Coffey Esq.
Dept. of Philosophy
St. Louis University
St. Louis
Missouri
U.S.A.

To Vivienne Koch
22 December 1948

Dear Vivienne,

This will introduce a very good friend of mine, George Reavey, of whom you may remember me to have spoken. He knows people we know, the Roberts and Jock.[1] I shall be very grateful for any kindnesses you may wish to extend to him.[2]

With all best wishes,

Yours very sincerely,

Denis Devlin

Typed letter signed. 1 leaf, 1 side. *Header*: High Commissioner for Ireland, Éire, 33-37 Regent St., London W1. *Address*: Mrs Vivienne Macleod, Department of English, Columbia University, New York. Unposted. George Reavey Papers, Container 49.5, HRC, UTx.

---

1. Laurance P. Roberts (1907–2002), American scholar of Asian art and director of the Brooklyn Museum (1938–46) and the American Academy in Rome (1946–60), and his wife Isabel Spaulding Roberts (1911–2005), a fellow art historian who worked in the educational department of the Brooklyn Museum and took over as chief curator during her husband's war service as captain in army intelligence in Washington (1942–6). Jock has not been identified.

2. Devlin wrote near-identical letters of introduction to Allen Tate and Robert Penn Warren.

To Alexis Leger
Christmas 1948

[*in Caren's hand*]

Cher Ami,

Nous espérons que vous allez bien et que Washington vous plaît toujours.

Nous sommes toujours dans le même appartement à Chelsea et la vie passe doucement sans secousses ni grands évènements.

Denis vient de finir un long poème que je trouve très beau.[1] C'est la première chose qu'il a faite depuis vos traductions. Nous n'avons pas encore vu le livre, mais nous espérons en voir un[e] copie bientôt.[2]

Nous avons passé cinq semaines très gaies et agréables en Italie cet été. Quel beau pays! Nous étions aussi à Paris mais seulement pour quelques jours. Espérons que vous viendrez en Europe un jour dans l'avenir pas trop lointain, et que vous viendrez nous voir. Moi-même, j'espère venir en Amérique et à Washington en Février (peut-être), et j'aurais peut-être alors le plaisir de vous revoir.

Très amicalement

Caren

[*in Denis' hand*]

J'ajoute, à ceux de ma femme, mes vœux les plus amicaux; j'espère que vous allez bien et que vous êtes entièrement remis de votre maladie de l'année dernière. Washington n'est pas le meilleur des endroits pour la santé; j'ai pensé que vous ne vous soigniez pas assez dans [ce] climat "extrémiste" –

J'ai lu Vents avec grandes délices – et en me félicitant d'avoir été votre collaborateur. Ce poème est tout beau, tout grand; et quel plaisir de voir que votre œuvre s'augmente et se fait entière.

Vous voyez que nous sommes finalement une république! – l'Irlande nominaliste![3]

Bien à vous

Denis

Co-authored Christmas card signed. Recto image of snow-covered London street scene: English policeman, and horse and poodles dressed for the winter weather. Les Collections Patrimoniales, FSJP.

[*Translation*]

[*in Caren's hand*]

Dear Friend,

We hope that all goes well with you, and that Washington continues to give you pleasure.

We are still in the same apartment in Chelsea and life passes without tremor or big events.

Denis has just come to the end of a long poem I find very beautiful. It's the first thing he has done since your translations. We haven't yet seen the book, but we hope to see a copy soon.

We spent five very cheerful and pleasant weeks in Italy this summer. What a beautiful country! We also went to Paris but only for a few days. Let us hope that you will come to Europe one day in the not too distant future, and that you will come and see us. Myself, I hope to come to America and Washington in February (maybe), when I will perhaps have the pleasure of seeing you again.

Very fondly,

Caren

[*in Denis' hand*]

I add, to those of my wife, my warmest greetings; I hope that you are well and that you are entirely recovered from last year's illness. Washington is not the best of places for one's health; I have thought that you don't take enough care of yourself in that "extremist" climate – I have read <u>Vents</u> with great delight – and congratulate myself on having been your collaborator. This poem is all beautiful, all great, and what a pleasure to see that your work is expanding and completing itself.

You see that we are finally a republic! – Nominalist Ireland!

All good wishes to you

Denis

---

1. The poem is *The Heavenly Foreigner*, see DD to Robert Penn Warren, March 1950.

2. *Exile and Other Poems* was published in the summer of 1949.

3. The Republic of Ireland Act, declaring Ireland's official designation as a republic and vesting the president of Ireland with executive powers over external relations, was signed on 21 December 1948 and ratified the following Easter.

To Marcella Comès Winslow
Christmas 1948

Dear Marcella,

It was such a pleasant surprise to get your letter and to learn about your exhibition of painting.[1] It was, I'm sure, a great success and I did appreciate most highly the honour of having my picture on the book of words; and it all gave me a painful whiff of nostalgia for Washington. I hear from one who has returned from those blessed groves that Dupont Circle has been ruined: I burnt with indignation.[2] I do think back so pleasantly on my time in Washington – not least on those parties in your Georgetown garden at the relaxed end of days in [s]ummer. – We are very well here in London in a high flat over the Thames, nevertheless, and the theatres and concerts are good.

I hope the children are well & flourishing – and please remember me to your sister – and my best wishes & regards.

Vale[,]

Denis

Autograph Christmas card signed. *Dating*: Excavations for the Dupont Circle underpass began in 1948. Devlin's message surrounds a printed greeting, reading 'With All Good Wishes for Christmas and New Year', and Caren's handwritten signature, 'from Denis and Caren Devlin'. Marcella Comès (Winslow) Papers, 1915–82 [and undated], Reel 2424, Archives of American Art, Smithsonian Institution.

---

1. Devlin possibly refers to an exhibition of Winslow's oil paintings at the United Nations Club in March 1948.

2. Dupont Circle is a historic district in north-west Washington DC. Plans to build an underground transit system in the area to ease traffic congestion, first released in 1947, caused great consternation among local residents. The streetcar underpass opened in 1949.

To Niall Montgomery
16 March 1950

The Slopes, Dún Laoghaire
Co. Dublin

Dear Niall,

Thanks very much indeed for your good wishes, in such splendid baroque. I've been meaning to phone you but have been so disorganised since I got back, if it can be called back – I've been away a lot on short trips. Would you have lunch with me, say Friday? I shall phone you Friday morning to see.

Yours

Denis

Autograph letter signed. 1 leaf, 1 side. Niall Montgomery Papers, MS 50,118/26/23, NLI.

To Robert Penn Warren
March 1950

Dear Red,

You will have heard through Cinnina [*for* Cinina] that we are leaving for Rome.[1] I wonder how this will affect your plans? It's a great shame just when we were looking forward to seeing you in Ireland this Summer – or rather to showing Ireland to you: as to seeing you we are assured since, I am sure, if you come to Europe you will come to Italy. You could still, especially if your boat reservations provide for disembarkation at Cork, come for a short visit. There are plenty of our friends who would be happy to meet you and try to make things easier, and my father, for instance, would lend you a car. Let me know what you think.

My next matter is closer to the profession. You will remember the long poem I was working on at Sirmione.[2] Well, it's long since finished and with John Palmer who is bringing it out in the Autumn number of the Sewanee; and I do thank you again for your recommendation of the poem to him. I approach you now with but little ceremony – yet the plumes of my obeissance [*for* obeisance] would frill the Atlantic! [–] for this: a poetry quarterly in Cork are devoting their summer number to my work, including <u>The Heavenly Foreigner</u> and they would like an introductory essay to set it up and set it forth.[3] Could you think of doing it? I ask this with trepidation, knowing how busy you are and aware also of the possibility that the subject may not offer material for the kind of study you would be interested in. However, I know that if you have the slightest doubt about it you will tell me and I shall take it as the frank conclusion to an objective negotiation! The essay, by the way, is to relate only to <u>The Heavenly Foreigner</u>. And if you agreed, it could go in the Sewanee too.

Caren and I send you and Cininna [*for* Cinina] our love,
                    Yours,
                         Denis Devlin

1. Emma 'Cinina' Brescia (?1906–69), Penn Warren's first wife, was an Italian tutor and translator whom he met at the University of California. Their marriage was at this time breaking down, and the pair divorced in 1951.

2. Sirmione is a resort town on Lake Garda in northern Italy. The Devlins spent June–July 1948 there, and were joined by RPW and Cinina.

3. The quarterly is *Poetry Ireland*, edited by David Marcus and published by Trumpet Books in Cork. The summer number published 'The Heavenly Foreigner' in its fullest form to date, and a selection of poems from *Lough Derg and Other Poems*. The accompanying introduction was ultimately supplied by Niall Sheridan. See *Poetry Ireland*, no. 10, July 1950, pp. 3–26.

Rome, 1950–9

CHRONOLOGY

1950

April	DD and CD arrive in Rome, accompanied by his sister Finola; DD takes up position of envoy extraordinary and minister plenipotentiary to Italy.
June	Sits on the jury for the XXVth Venice Biennale.
July	A version of *The Heavenly Foreigner* is published in *Poetry Ireland*, no. 10.
	DD and CD are received by the pope in a special audience.
October	A version of *The Heavenly Foreigner* published in *The Sewanee Review*, vol. LVIII, no. 4.

1951

March	DD accredited minister to Turkey.
May	An extract from *The Heavenly Foreigner* published in *World Review*, no. 27.
June	DD has a short stay in the Blue Sisters' nursing home in Rome, with a stomach complaint.
August	Devlins holiday in Austria.
Sept–Oct	DD and CD travel to Turkey, in order to formalise his new appointment.
October	Devlins take up residence on Via Valle Delle Camene, Passeggiata Archeologica, after the Irish legation

moves from its premises on Via San Martino della Battaglia.

November   DD visits Venice to negotiate an invitation for Jack B. Yeats to exhibit at the 1952 Biennale.

1952

May   DD is elected member of the Keats-Shelley Association in Rome.

June   Attends Venice Biennale (without Irish participation).

July   DD and CD spend a month in Ireland.

Autumn   Translations from the poetry of René Char, in collaboration with Jackson Mathews, are published in *Botteghe Oscure*, quaderno X, Fall 1952; DD's 'The Colours of Love' appears in the same issue.

DD visits Ankara.

1953

January   DD asked to edit a selection of contemporary Irish poetry for the *New World Writing* series; begins to solicit poems.

Spring   Robert Penn Warren and Eleanor Clark visit the Devlins in Rome.

June   DD represents Ireland at the Second International Congress for Christian Peace and Civilisation in Florence, and makes an Italian radio address on the importance of faith in Ireland.

[?August]   DD and CD's child, Stephen Devlin, is born.

October   'Ten Irish Poets', DD's contribution to *New World Writing*, is published.

November   Represents Ireland at the Conference of the United Nations Food and Agriculture Organization in Rome.

1954

May–June   DD attends the International Trade Fair in Padua.

June   Visit from Robert Penn Warren and Eleanor Clark.

July   Attends Trieste Trade Fair.

1955

Spring   'Mr Allen' is published in *Partisan Review*.

July–August   Devlins spend annual leave in the Dolomites and in Ireland.

1956

June   DD in hospital with a slipped disc and other ailments.

July   Visits Penn Warren and Eleanor Clark in Porto Ercole.

July–August   Devlins summer in Ischia.

September   DD named chairman of the Appeals Committee of the United Nations Food and Agriculture Organisation.

October	'The Tomb of Michael Collins' is published in *The Sewanee Review*, vol. LXIV, no. 4.

1957

March	DD accompanies President O'Kelly on a tour of Italy.
July–August	In hospital having suffered a haemorrhage and pneumonia.
Sept–Oct	The Devlins spend the autumn in Arosa, Switzerland, while DD convalesces.
December	'The Passion of Christ' is published in *Encounter*.

1958

June	DD visits Turkey to discuss Ireland's position on Cyprus.
August	Devlins holiday in the Dolomites and Hinterbichl, Austria.
November	DD made Ireland's first ambassador to Italy as the status of the Irish legation in Rome is raised to embassy.

1959

February	DD is awarded the Grand Cross of the Order of Saint Sylvester by Pope John XXIII.
April	Accompanies Seán Lemass, minister for industry and commerce, to meet Italian industrialists at the Milan International Trade Fair.

To Sheila Murphy, Department of External Affairs
23 June 1950

Dear Sheila,

The rolls of the Yeats' [*for* Yeats] film arrived and have been sent on to Venice.[1] The script, French translation, synopsis, list of particulars, three stills, and the publicity material have also been forwarded. We had already been notified by the Administration that the Yeats entry had been accepted and that the film would be shown, at some date as yet undetermined, during the exhibition.

For the final French text, I put together Sheehy-Skeffington's prose and the combined verse rendering of Caren and Cugnon.[2] I feel sure this made an excellent script, after the various little accidents which it met on the way.

I know you are waiting for my Biennale report.[3] I am sending it presto. Our pavilion was reasonably attractive and our exhibitors well hung, but there were numbers of big guns like Matisse, Kandinsky, Severini, Jacques Villon etc., and even the light artillery was abundant.[4] I had tremendous fun on the Jury. All the others were professors of Art-History and aesthetics – indeed the Administration who know me well by now keep calling me Professor as if my actual job were slightly bad form. Matisse – for whom I voted – got the Prize.[5] I also put in votes for our two by a courtesy process which we evolved.

> With best wishes.
>> Yours very sincerely,
>> D.D.

> Typed letter signed. 1 leaf, 1 side. *Address*: Miss Sheila Murphy, Department of External Affairs, Dublin. Marked "airmail", and with departmental ref. no. [?]/[?]/555B. Department of Foreign Affairs Papers, DFA/Rome Embassy/555B, NAI.

---

1. This short film, *W.B. Yeats: A tribute* (1950), was directed by Georg Fleischmann and J.D. Sheridan, and narrated by Cyril Cusack. It was rushed to Italy as an Irish entry to the Venice International Film Festival in August.

2. (Owen) Sheehy-Skeffington (see DD to Thomas MacGreevy, 26 [April] 1934, n. 4) translated the narration into French. In a telegram sent on 27 May 1950 Caren Devlin had been asked, at very short notice, to translate the verse. Cugnon (or Cougnon), apparently Caren's collaborator, has not been identified.

3. Devlin had served as an Irish commissioner on the jury of the Venice Biennale Arts Festival this summer.

4. Ireland's exhibition room represented paintings by Nano Reid (1900–81) and Norah McGuinness (1901–80), part of a group of modernist and abstract-expressionist painters who had come to prominence in the Irish Living Art Exhibitions of the 1940s. Reid and McGuinness were little known outside Ireland. Henri Matisse (1869–1954), French painter and sculptor known for his bold colourism and a cut-out composition method developed after illness late in life. Wassily Kandinsky (1866–1944), Russian painter and art theorist, associated with abstract expressionism and the *Blaue Reiter* movement, which was prominently represented in the 25th Biennale. Gino Severini (1883–1966), Italian painter and leading member of the futurist movement, which also received an exhibition in Venice this year. Jacques Villon, born Gaston Duchamp (1875–1963), French cubist painter and printmaker. A major Villon retrospective occupied the room immediately adjacent to Reid and McGuinness's exhibition.

5. The eighty-one-year-old Matisse was awarded the Grand Prize for painting this year.

* * * * *

To Sheila Murphy, Department of External Affairs
25 September 1950

Dear Sheila,

With reference to your letter of the 28th August about the showing of the Yeat[s] film in Venice, the Biennale people have informed us, after leaving several letters unanswered, that the film was shown on the evening of the 17th August in the category of the Cultural Films with "good success". We are further informed that the film obtained a "mention" prize. The Administration undertook with their letter of the 3rd September to send us the Diploma issued by the Exhibition in this connection, but it has not yet come to hand.

The newspaper refer[e]nce is practically nil, being confined to mention of the Film's showing in a few dailies. The Weekly Film Magazines were inspected for mentions, but without result.

I shall send on the Diploma as soon as it is received.

Yours sincerely

[Denis Devlin]

Typed letter unsigned (carbon copy). 1 leaf, 1 side. *Address*: Miss Sheila Murphy, Department of External Affairs, Dublin. Marked with departmental ref. no. [?]/50/555B. Department of Foreign Affairs Papers, DFA/Rome Embassy/555B, NAI.

* * * * *

To Sheila Murphy, Department of External Affairs
7 May 1951

Dear Sheila,

I received your letters 415/95 of the 6th and 30th April, regarding Irish participation in the next Biennale.

It is entirely a matter for the organising committee to Venice to decide whether or not to extend an invitation to Jack Yeats.[1] Frankfurter's support for the idea may turn out to be useful at a later stage, but he is now in New York and therefore not in a position to broach the subject.[2]

I can really only get you a decision one way or the other by going to Venice and discussing the question with Pallucchini.[3] The main difficulty, brought home to me in a conversation with people in the Art world here, is that Yeats is not known in Italy. As you will readily appreciate, a written request from me to invite an unknown artist to exhibit is unlikely to evoke an enthusiastic reply.

It happens that Caren and I plan to sail from Bari for Turkey about 15th of this month, but we could easily arrange to embark at Venice instead, going up a day earlier to interview the Biennale people. The extra cost would not be great, and certainly much less than if I had to make a special trip. Perhaps you would let me know by cable if I may go ahead so that I may have time to make the necessary appointments.

As it will be essential to have some examples of Yeat's [*for* Yeats's] work, I should be grateful if you would airmail me at once a copy of McGreevey's [*for* MacGreevy's] book and anything else you can lay your hands on.[4]

Yours sincerely,

[Denis Devlin]

Typed letter unsigned (carbon copy). Marked "air mail", and with departmental ref. no. 302/51/555A. Department of Foreign Affairs Papers, DFA/Rome Embassy/555A/1, NAI.

---

1. Jack B. Yeats (1871–1957), Irish artist renowned for his paintings of landscapes and daily life in Ireland; brother of William Butler Yeats.

2. Alfred M. Frankfurter (?–1965), president of the Arts Foundation of New York and the organiser of America's 1950 Biennale exhibition.

3. Rodolfo Pallucchini. See letters dated 3 November 1951, 14 December 1951, 9 February 1952, and Correspondents' Biographies.

4. MacGreevy published a book-length essay on Yeats, *Jack B. Yeats: An appreciation and an interpretation* (1945). See DD to Thomas MacGreevy, 15 March 1936, n. 7. In the same year, his *Pictures in the Irish National Gallery* (Cork: Mercier Press, 1945) included a profile of Yeats' 'Portrait of John O'Leary'. It was followed by *Illustrations of the Paintings: National Gallery of Ireland* (Dublin: National Gallery of Ireland, 1951).

* * * * *

To Sheila Murphy, Department of External Affairs
18 May 1951

Dear Sheila,

With further reference to your letters 415/95 of 6th and 30th April, I have had to postpone my departure for Turkey until the end of the month. I doubt that I can manage the Venetian visit on the outward journey, but on my way back I may be able to arrange to disembark at Venice. It will then probably be late June. In any event, if you can get me the sanction I asked for in my letter 302/51/555A of 7th May, I shall do my best.

An airmail reply will be sufficient.

Yours sincerely,

[Denis Devlin]

Typed letter unsigned (carbon copy). Handwritten corrections. 1 leaf, 1 side. Marked "air mail", and with departmental ref. no. 343/51/555A. Department of Foreign Affairs Papers, DFA/Rome Embassy/555A/1, NAI.

To Shiela Healy (née Devlin)
8 June 1951   The Blue Sisters, Rome[1]

Dear Sheila [*for* Shiela],

    This is a very temporary address. It's me stummick. How is your leg? I assume you are out of the <u>Bon Secours</u> now and back with the [c]ost of living whose mystifications you show such a grasp of in your nice letter.[2] I do hope you will soon get better from the malady, whatever it is – is it what Moya had? I exhort you to resistance. I encourage you, my friendess! You'll just have to put your foot down. (scusi, sa!)[3]

    There's the most spoffofficial and spyrogrillgrill roaring & rumpus going on where racing cars are practising on the Passegiata Archeologica about 200 yds from my room – Alfa Romeos & Maseratis & Ferraris tearing up & down the asphalt, snorting & growling & generally showing off. The street I mention is the last lap of the bi[g] race, which is tomorrow, and in true Italian fashion the drivers are only practising to win – or not so much to win as to be seen winning.[4]

    So they start at the end of the last lap, pretending to themselves that they've already done the previous 300 [?nicks] or so, and belt along to the winning tape under the eyes of all the small boys – and many of the men – in Rome. You see how little fun it would be practising in the country. It would mean you couldn't win the race in imagination; it would mean no small boys; it would mean you wouldn't drive half-Rome quite crazy with noise for 3 days. By Moses! I wish I was Goliath & I would go down there & take up every one of those superchargers by its exhaust pipe & smash it among the ruins of the Forum.

    I've described my uninteresting condition in letters to Pop & Mom (how they'd hate to be called that, even in fun)[.] It just came when we were all ready to go to Turkey: I had even started on a little thing – a little thing of my own – a little Noel Coward number which begins

    "I'm going to have a Turkish Bath in Turkey

    'Cos I never had a Roman bath in Rome"[5]

After that it gets a bit bogged down in "my sweet Turkish delight" which "ain[']t so bad a sight" but I'm afraid it lacks the Cowardian polish & smoothness because the way I have it you have to say "Turk*i*sh". It's all right I have my serious sides too.

>Kindest regards to Kevin
>>Love
>>>Denis

Now the loudspeakers are down on the last lap, practising too. They're trying to shout down the Alfa-Romeos. They can't make it but my God they're TRYING!
>Blessings.

Autograph letter signed. 2 leaves (1 folded), 6 sides. *Header*: Légation d'Irlande, Rome. *Address*: Mrs. Kevin Healy, c/o The Slopes, Dunlaoghaire, Co. Dublin, IRLANDA. Private collection, Caren Farrell.

---

1. The Blue Sisters was another name for the Little Company of Mary, a Catholic religious institute for women dedicated to caring for the sick. In 1909 the English founder of the order, Mary Potter, set up the Calvary hospital on the Via Santa Stefano Rotondo in Rome, the first Catholic hospital in the city.

2. Bon Secours is a private hospital in Glasnevin, Dublin.

3. scusi, sa! (It.): sorry, you know!

4. The Gran Premio di Roma, a sixty-lap, 200 km circuit race, was held on 10 June 1951.

5. Noël Coward (1899–1973), English playwright, actor and songwriter, known for his comedies of manners and popular songs.

To Máire MacEntee, Department of External Affairs
19 September 1951

Dear Máire,

Thank you for your letter of the 7th September on the subject of obtaining an invitation for Jack B. Yeats to exhibit at the Biennale. The enclosures are excellent and will be a great help in my approach to the authorities in Venice. In fact, I do not think I could do anything without them, as I could see last year that they were quite vague there about our great man. So they will have to be persuaded at second hand and by names like Herbert Read, since the reproductions obviously will not persuade them.

I find it is not convenient no[w] for me to go, as I had proposed, on the way to or from Turkey, on which high-fantastickal assignment I depart in a few days. I shall be back in about two weeks and then go up to Venice.

How do you think Yeats will stand up to the clarifying Italian sun?

Yours sincerely,

[Denis Devlin]

Typed letter unsigned (carbon copy). 1 leaf, 1 side. Marked with departmental ref. no. 567/51/555A. Department of Foreign Affairs Papers, DFA/Rome Embassy/555A/1, NAI.

To Robert Penn Warren

1 October 1951   Ankara Palais, Ankara

Dear Red,

We only hope, Caren and I, now that you are coming, that that arm doesn't stop you.[1] I'm sorry about it and I hope it doesn't get any worse. But if it does couldn't you drop into Switzerland and get it "cut" there? The Switzers are supposed to be all right at these jobs. I say this that your way not be deflected from the path of Rome – at least not too much. We want to hear about West England and your holiday generally in France; and long draughts of MS poetry are looked forward to with the greatest interest. I'm glad you have taken up the long poem again – I think you had already planned it in Sirmione?[2]

We had a pleasant holiday in Austria, the idea mostly being to get out of the heat for a while – de l'air frais et du footing in the Tirol and hard Séamus on hard benches in Salzburg.[3]

I'm now, improbably, here, waiting to present, tomorrow, my letters of evidence – I'm Minister to Turkey now as well as Italy. We shall continue to live in Rome, coming here for spells of duty from time to time. Caren is not with me and I shall be back in Rome in about ten days.

Excellent, the <u>Nostromo</u> essay, which has made me want to read the Conrad – Conrad tout court.[4]

And be careful with the arm because noialtri are certainly watching out for you all.

        Yours ever,
          Denis

Please remember me kindly to the Beaches – I met them in Washington when they came to see you.[5]

I suppose this letter will be following you round too.

IMPORTANT
NEW ADDRESS: LEGAZIONE D'IRLANDA
3 VIA VALLE DELLE CAMENE
(PASSEGGIATA ARC[H]EOLOGICA)

Autograph letter signed. 2 leaves, 2 sides. *Header*: Légation d'Irlande, Rome. Postscript written up left-hand margin and above header on second leaf. Robert Penn Warren Papers, Box 21, Folder 210, Beinecke, YU.

---

1. A damaged nerve in his left arm was the cause of recurring discomfort for Penn Warren at this time. Randy Hendricks and James A. Perkins, editors of Penn Warren's letters, suspect that this was related to a basketball injury from the summer of 1950 (see *SLRPW*, vol. III, p. 388). Penn Warren had spent the late summer writing in England; the planned driving trip to visit the Devlins in Rome, via France, was cut short owing to the arm injury (see RPW to Allen Tate, 12 November 1950, *SLRPW*, vol. III, pp. 416–18).

2. In the early 1950s Penn Warren was working on *Brother to Dragons: A tale in verse and voices* (New York: Random House, 1953), his first book of poetry since 1942.

3. de l'air frais et du footing (Fr.): some fresh air and jogging. The reference to 'hard Séamus' is unclear, but it might be a pun alluding to Jameson Irish whiskey (Séamus = James), which was commercially available in Europe in the 1950s (see DD to William Fay, 18 May 1954).

4. Penn Warren wrote an introduction to the Modern Library edition of Joseph Conrad's *Nostromo* (New York, 1951). Conrad tout court (Fr.): simply Conrad.

5. Joseph Warren Beach (1880–1957), critic and recently retired professor of English at the University of Minnesota (1917–48), and his second wife, the writer Dagmar Doneghy Beach (1888–1966).

To Seán Nunan, Secretary, Department of External Affairs

13 October 1951

I have the honour to inform you that Prof. Dino Gribaudi of the University of Turin has asked me for some up-to-date and well-chosen photographs, illustrating the country, people and economic development in Ireland, for inclusion in his text books on geography which are the most widely diffused in Italian schools.[1] This, I feel, is a splendid opportunity for us. I should accordingly be grateful if you would give the request a high priority. From Professor Gribaudi's letter, I gather that he would particularly welcome photographs of economic interest and peculiar to Ireland. I suggest that you select fifteen or so in all which might include photographs on some of the following subjects: Turf industry and turf generating station; large cooperative creamery; horse breeding industry; cottage industry; Guinness's (view showing size).[2] A background note for each photograph would be very useful.

> [Denis Devlin]
> Minister Plenipotentiary

Typed letter unsigned (carbon copy). 1 leaf, 1 side. Marked with departmental ref. no. [?]13/51/340. Department of Foreign Affairs Papers, DFA/Rome Embassy/340, NAI.

---

1. Ferdinando Gribaudi (1902–71), professor of economic geography at the University of Turin.

2. A modernist power house on the site of the Guinness brewery at St James's Gate, designed by the English architect F.P.M. Woodhouse, had been completed in 1950.

To Rodolfo Pallucchini

3 November 1951   3 Via Valle delle Camene

Egregio Prof. Pallucchini,

Io ebbi il piacere d'incontrarmi con Lei, come membro della Giuria in qualitá di Commisario Irlandese, alla Esposizione della scorsa estate.

Saró a Venezia la prossima settimana e vorrei sapere se potrei avere con Lei uno scambio di vedute circa le possibilitá di una eventuale partecipazione dell'Irlanda alla prossima Esposizione. Le sarebbe possibile concedermi un appuntamento per lunedi 12 novembre, o altrimenti per qualsiasi altro giorno della medesima settimana, con esclusione del sabato? Le sarei assai grato per una Sua cortese conferma.

Con i migliori ossequi,

[Denis Devlin]

Ministro d'Irlanda in Italia

Typed letter unsigned (carbon copy). 1 leaf, 1 side. *Address*: Prof. Rodolfo Pallucchini, Segretario Generale de l'Ente Autonomo della Biennale, S. Marco – Ca'Giustinian, Venezia. Marked with departmental ref. no. 1990/51/555A. Department of Foreign Affairs Papers, DFA/ Rome Embassy/555A/1, NAI.

[*Translation*]

Dear Prof. Pallucchini,

I had the pleasure of meeting you, as a member of the jury in the role of Irish Commissioner, at the Exhibition last summer.

I will be in Venice next week and I would like to know if I could have a discussion with you about the possibility of Irish participation at the next Exhibition. Would it be possible to grant me an appointment for Monday 12th November, or otherwise for any other day of the same week, with the exception of Saturday? I would be very grateful for your kind confirmation.

With the best regards,

[Denis Devlin]

Irish Minister to Italy

To Máire MacEntee, Department of External Affairs
17 November 1951

Dear Máire,

I have just got back from Venice where I saw the officials of the Biennale d'Arte Figurativa Moderna with a view to securing an invitation for Mr. Jack B. Yeats to be represented in a "retrospective" one-man exhibition. The discussion was not without its embarrassing side as I was asking them to invite a painter whom, frankly, they know nothing whatever about, except vaguely by name. I could not even say that Yeats would accept if invited. However, I was received very politely; I talked at length about Yeats and the officials showed an agreeable willingness to meet our wishes.

The Biennale cannot now give Yeats a pavilion to himself. They have reduced the number of one-man pavilions for next year and they are so hard pressed for space, as a result of an increase in the number of countries being represented, that they will probably have to house part of the exhibition in the city[,] i.e. far from the exhibition grounds which are in the suburbs. They offered the following solution, however; they would try to give us an extra room beside the room assigned to Ireland as a whole; this extra room would be entirely devoted to Yeats. To get this plan going, we arranged that I would write a personal letter to the Secretary-General suggesting the plan as if it were my own idea, hence not involving either our Government or the Biennale.[1] I cannot, however, write such a letter without knowing whether this suggestion would be acceptable to Yeats. Would you therefore consult him and let me know. The matter is extremely urgent as I want to get the letter to the Secretary-General as soon as possible before he can have an excuse in saying that we delayed. In any case he asked me to write this letter within a few days.

The idea should commend itself; there seems to be little difference between a one-man pavilion and a one-man room. Last year Matisse who had a "retrospective" show was in a room by himself but right beside the other French painters. When I asked for the pavilion in the first place, by the way, I was asked whether our Government would assume financial responsibility. I was not sure but anyhow I said no. Details will have to be settled later but in the meantime could you let me know Yeats' decision immediately, by telegram preferably.

> With kind regards,
> > Yours sincerely,
> > > D.D.

x   except that it won't mean an invitation from the Biennale – we would be choosing Yeats.

> Typed letter signed. Handwritten corrections. 2 leaves, 2 sides. The 'x' of the postscript might respond to a deletion in the final paragraph ('there seems to be ~~no~~ little difference …') which is overwritten with an 'x'. Marked with departmental ref. no. 672/51/555A. Department of Foreign Affairs Papers, DFA/Rome Embassy/555A/1, NAI.

---

1. Rodolfo Pallucchini was the secretary-general of the Biennale. See previous letter, and Correspondents' Biographies.

To Robert Penn Warren
11 December [1951]

[*co-authored with Caren*]

All our best wishes for a happy Christmas and New Year to you, dear
Red. We hope your arm is quite better again, and that this year we
can look forward to our talks and walks and drinks and fun together.
I never got to the States as I had planned – but might go in February
or March.
>   Love,
>   Caren

and from me too all best wishes – is the poem going well? Hoping to
see you next year and surely before I find myself transferred!
>   amichevolissimi auguri![1]
>   Denis

Autograph (co-authored) postcard signed. Robert Penn Warren Papers,
Box 21, Folder 409, Beinecke, YU.

---

1. amichevolissimi auguri: corrupted Italian, translating as something like 'friendliest
wishes'.

To Rodolfo Pallucchini

14 December [1951]   Roma

Egregio Prof. Pallucchini,

Desidero informarLa che ho inviato oggi alla Presidenza della Biennale una lettera ufficiale di accetazione dell'invito rivolto al mio Paese per partecipare alla XXVI Esposizione.[1]

Sono stato informato dal mio Governo che esso intende nominare Jack B. Yeats, il piú eminente fra i pittori irlandesi, a rappresentare l'Irlanda alla Biennale. Il mio Governo desidererebbe che tale Artista rendesse onore a questa che é fra le piú importanti esposizioni del mondo, ed avesse nel contempo la possibilitá di mostrare la pienezza della sua arte in questa mostra, la prima in Europa dopo quella tenuta alla Tate Gallery a Londra nel 1948 e ancor oggi assai celebrata.[2]

Sarebbe pertanto desiderio del mio Governo che convenienti spazio e posizione venissero accordati alla mostra irlandese. Posso permettermi di aggiungere che una sala, come quella che rispondeva perfettamente alle esigenze della mostra irlandese lo scorso anno, non renderebbe giustizia né alla Biennale, né all'Artista? Ritiene Lei che vi sia la possibilitá di assegnare, in questa occasione, due sale all'Irlanda? Jack B. Yeats, alla sua mostra a Londra, che io vidi di persona, esposa 80 quadri; così pure alla sua mostra retrospettiva che tenne nel 1951 al Boston Institute of Contemporary Art, alla Phillips Gallery di Washington[,] ed alla Toronto Art Gallery, egli espose un considerevole numero di quadri.[3] Credo pertanto che due sale si rendano necessarie; in realtá il mio Governo mi aveva richiesto se fosse stato possibile ottenere un padiglione per la mostra irlandese.

Sempre parlando personalmente, vorrei sapere se sia intervenuto qualche altro elemento – dopo l'ultima volta che La vidi – che offra nuove possibilitá all'acquisto di un padiglione da parte nostra.

In attesa di una Sua cortese risposta, La prego di gradire i miei piú cordiali saluti,

[Denis Devlin]

Typed letter unsigned (carbon copy). 2 leaves, 2 sides. *Address*: Prof. Rodolfo Pallucchini, Segretario Generale de l'Ente Autonomo della Biennale, S. Marco – Ca'Giustinian, Venezia. Marked "espresso", and with the departmental ref. no. 2203/51/555A. Department of Foreign Affairs Papers, DFA/Rome Embassy/555A/1, NAI.

[*Translation*]

Dear Prof. Pallucchini,

I would like to inform you that today I sent to the President of the Biennale an official letter of acceptance for the invitation addressed to my country for participation in the XXVIth Exhibition.

I have been informed by my government that it intends to nominate Jack B. Yeats, the most eminent of Irish painters, to represent Ireland at the Biennale. My government would wish that such an artist honours this which is among the most important exhibitions in the world, and had at that same time the opportunity to show the fullness of his art in this exhibition, the first in Europe after that held at London's Tate Gallery in 1948 and still very much celebrated today.

It would therefore be my government's wish that convenient space and location were granted to my country's exhibition. Would you permit me to add that one room, like that which perfectly met the needs of the Irish exhibition last year, would not do justice to the Biennale, nor the artist? Do you think there would be the possibility of assigning, on this occasion, two rooms to Ireland? Jack B. Yeats, at his London show, which I saw in person, exhibited 80 paintings; so too at his retrospective exhibition which he held in 1951 at the Boston Institute of Contemporary Art, at the Phillips Gallery in Washington[,] and at the Toronto Art Gallery, he exhibited a considerable number of paintings. I therefore believe that two rooms become necessary; in fact my government asked me if it was possible to obtain a pavilion for the Irish exhibition.

Speaking personally as always, I would like to know if some other element has intervened – since the last time I saw you – that offers new possibilities for the purchase of a pavilion on our part.

In awaiting your kind reply, please accept my best regards,

[Denis Devlin]

---

1. Giovanni Ponti (1896–1961), Italian academic and Christian Democrat politician, was president of the Biennale from 1946 to 1953.

2. The Jack B. Yeats exhibition at the Tate Britain in London ran from 14 August to 15 September 1948.

3. 'Jack B. Yeats: A first retrospective American exhibition' opened at the Boston Institute of Contemporary Art in March 1951 and travelled to Washington, San Francisco, Toronto, Detroit and New York.

To Máire MacEntee, Department of External Affairs
23 January 1952

Dear Maire [*for* Máire],

Further to my telegram 5 about Ireland's participation in the Biennale, I have been trying to get some information from the Legations of a number of countries here on the duties and functions of the [C]ommissioners in Venice: I regret without result, since these countries turned out to have Consuls in Venice, through which all Biennale work was done, or else their cultural bodies deal directly with the Biennale authorities. The official Regulations of the Exhibition have now come to hand and I give below a translation of the Articles affecting Commissioners. The description of the Commissioners' functions fits in with what I had to do as Commissioner in 1950. Briefly these functions are to supervise the setting up of his country's pavilion and to act as a member of the International Jury which awards the prizes. However, the first function is not essential as the Biennale people will hang the pictures if requested; they did so in our case in 1950.

The Biennale authorities while asking us to appoint a Commissioner have given no indication of wanting any particular type of person; and my suggestion of the name of the Director of the National Gallery was entirely personal and unknown to Mr McGreevy; it was intended as an indication of the type of Commissioner who would be suitable. For instance, taking for granted the advisability of some general knowledge of painting it would be worse than useless to send somebody, however scholarly, who could not speak French and had not some sort of position at home as well as some experience of the world in which the Museum Directors and art critics move, who make up the International Jury. The proceedings of the Jury are conducted in French.

As to the expenditure involved, if you send a Commissioner, he should, I think[,] be in Venice for the hanging, that is four or five days before the Jury starts its proceedings. The Jury sits for a period of two days before the opening and three days after and Commissioners are accorded the hospitality of the Biennale authorities during the period of the sitting of the Jury. After that period Commissioners would stay on at their own or their governments' expense. Your outlay would then have to cover the four or five days before the Jury sits and any time the Commissioner staid [*sic*] on afterwards. This would involve travel to and from Venice, hotel expense and subsistence for, say, a minimum of five days. I did not have an entertainment allowance but I think the Commissioner appointed should probably have one: the amount could best be decided by you in consultation with Establishment on the basis of precedents for international conferences. The hotel and subsistence allowances should be on a par with those sanctioned for heads of Mission: I noticed last time that the Commissioners staid [*sic*] in the same hotels as did the Ambassadors and Ministers who, by the way, all go to Venice for the opening. Generally speaking, the precedents can be found in my report 399/50/555A of the 4th July 1950 and claim 487/51/555A of 1st August 1951.

The following is a translation of the relevant portion of the Regulations of which I attach a copy in the original Italian:

"The Government of each participating nation shall nominate its own Commissioner, who shall superintend the preparations and arrangements connected with his country's section in agreement with the Secretary General of the Biennale and in conformity with the general organisational plans for the whole exhibition.

"Any foreign Commissioner who may find it impossible to be on the spot for the preparation of his section may, as an exceptional measure, delegate his duties, for this preparation, to the Secretariat of the Biennale.

"The members of the International Jury are: the Commissioners appointed by the Governments of the nations participating in the Biennale; two of the Italian members of the International Committee of Experts/etc."

The Biennale authorities have not yet made a definite decision about the space which they will assign to us and I send you a translation of the most recent communications received from the Secretary General, dated 8th and 10th January in the matter. You will see that the outlook is not too hopeful and that we are not likely to be given a pavilion. I had written – as well as talked – to them at length about Yeats' fame and his successful exhibitions in London, America and Canada. As mentioned in my telegram, I replied to the attached letters to the effect that you were unlikely to be in a position to undertake the building of a new pavilion. I asked them, however, to give a rough estimate of the cost and am awaiting their reply. I have arranged to see Venturi and I am getting in touch also with Roberto Longhi and Marino Marini who are also on the Committee and whom I met.[1] It is discouraging though that the intervention of Ponti whom I know well has not apparently produced much change in the situation.

> Yours Sincerely,
> [Denis Devlin]

Typed letter unsigned (carbon copy). Handwritten corrections. 3 leaves, 3 sides. *Address:* Máire MacEntee, Department of External Affairs, Dublin. Marked "airmail", and with departmental ref. no. 49/52/555A. Department of Foreign Affairs Papers, DFA/Rome Embassy/555A/1, NAI.

---

1. Lionello Venturi (1885–1961), Italian art historian and critic. Roberto Longhi (1890–1970), Italian art historian and curator, scholar of Caravaggio. Marino Marini (1901–80), Italian sculptor and recipient of the Biennale's Grand Prize for Sculpture in 1952. These men were all part of the Biennale's Commission for Figurative Art, which had been set up by Pallucchini in 1948.

To Máire MacEntee, Department of External Affairs
26 January 1952

Dear Maire [*for* Máire]

Further to my recent letter, is it yet known what number of pictures Yeats would send to the Biennale? I evaded the question (in conversation) but I told the President of the Committee about the London and American exhibitions, saying that Yeats had exposed about eighty canvasses in London. This might eventually clear up the question of the number of rooms since if you were only sending forty or so pictures and Pallucchini gave us one of the larger rooms, then one room would be sufficient. I am not saying this, of course, for the present.

I enclose [a] rough plan of the main pavilion in 1950 showing relations between the sizes of various rooms and numbers of pictures exposed.

Yours sincerely,

[Denis Devlin]

Typed letter unsigned (carbon copy). 1 leaf, 1 side. *Address:* Máire MacEntee, Department of External Affairs, Dublin. Marked "airmail" and with departmental ref. no. [?]/52/555A. Department of Foreign Affairs Papers, DFA/Rome Embassy/555A/1, NAI.

To Seán Nunan, Secretary, Department of External Affairs
30 January 1952

With reference to your minute 408/200 of 14th December 1951, I enquired whether Italy recognises the Federal Republic of Germany as the sole successor State of the former Reich.[1] Officials told me that Italy would adopt the same view as the U.S.A., France and Great Britain and that they would write to their Missions in these countries for information.

In the course of conversation, I learned that the Federal Government has assumed responsibility for the debts of the former Reich.

A memorandum sent to all Italian Offices abroad states that the agreed policy of the Brussels Pact countries is not to recognise de jure or de facto the East German regime.[2] Trade is to be kept entirely in private hands and official dealings where necessary are to be direct with the Russian Government.

[Denis Devlin]
Minister Plenipotentiary

Typed letter unsigned (carbon copy). 1 leaf, 1 side. *Address:* Secretary, Department of External Affairs, Dublin. Department of Foreign Affairs Papers, DFA/Rome Embassy/495B, NAI.

---

1. The Potsdam Agreement (1945) at the end of the Second World War had divided Germany into four Allied occupation zones. The Federal Republic of Germany constituted the three zones to the west, occupied by the United States, the United Kingdom and France. The east zone, which became the German Democratic Republic, was occupied by the Soviet Union.

2. The Brussels Pact, or the Treaty of Brussels, signed in 1948 by Belgium, France, Luxembourg, the Netherlands and the United Kingdom, founded the Western Union – a commitment to economic, social and cultural cooperation as well as a bulwark against the threat of communism.

To Robert Penn Warren
2 February 1952

[*from Caren Devlin*]

My dear Red,

I am most terribly sorry that the letter herewith enclosed was both opened and so long delayed. I am afraid it was due to some mix-up in the office. The reason it was opened, I suppose, is that one of the secretaries, as usual in a rush, looked at the written part "Denis Devlin", and did not think again about opening it. Anyway, I'm sorry about this.

Thank you so much for your letter. We enjoyed so much hearing all your news – and are looking forward to next summer, with you here, a most delightful prospect. Denis, concerning your remark about his 'never writing letters', a fact that is absolutely and undeniably true, does however state that he wrote you a magnificent epistle* of 3 pages last November – [d]id you ever get it? I will not fail to let you know when I come over; seeing you, is a thing I am looking forward to most particularly, and I do hope we will manage somehow to meet. Your poem, I hope you will bring over, and read to us, and work on here, while gazing over poplars and pines and arch[a]eological remains (all of which are to be seen, from your prospective window). Denis is at present working on translations of René Char, and a longish poem, both for 'Botteghe Oscure'.[1]

More soon! Much love to you from both of us,

And promise you will come over, fate and work permitting.

Caren

* A terrific effort, and one he has not repeated since to anyone. It seems to be his "maladie", not writing letters.

Autograph letter signed. 1 leaf, 2 sides. Asterisked addition is indicated by an arrow pointing to the top of the verso. Robert Penn Warren Papers, Box 21, Folder 409, Beinecke, YU.

---

1. René Char (1907–88), French poet associated with the surrealists. Devlin was collaborating with the American poet-critic Jackson Mathews (1907–78) on a clutch of translations from Char's *Fureur et mystère* (1948), which were published in the Italian journal *Botteghe Oscure*, quaderno X, Fall 1952, and as a separate limited edition pamphlet. Devlin's long poem 'The Colours of Love' appeared in the same issue.

To Victor Mallet, British Ambassador in Rome

6 February 1952   Rome

My dear Ambassador,

It is with deep regret that I learn of the sudden and tragic death this morning of His Majesty King George VI. May I offer you my most sincere sympathy in this great loss which your country has sustained.

Accept, Sir, the expression of my highest consideration.

[Denis Devlin]

Irish Minister.

Typed letter unsigned (carbon copy). 1 leaf, 1 side. *Address*: His Excellency, Sir Victor A.L. Mallet, British Ambassador in ROME. Department of Foreign Affairs Papers, DFA/Rome Embassy/1205B, NAI.

To Rodolfo Pallucchini
9 February 1952   3 Via Valle delle Camene

Egregio Professore,

Desidero informarla che ho provveduto immediatamente ad inoltrare a Dublin il preventivo cortesemente inviatomí dal Rag. Romolo Bazzoni il 25 gennaio u[ltima] s[corso] per la construzione di un padiglione irlandese alla Biennale di Venezia. Il mio Paese è molto sensibile all'onore fattogli offrendogli un posto permanenta alla Biennale, ma, purtroppo, le Autorità Irlandesi hanno confermato di avere già fissato il bilancio per le spese culturali per l'anno finanzario in corso, e non vi sarebbe perciò più tempo sufficiente per esaminare in tutti i suoi dettagli la gradita offerta ed arrivare ad una decisione prima della Biennale di quest'anno.

Sono stato informato che Dublino desidererebbe inviare 40 quadri, di dimensioni piuttosto vaste, del pittore Yeats. So benissimo che malgrado le innumerevoli difficoltà di spazio che lei deve affrontare, lei farà tutto il possibile, dato le circostanze, per assicurare due stanze, o una molto grande, all'esposizione irlandese.

La prego di gradire i miei più cordiali saluti.

[Denis Devlin]

Typed letter unsigned (carbon copy). 1 leaf, 1 side. *Address*: Prof. Rodolfo Pallucchini, Secretary General, Biennale d'Arte di Venezia. Marked with departmental ref. no. [?]/52/555A. Department of Foreign Affairs Papers, DFA/Rome Embassy/555A/1, NAI.

[*Translation*]

Dear Professor,

I wish to inform you that I immediately proceeded to forward to Dublin the quote kindly sent to me by accountant Romolo Bazzoni on 25th January last for the construction of an Irish pavilion at the

Venice Biennale. My country is very sensitive to the honour given by offering to it a permanent post at the Biennale, but, unfortunately, the Irish authorities have confirmed that they have already fixed the budget for cultural expenses in the current financial year, and therefore there would not be sufficient time to examine the kind offer in all its details and arrive at a decision before this year's Biennale.

I have been informed that Dublin would like to send 40 paintings, of rather large dimensions, by the painter Yeats. I know very well that despite the innumerable difficulties with space that you must be faced with, you will do all that is possible, given the circumstances, to secure two rooms, or a very large one, for the Irish exhibition.

Please accept my best regards.

[Denis Devlin]

To Máire MacEntee, Department of External Affairs
13 February 1952

Dear Móira [*for* Máire],

My telegram of today will have given you the bad news from Venice, which was received in a letter from Pallucchini this morning. He says that independently of the question of a Pavilion he had been keeping in mind the reserving of a place for Ireland "in the distribution of rooms granted by hospitality". He offers us a room in an excellent position with a wall length of 24 metres suitable therefore to hold 20 or 22 paintings and some sculpture. He adds (I translate):

"I will not hide from you that it has been possible for me to reserve this room, which has the same characteristics as that of the other year and which comes in order of location immediately after, only with the greatest difficulty, in view of the great number of requests for participation on the part of countries which have not got their own building; for this reason I would be very grateful if you would let me know as soon as ever possible whether the construction of a Pavilion has been decided upon, since this, while affording greater elbow-room to the Irish exhibit, would make it possible for the Biennale to satisfy one of the other applicant nations."

This letter evidently crossed mine informing Pallucchini of your negative decision about the Pavilion.

You will see that the tone is pretty final. I think there was a slight possibility of getting a larger space while the Swedes were considering building a Pavilion but it vanished when they decided against; and they then had first option on the space they had last year. Anyhow, Pallucchini was never very forthcoming and he is the one who counts. Perhaps he should have been invited to Dublin to see Yeats['s] work or perhaps a few paintings should have been sent to him to see; certainly the black and whites in McGreevy's [*for* MacGreevy's] book would not have convinced him.

I think I have used all the themes of persuasion and I would not advise insisting further; in fact, in view of our position as the invited party, I feel I have gone further than propriety would permit. (Pallucchini gently reminds us of his position in his letter: see the sentence quoted in the first paragraph above). As the space now offered is less than half what would be required for Yeats' 40 pictures, I suppose he will now withdraw (though Jacques Villon had a similar sized room last year). But if he does I think we should not: it would look pettish and indignified [*sic*]. You could assemble four or five of the younger (men!) painters only too easily, I am sure.[1]

Pallucchini points out that all data must be in Venice before 15th April, for the catalogue, and that the works should arrive at the beginning of May. He enquires whether they are "to have the pleasure" of having me as Commissioner this year and could I let him know soon.

[Denis Devlin]

Typed letter unsigned (carbon copy). 2 leaves, 2 sides. *Address:* Miss Máire MacEntee, Department of External Affairs, Dublin. Marked "airmail" and with departmental ref. no. [?]/[?]/555A. "P.T.O." typed between two leaves. Department of Foreign Affairs Papers, DFA/Rome Embassy/555A/1, NAI.

---

1. Devlin's sexist joke is a reference that would have been well understood by those in the department. Ireland's 1950 Biennale exhibition of the painters Nano Reid and Norah McGuinness had not been very warmly received; members of the Cultural Relations Committee within the department believed that the Biennale authorities were denying Ireland exhibition space as a response to the 1950 entry (Letter from Brian Durnin to DD, 2 April 1952, DFA/Rome Embassy/555A, NAI).

To Seán Nunan, Secretary, Department of External Affairs
22 March 1952

Dear Secretary,

I received this morning your letter 415/95 Pt. II of 18th March, regarding our participation at this year's Venice Biennale.

I am frankly at a loss to understand how the misunderstanding arose that two rooms had been or would certainly be offered by the organisers to accommodate the Irish exhibit consisting entirely of paintings by Mr. Jack B. Yeats. In correspondence and conversation, the President, Professor Ponti, and the Secretary General, Professor Pallucchini, made it clear that their firm offer consisted of one room; the alternative suggestions about a pavilion and two rooms came from us. The Biennale authorities took our requests under consideration; they constantly stressed, however, that they were hard put for space, and at no time did they give any undertaking that they could assign us what we consider adequate hanging-room for a representative selection of Yeats' paintings. This situation is reflected in my despatches, and in my telegram of the 30th January, my last communication to you before the Biennale's decision was received, I clearly asked whether I should "continue endeavour obtain loan pavilion or concentrate on effort obtain two rooms".

I fully share the disappointment which Mr. Yeats and his admirers feel. I also appreciate the reasons for his declining to send a small number of pictures which would inadequately represent his work and his stature as a painter. However, I feel I must point out that Ireland has been invited to participate and has been offered hanging-space in the central pavilion of one of the world's most important Art Exhibitions. It must be remembered that our position is very different from that of a country which owns its own pavilion and exhibits as of right. Also, as I mentioned above, the Biennale authorities never promised to give us two rooms. For these reasons, I feel very strongly that it would be unworthy to reject out of hand the honour done to

Ireland in inviting our participation and I would earnestly reque[st] you to consider whether the work of some of the younger painte[rs] might be chosen for this year's Exhibition.

With regard to your final paragraph, I assume the Italian Minister's representations were not a "protest" at the Biennale's decision.[1]

Finally, may I say that I am very grateful for your remarks about my effort to obtain greater space.

Yours sincerely,
DD

Typed letter signed. Handwritten corrections. 2 leaves, 2 sides. *Address*: Seán Nunan, Esq., Secretary, Department of External Affairs, Dublin. Marked "airmail", and with departmental ref. no. [?]/52/555A. Some text on the right-hand margin has been cut off. Department of Foreign Affairs Papers, DFA/Rome Embassy/555A/1, NAI.

---

1. In the letter Devlin is responding to, Nunan had written: 'You may wish to know that the Italian Minister here made representations to the Italian Authorities on the matter.' (Seán Nunan to DD, 18 March 1952, DFA/Rome Embassy/555A). The Italian minister in Dublin at this time was Signor Guido Borga (dates unknown).

To Classe V, Scuole Elementari di Palidano
3 April 1952

Cari Bambini,

Ho letto con vero piacere la vostra lettera, piena di espressioni di simpatia e di amicizia per il mio Paese, e sono ben lieto di aderire al vostro desiderio di aumentare la vostra biblioteca con pubblicazioni e riviste che parl[a]no dell'Irlanda e ne illustrino le varie attivitá. Parte di esse sono in lingua inglese, ma il vostro Maestro le tradurrá per voi, nel corso di quei viaggi immaginari che riempiono la vostra fantasia e le vostre menti durante le ore di storia e di geografia. L'Irlanda non [è] una grande isola, ma la sua popolazione è effettivamente laboriosa e cordiale, e la sua natura assai bella. Non credo di avere, purtroppo, tutto quello che desiderereste leggere, ma ció che vi mando potrá servire per la prima tappa del Vostro viaggio verso l'Isola di Smeraldo come appunto l'Irlanda [è] chiamata, dal colore smagliante dei suoi prati.

Con il piú vivo augurio di ogni bene e per la migliore riuscita dei vostri studi,

Cordialmente,

[Denis Devlin]

Ministro d'Irlanda in Italia

Typed letter unsigned (carbon copy). 1 leaf, 1 side. *Address*: Alla Classe V Elementare, Scuole di Palidano (Mantova). Marked with departmental ref. no. 514/52/340. Department of Foreign Affairs Papers, DFA/ Rome Embassy/340, NAI.

[*Translation*]

Dear Children,

I read your letter with real pleasure, full of expressions of sympathy and friendship for my country, and I am happy to grant your wish to increase your library with publications and magazines that talk about Ireland and illustrate its various activities. Some of them are in English, but your Master will translate them for you, during those fantasy journeys which fill your imagination and your mind during your history and geography lessons. Ireland is not a big island, but its population is indeed hard-working and friendly, and its landscape very beautiful. I don't believe I have, unfortunately, everything you would like to read, but what I am sending will be able to serve for the first leg of your journey to the Emerald Isle as Ireland is called, because of the dazzling colour of its meadows.

With the most lively wishes for all the best and for the greatest success of your studies,

> With regards,
> [Denis Devlin]
> Irish Minister to Italy

To Eleanor Clark
9 May 1952

Dear Eleanor,

We are most grateful to you for sending us <u>Rome and a Villa</u>.[1] It is a beautiful book; my warm congratulations on it, on having done it so well and completed something that obviously had to find its own form. I'm delighted, too, that it is having success and that the reviews are favourable, even though the two or three I've seen have been quite inadequate, reading you as one whose object was to inform travellers about Rome. How absurd! [W]hen your book is quite original – it strikes me, among other things, as a novel whose characters are architecture, the populus romanus and time. Probably the quarterlies will be more perceptive. – The <u>Hadrian's Villa</u> re-read is splendid; so is <u>Fountains</u> in how they unite 'the sensibility of stone' with wisdom, with sagesse.[2] And I'm completely won by your cats of the Piazza Vittorio. The Belli chapter I admire immensely as a work of elucidation, of revelation.[3] It should certainly be published in Italian – shall I ask Praz's views?[4] Now Belli is forever yours, your plume, your Lazarus –

Caren is flying to New York on the 20th of this month. I wrote poetry during the winter, some of which will be in the next <u>Botteghe Oscure</u> as well as translations of René Char, who is the great passion with the Principessa these days.[5] After that, no more translation for me. We have been to Ninfa more than usual.[6] I have been to Turkey. We go to Ireland end [of] July for a month, but we shall see you before that – it's fine to hear that you are to come in June, may the auspices remain favourable!

Many congratulations & good things from Rome and the Romans to their new poet!

Yours ever

Denis

Autograph letter signed. 4 leaves, 4 sides. *Header:* Légation d'Irlande, Rome. Eleanor Clark Papers, Yale Collection of American Literature (MSS 315), Box 28, Folder 363, Beinecke Rare Book and Manuscript Library, Yale University.

---

1. Clark's *Rome and a Villa* was first published by Doubleday, Garden City, NY, in 1952.

2. sagesse (Fr.): wisdom/good sense.

3. Clark devoted a chapter to Giuseppe Gioachino Belli (1791–1863), the Italian poet known for his sonnets in Romanesco.

4. Mario Praz (1896–1982), Italian literary critic and professor of English literature at the University of Rome.

5. Marguerite Caetani (née Chapin) (1880–1963), princess of Bassiano, the American-born, Rome-based founder and editor of *Botteghe Oscure*, which ran from 1948 to 1960.

6. The Gardens of Ninfa in Cisterna di Latina, a short distance south-east of Rome, had been part of the Caetani family's domain since the sixteenth century. Marguerite Caetani, a keen gardener, often entertained guests at Ninfa, and when the publication of *Botteghe Oscure* ceased, she retired there for the last years of her life.

To Thomas MacGreevy
15 May 1952

My dear Tom,

I've had a pleasant letter of regret from the Biennale authorities and our effort at participation is ended. What a pity! the more so as the final negative decision may have been based on the misunderstanding which took place early on and of which you must have heard by now. For the Biennale never offered two rooms, they offered one and I kept pressing for two; and they agreed to consider my request. I don't know how Mr. Yeats decided on the figure of 40 as the number of exhibits but it occurs to me as being just possible that if he had not thought he was being given space for 40, he might have fixed on 30 and 30 pictures would have fitted into the room I got in the end. The Biennale people said that 30 was the average with them for individual shows. But if Yeats thought he would not be adequately represented by less than 40 pictures, that, of course, is another matter.

Since we were guests asking for more there was always the feeling: "If you think so much of this great painter of yours, why don't you build a pavilion for him." (I got an estimate for the building and decoration of a suitable pavilion: it was 8½ million lire, approx. £4,500.) Another stroke against us was, I feel sure, the undistinguished quality of our 1950 exhibit. Finally, the Secretary General, Palucchini [*for* Pallucchini], may have sought an opinion of the foreign experts who advise the Biennale selection committee: I failed to identify these experts but if they include the British Commissioner who was on our Board in 1950, that opinion would not have been entirely pro-Yeats.[1] But, underlying all these, the principal disadvantage was that the Biennale authorities simply did not know Yeats. (For that matter, until after the war the Italians knew precious little about any modern painting[.]) That may be deplorable but so it was; and I think we should have approached the thing differently. Someone officially connected with painting in Ireland, such as yourself, should have been sent out by the Cultural Affairs Committee, taking with him two or three canvasses of Yeats to show to the Venetians, last year. Then my advocacy would have had solider ground to rest on. Well! – anyhow there would be far more sense to an exhibition in Paris. By the way, your book on Yeats, which I presented to Palucchini, now reposes in the archives of the Biennale.[2]

The National Gallery book is out, I see.[3] I have asked the Department to give me a copy (officially) for the Legation. I think they should supply one to all our Missions[.] – At the Radio last week I met a young man – Zavatti or something like it – who claimed acquaintance of you. As for Brian (whom I owe a letter to for nearly a year alas!) his address last was: RR 1., House Springs, Mo. also c/o Dept. of Philosophy, University of St. Louis, St Louis, Mo.

I have presented your salutations to Rome and am the bearer of Rome's salute to you.

Caren sends her love. All my best wishes[,]

Denis

Autograph letter signed. 2 leaves, 4 sides. *Header*: Légation d'Irlande, Rome. Thomas MacGreevy Papers, 8112/17–22, TCD.

---

1. The British commissioner who sat on the jury with Devlin in 1950 was Sir Eric Maclaglan (1879–1951), art historian and museum curator. Maclaglan's area of specialism was early Christian and Italian Renaissance art, but he was also a keen follower and collector of modern and abstract art.

2. See DD to Sheila Murphy, Department of External Affairs, 7 May 1951, n. 4.

3. Ibid.

To Seán Nunan, Secretary, Department of External Affairs
May 1952

I have the honour to state, for information, that I have been elected member of the Committee of the Keats-Shelley Association in Rome.[1] Other members are: the British Ambassador, Mr. Kennedy Cook [*for* Cooke], head of the British Council here, Mr. Roberts, director of the American Academy, Professor Mario Praz, Professor Van Buren and Avvocato Giustinani.[2]

Denis Devlin

> Typed letter signed. 1 leaf, 1 side. *Header*: Légation d'Irlande, Rome. *Dating*: Administrative annotation regarding the cataloguing of the letter is dated 24/5/52. Department of Foreign Affairs Papers, DFA 5/338/412, NAI.

---

1. The Keats–Shelley Memorial Foundation is the charity supporting the Keats–Shelley House in Rome's Piazza di Spagna.

2. Sir Victor Mallet (1893–1969) was British ambassador to Italy at this time. Brian Kennedy Cooke (1894–1963), a civil servant appointed British Council representative in Italy in 1950. Laurance P. Roberts, see DD to Vivienne Koch, 22 December 1948, n. 1. Mario Praz, see DD to Eleanor Clark, 9 May 1952, n. 4. Albert Van Buren (1878–1968), classical archaeologist and curator and librarian at the American Academy in Rome. Avvocato Giustinani has not been identified.

To Brian Durnin, Department of External Affairs
19 June 1952

Dear Brian,

The Biennale opened a few days ago with great pomp and circumstance, reviving [m]y disappointment that we are not taking part and reminding me that I wanted to thank you for all your efforts towards reaching a satisfactory solution of the difficulties in the way of our participation. I had already guessed that the mistake occurred before you took over Cultural Relations. It is a pity that such a small slip should have had such important consequences.

However, the attitude of the Biennale authorities has been pleasant and they will probably invite us again for the next exhibition. I quote the following extract from the Secretary General's closing letter. You will note the hint about building our own pavilion. "I wish to express our lively disappointment at the fact that Ireland will not participate this year in the Biennale.

"We had made every effort to grant larger space but I see that the painter Yeats still considers the room too small.

"We hope that your participation will become effective at the Biennale of 1954 and above all that the Irish Government will decide to build a pavilion for itself so as to give to its exhibit the amplitude and importance which are desiderated and which we ourselves would be most pleased to see".

Kindest regards,
Yours sincerely,
[Denis Devlin]

Typed letter unsigned (carbon copy). 2 leaves, 2 sides. *Address:* Brian Durnin, Esq., Department of External Affairs, Dublin. Marked with departmental ref. no. [?]/52/555A. Department of Foreign Affairs Papers, DFA/Rome Embassy/555A/1, NAI.

To Brian Coffey
16 September 1952

My dear Brian,

I have made a preliminary enquiry with I.T.A.[1] When they reply, I shall write to you again and you can then write to their New York Office. I will write then in support. I have put it that your contract at St. Louis is up, that you are going to another University next year and that you wish to tide over the transition period in a temporary post.[2]

I spoke to Allen Tate, who is an old friend, about you. He thought you should try St. Thomas College, Minnesota, of which he thinks highly as a religious university; most of the staff are laymen and the President, a Father O'Neill, I think, a secular, wants to make of it the perfect and noble Catholic University (that eternal will-o-the-wisp!).[3]

The whole business must be terribly distressing you but I am sure your stand is right and that if it weren't for the family, you would not mind so much but would enjoy the fight. It would be fine if you got into Yale. I know the Professor of Drama there, Robert Penn Warren, and spoke to him when he passed through Rome two weeks ago, avoiding any reference to details or reasons for your present situation. I don't think he has any influence with the Governors, but anyhow he said he would like to mee[t] you.

Remember me kindly to Bridget. Caren sends her wishes too. I hope something may come of this but, as most bodies nowadays are closed corporations, I'm not too sanguine. I'll write as soon as I hear from I.T.A.

> Yours ever,
> Denis

Typed letter signed. 1 leaf, 1 side. *Header*: Légation d'Irlande, Rome. Brian Coffey Papers, Box 30, Folder 22, UDel.

1. Devlin possibly refers to the Irish Tourist Association (est. 1924, liquidated 1964), a private organisation which set up a bureau in New York. The ITA was succeeded by the Irish Tourist Board (An Bord Fáilte), which became Bord Fáilte Éireann. It is not clear what kind of service Devlin envisaged the ITA could provide for Coffey.

2. Coffey resigned from his post at St Louis University this year; his reasons for re-signing are unclear, but his correspondence suggests it was on principled grounds. In a letter from Coffey to Devlin written the following year, preserved in Coffey's University of Delaware archive, he explains: 'The last year has been a dreary affair. I applied to more than 150 universities without success.' He goes on to describe the low-paid factory work he has taken on to keep the family afloat, and the illness and premature labour his wife Bridget has suffered (Brian Coffey to DD, 5 October 1953, Brian Coffey Papers, Box 30, Folder 22, UDel).

3. The president at St Thomas College at this time was the Very Rev. Vincent J. Flynn (1901–56); Father Joseph O'Neill (dates unknown) was a contemporary dean.

To Raymond McGrath, Office of Public Works
20 December 1952

Dear Mr McGrath,

Thank you for your letter of the 17th November. I too am sorry that I was not here to see you during your visit to Rome. My sorrow was in fact compounded with anger and frustration since I had been looking forward so much to your visit so that we could have a talk about the legation from all the points of view which interest your Office. When I knew you were coming, however, it was too late to put off my commitments for my stay in Ankara.

On the question of future accommodation, I am afraid my ideas are not yet definite. I think our present premises are most satisfactory from every point of view (except for the landlord's furniture) but I realise of course tha[t] a State-owned property would be a great financial saving to the Government in the long run. I did strongly recommend the latter solution at the time of the sale of the old San Martino property but at the time for some reason the authorities did not want to buy and I was instructed, as you probably know, to get rented premises.[1] I shall think the thing over for a while though and write to you in a few months.

In the meantime there is one very urgent item of furnishing need-ed, for which I applied many months ago and that is curtains for the reception rooms. The old San Martino curtains now in the dining room and small drawing room, though my wife has had them cleaned and patched, are in a sad state of shabbiness. The landlord's white net [c]urtains whic[h] in themselves look cheap in such a room, have holes and tears and the landlord will not replace them. I should be very grateful if you would see whether your Office can agree to grant the sanction I had applied for[, for] getting new curtains.

All the best greetings of the season and please remember me kindly to your wife.

> Yours sincerely,
>
> [Denis Devlin]

---

1. The Irish legation in Rome was previously situated on Via San Martino della Battaglia. Devlin oversaw the transfer of premises in the summer and autumn of 1951.

To Brian Durnin, Department of External Affairs
20 December 1952

Dear Brian,

I am rather puzzled by your letter of the 31st October asking me to make discreet enquiries as to whether there is any good reason why the statuette awarded by the Catholic Stage Guild to Vittorio De Sica should not be presented.[1] The Guild's criteria in deciding on these awards are surely drawn up with reference to a community which does not embrace the whole Irish population. I[t] would seem to be therefore that the Guild should properly make any such "discreet" enquiries through its own private channe[l]s rather than through the Mission which represent[s] the whole of the Irish people.

However, the factual point is that the award was announced publicly from Dublin.[2] Local papers reported it here and De Sica's secretary telephoned the Legation to express his principal's pleasure and gratitude. It is, of course, a matter for the Guild, but it seems to me that it would be difficult to decline now to go through with the presentation.

> Yours sincerely,
> [Denis Devlin]

Typed letter unsigned (carbon copy). 1 leaf, 1 side. *Address*: Brian Durnin, Esq., Department of External Affairs, Dublin. Marked with departmental ref. no. 711/52/915A. Department of Foreign Affairs Papers, DFA/Rome Embassy/915, NAI.

---

1. Vittorio De Sica (1901–74), Italian director and actor and a leading figure in the neorealismo movement. The Catholic Stage Guild of Ireland was an organisation founded in 1945 to represent the Catholic Church's relationship to the entertainment industry. The guild presented annual awards to international artists in every field of the entertainment industry, raising the profile of the church and its associated endeavours in the world's media. See Alex Cahill, *The Formation, Existence, and Deconstruction of the Catholic Stage Guild of Ireland* (Newcastle upon Tyne: Cambridge Scholars Publishing, 2017). The controversy regarding De Sica's award is illuminated in DD to Brian Durnin, 28 February 1953.

2. De Sica's award (the St Patrick statuette for contributions to film) had been announced on 12 November 1951 at the Adelphi Cinema in Dublin; it was reported in *The Irish Times* the following day.

To W.R. Rodgers
13 February 1953

3 Via Valle delle Camene
Passeggiata Archeologica

Dear Bertie,

I have been asked by <u>New World Writing</u>, an American publication rather like the old Penguin <u>New Writing</u>, to prepare a small anthology of contemporary Irish poetry and I should like to include one of yours.[1] I am allowed only about eight pages, inclusive of a short introduction, so that fairly short poems from each writer would be the rule.[2] Could you let me have about three from which to choose? And could you let me have them with great speed as the publishers in their American way have set me a very close dead end.

The Publishers inform me that they will pay the poets at their regular rates of 50c. a line with a minimum payment of $10. Work already published in America will not be eligible, and while the publishers have no objection to work published in Ireland or in England, they would naturally prefer unpublished poems. Postage will be refunded by me.

With best wishes,
Yours sincerely,
Denis Devlin

The editor asked especially that I get a poem from you.
D.

Typed letter signed. Handwritten postscript. 1 leaf, 1 side. *Header:* Légation d'Irlande, Rome. *Address:* W.R. Rodgers, Esq., C/o British Broadcasting Corporation, Broadcasting House, London W1. (Gran Bretagna). W.R. Rodgers Papers, Public Record Office of Northern Ireland, Belfast.

---

1. An identical request sent to Robert Greacen (see Correspondents' Biographies and DD to Robert Greacen, 20 March 1953) on 5 January 1953, preserved in the Robert Greacen Papers, is not included here. Devlin had in fact sent an identical letter to W.R. Rodgers on the same date, and after no response sent this follow-up with the personalised postscript.

2. *New World Writing*, under the general editorship of Arabel J. Porter, described itself as 'The New Cross Section of Current World Literature'. Each of these affordable paperback editions gathered a wide range of international contemporary poetry; Devlin was asked to put together and introduce a selection of 'Ten Irish Poets' for the '4th Mentor Selection' (The New American Library, October 1953). W.R. Rodgers apparently didn't respond to Devlin's request, and was not included in the final selection.

To Brian Durnin, Department of External Affairs
28 February 1953

Dear Brian,

Further to correspondence on the Catholic Stage Guild's award to De Sica, I would say from information which has come my way that there would seem to be no reason, politically speaking, why the award should not be presented with some ceremony at the Legation. It is said that De Sica has never been a Communist sympathiser and that he refused an offer of the Stalin Prize. It is true that, in his movies, he has shown some preoccupation with the social themes of the day and this has perhaps given rise to the rumours you mention.

However, at this stage, because of the long time which has passed between the assignment of the award and the present, I would rather not be asked to present the statuette formally on behalf of the Guild. If you will have it sent to the Legation I will be glad to see that it is delivered to Mr. De Sica.

Yours sincerely,

[Denis Devlin]

Typed letter unsigned (carbon copy). 1 leaf, 1 side. *Address:* Brian Durnin, Esq., Department of External Affairs, Dublin. Marked with departmental ref. no. 109/53/915A. Department of Foreign Affairs Papers, Dublin, DFA/Rome Embassy/915, NAI.

To Robert Penn Warren
3 March 1953

Dear Red,

How is the poem coming? You haven't sent me the proof and I hope it's not because of my culpable but insignificant epistolary scarcity. Since last summer we have been in Ireland, Turkey and hospital: each of us has had an operation with all the seccatura of doctors[,] medicine & convalescence, so that if I don't watch myself I'll turn into a hypochondriac.[1] I would like to see & ponder the poem before you come, so please send me a copy.

About that coming which will be hailed with great joy, someone here has heard that it has been brought forward from April to the end of March. Is this so? I ask because Paul Geier of your Embassy asks me: he is in charge of Cultural Affairs and would propose to you to attend the Fiera del Libro in Taormina from the 25th to 29th March.[2] You would be there as a famous American author, guest of the Fair people and you wouldn't have to give any lectures, just be all handsome and dignified for your country. It may seem a strange way to send you the invitation but Geier knows we are friends and just asked me to pass it on.

Your man of business at the Rocca did not approach me so I presume he made a clear bargain.[3] Would you tell Eleanor?[4]

We are having a wonderful intoxicating Spring or pre-Spring and one feels as elevated as twenty years ago, matterdamn senescence, matterdamn the bomb! And then some fatuous relic of a doctor tells me I may perhaps have a couple of glasses of <u>white</u> wine!

And we are looking forward to your coming, both. We'll have fine times and talks. And Eleanor, do bring a pair of good strong oars and a tiller – did you ever think o[r] do you know what a speleoscopy is?[5]

Love from Caren & me to you both

– Denis

Autograph letter signed. 2 leaves, 4 sides. *Header:* Légation d'Irlande, Rome. Robert Penn Warren Papers, Beinecke, YU.

---

1. seccatura (It.): nuisance.

2. Paul Esselborn Geier (1914–81) served in the US embassy in Rome between 1949 and 1953. 'Fiera del Libro' is the generic term for Italian book fairs.

3. La Rocca, or Rocca Spagnola, is a hilltop fortress above Porta Ercole in Grosseto, Tuscany. Penn Warren and Eleanor Clark spent summers at La Rocca with their family in the 1950s.

4. Penn Warren married Clark in December 1952. The nature of the 'business' is unclear.

5. Devlin may be referring to a procedure for diagnosing tuberculosis.

To Seán Nunan, Secretary, Department of External Affairs
11 March 1953

Dear Sean [*for* Seán],

When consulting the Estimates for 1952-3 recently in connection with representations about my allowances which I intend submitting, I noticed a feature concerning my salary which I do not understand. I am referring to the salary alone, as distinct from the allowances.

According to the Estimates, the salaries of the other Heads of Mission jumped, as between the year 1951-52 and 1952-3, from round £300 to £500. Mine increased by £103. There may be a reasonable explanation but you will understand that I am worried. It cannot be a question of my seniority since, of the two colleagues of my own year, one shows an increase of £295, the other of £310 – and the latter is a Minister, not an Ambassador. It cannot be connected either with the withholding of the (previous) award in certain posts, since my colleague in Rome shows a similar increase; and he for practical purposes is a resident of Italy, hence cost of living factors are identical between us.

I am sorry to bother you with this problem but it looks like a case of discrimination against me, which I cannot explain. I would very much appreciate a line from you.[1]

Yours very sincerely,

Denis Devlin

Typed letter signed. 1 leaf, 1 side. *Header*: Légation d'Irlande, Rome. *Address*: Sean Nunan, Esq., Secretary, Department of External Affairs, Dublin. Marked "Personal and Confidential", "air mail", and with departmental ref. no. 133/53/114B. Department of Foreign Affairs Papers, PS 35/25 (Folder 2), NAI.

---

1. In Nunan's response he writes that in 1952–3, officers in Rome, in common with those in Paris, Brussels, Lisbon and Madrid, did not receive the percentage award increase of the previous year. This followed a directive from the Department of Finance regarding exchange compensation relative to local cost of living. See Seán Nunan to DD, 13 March 1953, Department of Foreign Affairs Papers, PS 35/25 (Folder 2), NAI.

To Brian Durnin, Department of External Affairs
14 March 1953

Dear [Brian],

With reference to your letter 338/146 of the 10th of March, 1953, the statuette of Saint Patrick arrived safely in the last bag. Unfortunately, however, De Sica's name is misspelt (Di Sica) in the inscription on the pedestal.

The best thing to do, I think, is to have another pedestal made in Ireland. If the Catholic Stage Guild decides on this course, I shall return the statuette to you by bag. A much less satisfactory way out would be to have the I changed to E. This could be done, but I am afraid that the result would be clumsy.

> Yours sincerely,
> [Denis Devlin]

Typed letter unsigned (carbon copy). 1 leaf, 1 side. *Address*: Brian Durnin Esq., Department of External Affairs, Dublin. Marked with departmental ref. no. 140/53/915A. Department of Foreign Affairs Papers, DFA/ Rome Embassy/915, NAI.

To Austin Clarke
20 March 1953

Dear Austin Clarke,

Thank you for the poems of which I am taking one, or two, if space permits.[1] I have not yet finally arranged a selection. Publication has now been advanced to the next issue, because we were too late to appear in the last, despite the promptness with which you were kind enough to reply. The next issue will appear in June. The publisher will get in touch with you direct about the fee, shortly.

I think that your poem THE JEWELS is a magnificent one, and I am including it in my selection.[2] I would also like to include at least one other of your shorter poems, if possible. As for the rest, I thought of showing them to Princess Caetani the editor of BOTTEGHE OSCURE, which you may have seen.[3] It is distributed in England, America, France, etc. This would also be a dollar earner if it comes off.

With best wishes.

Yours, very sincerely,

Denis Devlin

Typed letter signed. Handwritten corrections. 1 leaf, 1 side. *Header:* Légation d'Irlande, Rome. Austin Clarke Papers, MS 38,654/1, NLI.

---

1. See DD to W.R. Rodgers, 13 February 1953, n. 2.

2. Devlin chose 'Respectable People', along with 'The Jewels', for his selection from Clarke's work.

3. See DD to Eleanor Clark, 9 May 1952, n. 5.

To Robert Greacen
20 March 1953

Dear Mr Greacen,

Thank you for the poems, of which I chose JAMES JOYCE. Publication has now been advanced to the ne[x]t issue, because we were too late to appear in the last, despite the promptness with which you were kind enough to reply. The next issue will appear in June. The publisher will get in touch with you direct about the fee, shortly.

Enclosed you will find the other poems you sent me.

> Yours very sincerely
> Denis Devlin

P.S. Can you please send me a short autobiography with titles and publishers' names of your books.

Typed letter signed. 1 leaf, 1 side. *Header*: Légation d'Irlande, Rome. Robert Greacen Papers, MSS 7940/1–24+7a, Misc Box XXXVI, TCD.

To Austin Clarke
22 May 1953

Dear Austin Clarke,

This has just come in this morning's mail, and I am forwarding it to you at once. All you have to do is sign the thing and return it direct to the publishers, and they will send the cheque directly to you. I have also sent the remaining poems to Princess Caetani, who said she will get in touch with you herself.[1] Sorry for the delay of all of this.

With all best wishes and many thanks for your collaboration,
I remain yours sincerely
Denis Devlin

Typed letter signed. Handwritten corrections. 1 leaf, 1 side. *Header:* Légation d'Irlande, Rome. Austin Clarke Papers, MS 38,654/1, NLI.

---

1. Clarke's poetry never appeared in *Botteghe Oscure*.

To Richard Hayes, Department of External Affairs
15 June 1953

Dear Mr Hayes,

I have your letter of the 2nd of June (No. 338/146) in regard to the statuette of St. Patrick awarded to De Sica by the Catholic Stage Guild. I found that it would have cost far too much to replace the plinth so I had the lettering changed; you could inform Father Sylvester that the result is satisfactory and that the base looks well.[1] The cost is 850 lire. It was paid out of official funds and I assume you will recover at your end.

De Sica has been away a lot but I hope to make the presentation shortly.[2] I shall let you know.

Yours sincerely,

[Denis Devlin]

Typed letter unsigned (carbon copy). 1 leaf, 1 side. *Address:* P.J. [*for* R.F. – Devlin may be confusing him for Dr R.J. Hayes, Director of the National Library] Hayes, Esq., Department of External Affairs, Dublin. Marked with departmental ref. no. 291/53/915A. Department of Foreign Affairs Papers, DFA/Rome Embassy/915, NAI.

---

1. The Rev. Father Sylvester (dates unknown) was chaplain to the Catholic Stage Guild.

2. The departmental correspondence does not show why Devlin changed his mind about presenting the award to De Sica (see DD to Brian Durnin, 28 February 1953).

To Theodore Roethke
23 June 1953

Dear Roethke,

I am sorry we did not meet again before I left Rome & before you leave for Ireland.[1] I got up too soon and my foot went back on me, which laid me low again for a spell. It's getting better now, though.

I hope you are keeping well and are managing to see a lot of Rome.

But perhaps you are ready for the quietness of Ireland – with which I hope you will not be disappointed. If you wanted to – or Mrs Roethke did – glide slowly into the simplicity of life in Western Ireland, you might like to start by staying in the bigger hotels of which there is in Kerry, Parknasilla, in Galway, Mallaranny, and in Donegal, Rosapenna.[2]

You might like to look up my friends Donagh MacDonagh & Niall Sheridan (details opposite) I think you would find them congenial.

I look forward to seeing you again. I enjoyed our talk and I assure [you] I am very often less vociferous.

With kind regards to your wife

Yours very sincerely

Denis Devlin

[*addendum, in Caren's hand*]

Donagh MacDonagh
Barrister-at-law
141 Strand Road   Telephone:
Sandymount   DUBLIN 63204
County Dublin

Niall Sheridan (with Tourist Board)
    'THE CRAG'   Telephone: 84357
    TORCA HILL
    <u>DALKEY</u>, (Co. DUBLIN)

Autograph letter signed. 1 leaf (folded), 4 sides. *Header*: Secondo Convegno Internazionale per la Pace e la Civiltà Cristiana, Firenze, Palazzo Vecchio, 21-27 Guigno 1953. Theodore Roethke Collection (0418–001), Box 4, Folder 28, University of Washington Libraries Special Collections.

---

1. In 1953 Roethke and his wife Beatrice were living in Rome, where he was teaching on a Ford Foundation Fellowship. Roethke's letters show that they were hoping to be joined by Dylan Thomas on their trip to Ireland (see TR to Dylan Thomas, 5 July 1953, *Selected Letters of Theodore Roethke*, ed. Ralph J. Mills (London: Faber, 1970), p. 191).

2. The Parknasilla Estate near Sneem in County Kerry, and the Mulranny Hotel in Mulranny (also spelt Mallaranny), County Mayo, opened as tourism-boosting railway hotels in the 1890s after securing contracts with the Great Southern and Western Railway Company. There has been a hotel and golf resort in Rosapenna, Sheephaven Bay, County Donegal since 1893.

To Seán Nunan, Secretary, Department of External Affairs
16 March 1954

Dear Sean [*for* Seán],

May I just let you know about a personal view of mine on my present post?

Rumours have, inevitably, come my way in connection with forth-coming appointments in the Service. I would not normally bother you on the basis of stories that go the rounds on occasions like this; but one of the rumours going round happens to concern my personal attitude to my post and might give the wrong impression. I hear, in fact, that I am said to be expressing dislike of Rome and desire for a change.

I have no wish to appear intrusive and quite realise that the general matter lies with you at head-quarters; however, insofar as there may be question of my personal views, I think it not out of place for me to let you know that I am quite content to be in Rome and have no desire for a transfer.

> With all best wishes,
> Denis Devlin

Typed letter signed. Handwritten corrections. 1 leaf, 1 side. *Header*: Légation d'Irlande, Rome. *Address*: Sean Nunan, Esq., Secretary, Department of External Affairs, Dublin. Marked Personal and Confidential. Department of Foreign Affairs Papers, PS 35/25 (Folder 2), NAI.

To William Fay, Department of External Affairs
18 March 1954

Dear Bill,

With reference to our telephone conversation yesterday concerning a proposed Irish delegation to the Padua Fair a matter may arise which has already caused some difficulty – I mean the provision of Irish Whiskey for the delegates. In this connection I intended to write in reply to your letter 408/454 of the 25th March concerning a case of John Jameson sent to me by air for our delegation to the Congress of Agrarian Law at Florence. I ran into the same difficulties when the Fógra Fáilte delegation came here for the Arts Congress last October.[1] The point was that these goods were despatched too late: I enclose [a] copy of my letter of April 15th to Mr O'Shiel which will explain the reasons.[2]

You will see that 2 to 3 weeks are required for [t]he clearance of goods benefiting by diplomatic franchise. I think it would be advisable therefore to war[n] Mr Lane that it is now too late to send whiskey to me for the delegation's purpose in Padua.[3] Unfortunately, I have no Irish whiskey in stock at present. Jameson is on sale in Rome commercially but the authorised diplomatic suppliers do not provide it. If it were brought as a sample, duty would be payable unless it was re-exported at the end of the Fair.

Yours sincerely,

[Denis Devlin]

Typed letter unsigned (carbon copy). 1 leaf, 1 side. *Address*: W.P. Fay Esq., Department of External Affairs, Dublin. Marked "Airmail", and with departmental ref. no. 292/54/555G. Department of Foreign Affairs Papers, DFA/Rome Embassy/555G, NAI.

---

1. Fógra Fáilte was established in 1952 to run in conjunction with An Bord Fáilte, taking responsibility for tourism publicity.

2. Kevin O'Shiel (1891–1970), Irish politician and civil servant, at this time working for the Irish Land Commission.

3. Gerry Lane, dates unknown, president of the Irish Exporters Association.

To William Fay, Department of External Affairs
2 June 1954

Dear Bill,

I have been invited, as in previous years, to the Fair of Trieste which opens on the 17th of June. I intended to decline as usual when the thought of your interest in the Padua Fair made me hesitate; and I wondered whether, since a new drive on the Italian market is being contemplated, my attendance might be considered desirable at home.

I am also asked to give a press conference on the Irish economy and on Ireland's economic relations with Italy and Central Europe. This could be prepared in the Department or I could simply extract suitable passages from Mr. Lane's speech at Padua.[1] I have to go to Florence (officially) on the 20th: I could go straight to Trieste on the 17th, stay for 2 days and return by way of Florence.

Such a visit would solely have propaganda value, of course, and direct contacts with business interests, such as Mr. Lane is presumably establishing, could not be expected and would indeed be out of place for me. The Fair has not the importance of Milan or Padua. If you think, however, within these limits, my acceptance of the invitation would be worth while, please let me know so that I may inform the Fair authorities accordingly.

Yours very sincerely,

[Denis Devlin]

Typed letter unsigned (carbon copy). 1 leaf, 1 side. Marked with "air mail", and departmental ref. no. 325/54/555H. *Address*: W.G. Fay Esq., Department of External Affairs, Dublin. Department of Foreign Affairs Papers, DFA/Rome Embassy/555H, NAI.

---

1. See DD to William Fay, 18th May 1954, n. 3.

To Frank Biggar, Department of External Affairs
18 June 1954

Dear Frank,

With reference to correspondence on the Department's file about the Padua Fair 415/110, you may like to have a short account of Mr. Lane's visit.

As had been arranged, I met him at Malpensa Airport, Milan, on Friday the 28th of May, and we took a train the same evening to Padua. Mr. Lane was very satisfied with the hotel, the Biri Stanga, which was comfortable and situated near the Fair grounds.

The office accommodation provided for the official trade representatives of foreign countrie[s] formed a separate section in the main pavilion. The offices were rather like stands but closed in front with a door and window: each was equipped with tabl[e]s and chairs, telephone and typewriter. Typists, interpreters, bank officials and a representative of the Ministry of Foreign Commerce were also in the Foreign Representa[t]ives Section.

In all, 12 foreign countries were represented besides Ireland – France, Belgium, Netherlands, Austria, Brazil, Syria, Great Britain, German[y,] Hungary, Dominican Republic, U.S.S.R., Czechoslovakia. Several of the representatives had not arrived when I left Padua. The British representati[ve] was from the British Chamber of Commerce in Milan.

You will probably have a report in some detail from Mr. Lane, so I can be brief. The Fair authori[ties] seem to have expected a steady flow of enquiries from Italian businessmen, but in fact nothing of the kind happened, at least in the first four days while I was there. Mr. Lane sized up the situation very quickly and decided that he would have to go out himself and talk to exhibitors and agents. I do not know what his final view may be of the value of the visit, but he certainly had made a number of contacts in the first days.

There was one major defect in organisation, namely, that the authoritie[s] did not fix any definite period during which the foreign representatives might be expected to be in attendance at their offices. The Fair opened at 9 a.m. and, with the exception of a break for lunch from 12.30 p.m. to 2 p.m., remained open until midnight. In theory, at least, the representativ[es] were available while the Fair grounds were open – though, of course, they usually went off about 6 p.m. In view of the small number of enquiries, it would have been quite sufficient if they had attended for two or three hours in the morning. Perhaps, the organisers thought that several people would come to staff each office; but, as you may have heard from Mr. Lane, no country sent more than one man.

Mr. Lane was to have read his paper in English on the 10th of June. The Fair authorities asked for 50 copies in Italian which we supplied: the translator's fee was Lire 4,000 and the cost of stencilling the 50 copies Lire 4,000 (both bills on the June accounts). I attach one copy of the paper in translation for your records. We amended the opening paragraphs to include an expression of gratitude to the organisers of the Fair for their hospitality and arrangements.

There is only one other matter I should mention here. Mr Lane seems to have had an idea that the Fair would provide him with free board and lodgings: what they did provide was free hotel accommodation but not free board. They also insisted on paying my hotel bill, although I had made my reservation independently and it had never been expected that they would pay for two Irish representatives.

Yours sincerely,

[Denis Devlin]

Typed letter unsigned (carbon copy). Handwritten corrections. 3 leaves, 3 sides. *Address*: Frank Biggar Esq., Department of External Affairs, Dublin. Some type missing from right-hand margins. Marked with departmental ref. no. 370/54/555G. Department of Foreign Affairs Papers, DFA/Rome Embassy/555G, NAI.

Top: Caren and Denis in Ostia, Rome, c. June 1954. Bottom: (from left) Rosanna Warren, Denis, Robert Penn Warren, Caren, in Ostia, Rome, c. June 1954.

To Seán Nunan, Secretary, Department of External Affairs
1 July 1954

I have the honour to refer to correspondence on the Trieste Fair (Mr. F[ay's] letter of the 10th of June). I accepted the invitation to attend the opening and went to Trieste on the 17th instant. I was shown round the Fair which, in its industrial machinery, machine-tool, chemical and radio-television industry section[,] seemed excellent; but in general much inferior in size, variety and importance to the Milan Fair.

I held the press conference as invited by the Fair authorities, reading a short paper on Irish-Italian trade exchanges. An outline was given of the import-export relations between the two countries, with emphasis on the comparativ[ely] favourable position of Italian exports. It was stated that we would be interested in increasing our activity in the Italian, and specifically the Trieste market. Reference was made to traditional items of Irish export, such as horses and tweeds, and to others such as scrap-metal and plaster boards for their importance in build[ing,] in which there is a boom in Italy at present. The President of the Fair then commented on the statement. He thought the marketing possibilities of horses were nil; tweeds were doubtful; seed potatoes interesting; and scrap-metal and plaster board worth exploring. These of course were personal opinions and the press [co]nference could have no immediate practical consequences but as propaganda [it] was not without value. There were about 35 journalists present and the local papers carried brief reports.

[Denis Devlin]

Minister Plenipotentiary

Typed letter unsigned (carbon copy). 2 leaves, 2 sides. *Address:* Secretary, Department of External Affairs, Dublin. Some text has not copied, or is cut off at the right-hand margin. Marked with "Airmail" and departmental ref. no. 411/54/555H. Department of Foreign Affairs Papers, DFA/Rome Embassy/555H, NAI.

To Patrick Little, Arts Council
25 August 1954

Dear Mr. Little,

I have just come back from annual leave and had previously been away from Rome on two or three congresses so I am afraid I have not been able to advance [the] export of your picture from Italy.[1] I have asked the Foreign Office, however, to put the matter in train and will keep you advised. It would be necessary to engage a shipping firm to take over the picture when the permission comes through; and I imagine the Government will want to have it u[n]packed for inspection before they agree to its transf[er].

With kind regards from myself and my wife,

Yours very sincerely,

[Denis Devlin]

Typed letter unsigned (copy). 1 leaf, 1 side. *Address:* P.J. Little, Esq., Director, The Arts Council, 45 St. Stephen's Green, Dublin. Some type cut off the left-hand side of the page. Department of Foreign Affairs Papers, DFA/Rome Embassy/129K, NAI.

---

1. On 30 June 1954 Little writes to Devlin thanking him and Caren for their recent hospitality in Rome, and asking what progress has been made in exporting a Domenico Piola (1627–1703) painting from Italy (Department of Foreign Affairs Papers, DFA/Rome Embassy/129K, NAI).

To Patrick Little, Arts Council
7 October 1954

Dear Mr. Little,

Further to my letter of 25ᵗʰ August, I have now received a communication from the Foreign Office indicating that prior to the exportation of your picture from Italy, it would be necessary to secure permission of the Office for the Exportation of Objects of Art and Antiquities which is a section of the Department of Public Instruction.[1] I think that at this stage your interests would be best served by my instructing an agent here to act on your behalf for the purpose of getting this permission and making the transport and packing arrangements. Could you let me know if you are agreeable with this procedure[?]

With kind regards to Mrs. Little and yourself,

Yours sincerely,

[Denis Devlin]

Typed letter unsigned (carbon copy). 1 leaf, 1 side. *Address:* P.J. Little, Esq., Director, The Arts Council, 45 St. Stephen's Green, Dublin. Department of Foreign Affairs Papers, DFA/Rome Embassy/129/K, NAI.

---

1. The Italian Ministero della Pubblica Istruzione (Ministry of Public Education) was the government body tasked with the administration of the national education system.

To Robert Fitzgerald
16 October 1954

Dear Robert,

Thank heaven we are not in Stockholm as I once feared we might be, so Caren and I will dine with you on the 20th, and see you again with great pleasure. It's fine that you are getting on so well with the Homer.[1]

> With warmest wishes to you and Sally
> Denis Devlin

Autograph letter signed. 1 leaf, 1 side. *Header*: Légation d'Irlande, Rome. Telephone numbers inserted by hand below header: Office 760242, House 778035. Robert Fitzgerald Papers, Yale Collection of American Literature (MSS 222), Box 8, Folder 344, Beinecke Rare Book and Manuscript Library, Yale University.

---

1. Fitzgerald and his family moved to Italy in 1953, while he worked on a version of the *Odyssey*. This was to receive the first Bollingen Award for poetry translation in 1961.

To Cesare Brandi

6 December 1954   3 Via Valle delle Camene
                                   (Via delle Terme di Caracalla)

Caro Direttore,

Ricevo in questo momento un telegramma dal Dott. Thomas McGreevy [*for* MacGreevy], Direttore della Galleria Nazionale di Dublino, il quale mi informa che lei ha gentilmente acconsentito a restaurare un quadro della galleria, la Madonna di Giovanni del Biondo, su tavola, della misura di 7 piedi.[1] Il quadro deve giungere all'aeroporto di Ciampino alle ore 14.40 di mercoledi, 8. corr.[,] con un'aereo della Panamerican, No. di volo TAO62, da Shannon. La Ditta Beverely [*for* Beverly] Smyth di Dublino è incaricata della spedizione.[2]

Il Dott. McGreevy mi ha pregato di informarlo del'arrivo del quadro e di pregarlo di volere cortesemente intervenire per assicurare un veloce disbrigo delle practiche doganali onde evitare che una lunga giacenza della tavola nella Dogana possa provocarne il deterioramento.

Se posso aiutarla il qualche modo, la prego de informarmi.

Ricordando sempre con piacere i nostri incontri in varie occasioni, la prego di gradire i miei più cordiali saluti.

(Denis Devlin)
Ministro d'Irlanda in Italia.

Typed letter unsigned (carbon copy). 1 leaf, 1 side. *Address:* Dott. Cesare Brandi, Direttore, Istituto Centrale del Restauro, 9, Piazza San Francisco di Paola, Roma. Marked "urgente-personale", and with departmental ref. no. [?]931/54/129K. Department of Foreign Affairs Papers, DFA/Rome Embassy/129K, NAI.

[*Translation*]

Dear Director,

I have just received a telegram from Dr. Thomas McGreevy [*for* MacGreevy], Director of the National Gallery in Dublin, which informs me that you have kindly consented to restore a painting from the gallery, the Madonna of Giovanni del Biondo, on a panel measuring 7 feet. The painting is due to reach Ciampino Airport at 14.40 on Wednesday, the 8th instant[,] with a Panamerican aeroplane, flight no. TAO62, from Shannon. The Beverely [*for* Beverly] Smyth Company in Dublin is in charge of the transportation.

Dr. McGreevy has asked me to inform you of the arrival of the painting and to ask you to kindly intervene to ensure its rapid processing through customs in order to avoid a lengthy retention of the panel in Customs which could result in its deterioration.

If I can help you in some way, please let me know.

Always remembering with pleasure our meetings on various occasions, please accept my best regards.

(Denis Devlin)
Irish Minister to Italy.

---

1. The painting is 'Virgin and Child with Angels' by Giovanni del Biondo (active 1356–99), purchased by the National Gallery of Ireland in 1931.

2. Beverly Smyth & Sons, a Dublin-based corporate relocation and international removal company.

To Patrick Little, Arts Council
25 February 1955

Dear Mr. Little,

I am sorry for the delay in writing to you about your picture, but we could not get a reply from the office for the Exportation of Objects of Art and Antiquities. We have now been told by telephone that a tax is payable on the export of the picture. We were informed that this would amount to 8% on a valuation up to 20,000 lire, 15% up to 100,000 lire and a 30% maximum. So I am afraid it will be necessary for you to make a declaration as to the value of the painting. This declaration is subject to the appraisal of the painting by the Italian authorities who, it seems, reserve the right to increase its value (for taxation purposes) if they think necessary.

Maybe, therefore, you could let me have your view as to its value. I hope then that we shall be able to get things moving a little faster.

      With kind regards.

           Yours sincerely,

               [Denis Devlin]

Typed letter unsigned (carbon copy). Blotting and typed corrections. 1 leaf, 1 side. *Address:* P.J. Little, Esq., Director, The Arts Council, 45 St. Stephen's Green, Dublin (Irlanda). Marked "air mail", and with departmental ref. no. 347/55/129K. Department of Foreign Affairs Papers, DFA/Rome Embassy/129K, NAI.

To Thomas MacGreevy
21 April 1955

Dear [Tom],

I wish to confirm what I told you on the telephone on Tuesday 19th April, namely that your Fra Angelico was taken from the customs on Thursday evening, 15th April, and delivered to the Vatican on the morning of 16th April.[1] The Secretary of the Legation went with the Onofri agent on 15th April to be present at the customs removal.[2] He saw the panel which seemed to be in perfect condition and which had to be photographed in order to comply with Italian import regulations.

I see from the papers that the exhibition was opened yesterday by His Holiness. I shall certainly try to get to see it before it closes.

    With kind greetings.

        Yours sincerely,

          [Denis]

Typed letter unsigned (carbon copy). Blotting and typed corrections. 1 leaf, 1 side. *Address*: Thomas McGreevy Esq., National Gallery of Ireland, Merrion Square, Dublin (Irlanda). Marked "air mail" and with departmental ref. no. [?]/55/129K. Department of Foreign Affairs Papers, DFA/Rome Embassy/129K, NAI.

---

1. The National Gallery of Ireland had agreed to loan to the Vatican 'The Attempted Martyrdom of Saints Cosmas and Damian' (*c.* 1439–42) by the Italian early Renaissance painter Fra Angelico (*c.* 1395–1455) for an exhibition held across the Vatican and Florence to mark the 500-year anniversary of Fra Angelico's death.

2. Lorenzo Onofri in Rome was the agency used by the Uffizi Gallery in Florence, presumably responsible for international transport.

To Thomas MacGreevy
10 June 1955

Dear [Tom],

Further to my letter of the 16th May, we were informed by O[n] ofri of the arrangements for the transport of the Fra Angelico collection from Rome to Florence.

The pictures were packed together and sent in two railway wagons on the morning of the 25th of May arriving in Florence just 5 hours later accompanied by representatives of the Italian police and three officials from the Institute of Fine Art in Florence.

The pictures, it seems, will be in Florence until September. Onofri has promised to let us know details of transport arrangements when the exhibition closes.

      With kind regards,
           Yours sincerely,
              [Denis]

Typed letter unsigned (carbon copy). Handwritten additions. 1 leaf, 1 side. *Address*: Thomas McGreevy Esq., Director, National Gallery of Ireland, Merrion Square W., Dublin (Irlanda). Marked "Airmail" and with departmental ref. no. [?]/55/129K. Department of Foreign Affairs Papers, DFA/Rome Embassy/129K, NAI.

To Patrick Little, Arts Council
23 June 1955

Dear Mr. Little,

I am writing to you concerning your picture, which, as I mentioned to you at Easter, was brought from the Embassy to Bolliger's office (the packing-transport firm). They had been expecting you to call at Easter to see it and have enquired if they are to go ahead with their applications for the necessary export licences for the Italian authorities. I have told them to do so on the basis of the £.100 valuation of the picture which you have given. I presume that you will have no difficulty in getting Department of Finance permission for the export of the necessary sterling to Italy to pay the taxes involved.

Yours sincerely,

[Denis Devlin]

Typed letter unsigned (carbon copy). Handwritten additions. 1 leaf, 1 side. *Address:* P.J. Little Esq., Director, The Arts Council, 45 St. Stephen's Green, Dublin, Irlanda. Marked with "Airmail", and departmental ref. no. 365/55/129K. Department of Foreign Affairs Papers, DFA/Rome Embassy/129K, NAI.

To Allen Tate
1 August 1955   Ortisei[1]

My dear Allen,

What a shame we are not in Rome to see you.[2] We are in the Dolomites on our way to Ireland for August; returning to Rome at the beginning of September, when we must meet instead.

It's beautifully cool here after Rome. Greatly looking forward to seeing you.

> Love from Caren,
> Denis

Autograph letter signed. 1 leaf, 1 side. *Header:* Irish Legation, Via Valle delle Camene 3, Rome. Allen Tate Papers, Box 25, Folder 27, PU.

---

1. Ortisei (or Urtijëi) is a town in Val Gardena, a valley in the Dolomites in South Tyrol, northern Italy, and a popular ski resort.

2. After having held a Fulbright professorship at the University of Rome in 1953–4, Tate returned for August–September 1955.

To Niall Montgomery
30 August 1955

Terribly sorry missed call
Country visit was deferred stop
till next time
all best [to] hop[1]
Denis

Telegram. *Address:* Niall Montgomery, Sunnyside, Dunmore East.

---

1. See DD to Niall Montgomery, 10 January 1940, n. 1.

To Thomas MacGreevy
25 October 1955

Dear [Tom],

You will by now have received my telegram sent yesterday 24 October concerning the return of the Madonna from the Centro di Restauro. We have been in constant touch with Gondrand over the past two weeks and I must say that we found it difficult to cooperate with him.[1] He seemed to multiply the difficulties for himself. Eventually he seemed at a loss to know how he would get the painting back to Ireland when he discovered that Panamerican no longer ran suitable planes directly Rome-Shannon.[2] When we suggested TWA, he told us they did not operate to Shannon![3] The last information he gave us on Saturday 23 October at one o'clock was that it would probably be several weeks before TWA could arrange to have a special fitting put on their plane to take the picture. The final blow came at 12.30 yesterday when he informed us that the picture had left on Sunday despite the fact that we had asked him repeatedly and confirmed to him in writing that he should give us details of the proposed flight schedule in good time for us to be able to inform you. He says, however, that he did telegram Beverly Smyth. I expect, nevertheless, that the picture had to remain longer in store-rooms than was good for it. Looking back on the whole business now, it seems to me that our exchange of telegrams concerning the method of payment was probably unnecessary and only arose on account of the extraordinary way in which Gondrand did his job.[4]

I regret to say that I must also tell you now that your other Fra' Angelico picture was sent on last Friday the 21st of October by direct BEA flight from Ciampino to London arriving at 17.30.[5] Onofri, who was the agent in this case, was told on four or five occasions during the Summer and most recently on 23 September that the Legation was to be informed before the final arrangements for the despatch of the picture were made. He did not do this an[d] it was only on our informal enquiry by telephone yesterday that he told us it had already gone. He apologised, of course, but the picture, it seems, was sent by him with the other Fra' Angelico paintings which were on loan here. Furthermore, Onofri did not inform Be[v]erly Smyth that the painting was en route. He said BEA would have done this. Onofri does not know what Aer Lingus flight took the picture from London to Dublin.

I regret very much the way that these two matters have turned out. I can only say that I hope, if you intend sending further pictures to Rome, that you will use as your agent Arthur Bolliger, Trasporti Internazionali, 49, Piazza di Spagna, whom we in the Legation always employ. Maybe you will think it worth while to mention this also to Beverly Smyth.

I have just received Gondrand's bill amounting to 61,223 lire. I [am] paying this – reluctantly enough – and I presume you will arrange to reimburse the Department. I have sent them a copy of this letter.

> [Denis]

Typed letter unsigned (carbon copy). 2 leaves, 2 sides. *Address:* Thomas MacGreevy, Esq., Director, National Gallery of Ireland, Merrion Square W., Dublin. Marked "Airmail", and with departmental ref. no. 1764/55/129K. Department of Foreign Affairs Papers, DFA/Rome Embassy/129K, NAI.

---

1. Gondrand is a national transport agency founded by the Gondrand Brothers in Milan in 1866.

2. Pan American Airways was the largest international air carrier in the United States, servicing Shannon airport from 1945.

3. Trans World Airlines was America's second largest international carrier.

4. The telegrams concerned whether the legation or Beverly Smyth should pay Gondrand's travel charges. See DFA/Rome Embassy/129K, NAI.

5. British European Airways, a British airline founded in 1947.

To Patrick Little, Arts Council
16 November 1955

Dear Mr. Little,

I have now received word from the Italian Foreign Office concerning the export of your picture. I regret, however, to have to say that they require information concerning the method by which the painting came into your possession as well as an estimate of the value. As regards the last point, of course, we can readily give them this information. Indeed, it could have been got from the Ministry of Public Instruction which, as you know, has already released its perm[it] for the export of the picture.

I am afraid that I am not sure on some points concerning this history of the painting and how it came into your possession. At any rate, I should be glad to have from you a note on the subject before passing on informat[ion] to the Italian authorities.[1]

I, of course, regret all these delays but, as you probably reali[se,] there is little I can do to avoid them.

           Yours sincerely,
             [Denis Devlin]

Typed letter unsigned (carbon copy). Over-typed corrections, handwritten additions. 1 leaf, 1 side. *Address*: P.J. Little, Esq., Director, The Arts Council, 45 St. Stephen's Green, Dublin. Marked "Airmail", and with departmental ref. no. 305/55/129K. Department of Foreign Affairs Papers, DFA/Rome Embassy/129K, NAI.

---

1. Little responds with a frustrated letter to Beverly Smyth, copied to Devlin, confirming that £100 was paid for the painting by his brother Con, after whose death Little was acting as executor. Little also notes that the painting (named in one letter as 'St Anthony in Ecstasy', not a recognised Domenico Piola) suffered damage during the war, rendering its value a matter of speculation (DFA/Rome Embassy/129K, NAI).

To Thomas MacGreevy
15 December 1955

My dear Tom,

I have your letters of the 6ᵗʰ and 8ᵗʰ of December. Thank you most kindly for your goodness in writing to the Secretary of my Department about the small and very willing efforts I was able to make in connection with the restoration of the Giovanni del Biondo "Madonna Enthroned".

I have arranged with Dr. Brandi for the formal presentation of the books on Tuesday morning the 20ᵗʰ of December at 11[.]30 and I hope you can send your telegram, as you proposed, in time.[1] Please send it to the Legation; the telegraph address is: "Hibernia, Roma". I am getting a press photographer; I shall uncover one book and hand it to Dr. Brandi. I think, by the way, that if there is a pres[s] reference or caption to the photograph, it should be clear that the gift of books is in return for work done by the Institute, mentioning Dr. Brandi's name. I sha[ll] instruct the press photographer in this sense. I have not open[ed] the books and sha[ll] have them delivered in their covers to the Institute immediately after the presentation.

In the friendly atmosphere which I hope will be created, I shall take up with Dr. Brandi his forgotten promises about the photographs.[2]

[Denis]

Typed letter unsigned (carbon copy). Handwritten corrections. 1 leaf, 1 side. *Address*: Thomas MacGreevy, Esq., Director, National Gallery of Ireland, Merrion Square W., Dublin. Some text cut off from the right-hand margin. Marked with departmental ref. no. 2050/55/129K. Department of Foreign Affairs Papers, DFA/Rome Embassy/129K, NAI.

---

1. Cesare Brandi had specially requested payment in kind in the form of art books for his institute's library, rather than financial remuneration, for the restoration work.

2. In an earlier letter MacGreevy had asked Devlin to remind Brandi of his promise to provide copies of photographs taken during the process of transferring and restoring the painting. See Thomas MacGreevy to DD, 6 December 1955, DFA/Rome Embassy/129K, NAI.

To Patrick Little, Arts Council
16 February 1956

Dear Mr. Little,

The representative of Arthur Bolliger called to the Legation to see me this morning and said that he expected that your picture would leave Rome within the next couple of days. I realize how glad you will be to get this news at last. In fact, the most recent delay was caused by the fact that the permit from the Ministry of Public Instruction had already expired when we got the permit from the Ministry of Foreign Affairs. It was, therefore, necessary to have it renewed. However, the Bolliger agent assured me (after I had signed no less than nine forms) that the road was now clear.

I have sent a copy of this letter to Beverly Smyth & Sons, Ltd., Dublin.

    With kind regards,
        Yours sincerely,
           [Denis Devlin]

Typed letter unsigned (carbon copy). Handwritten corrections and additions. 1 leaf, 1 side. *Address*: P.J. Little, Director, The Arts Council, 45 St. Stephen's Green, Dublin. Marked "<u>Airmail</u>" and with departmental ref. no. [?]/56/129K. Department of Foreign Affairs Papers, DFA/ Rome Embassy/129K, NAI.

To Robert Fitzgerald
7 June 1956

Dear Robert,

Thank you for Santayana's "The Idea of Christ in the Gospels" and for the dedication.[1] It was good of you to have braved the difficulties of finding it. I have merely glanced at it so far but I think it will help me. God knows I shouldn't be writing this poem at all.[2]

I hope you & Sally are well and enjoying Camogli.[3] We are going to Ischia for August. How are your poems going – apart from Homer?

> With affectionate regards
>
> Denis

Autograph letter signed. 1 leaf, 2 sides. *Header:* Légation d'Irlande, Rome. Robert Fitzgerald Papers, Box 8, Folder 344, Beinecke, YU.

---

1. George Santayana (1863–1952), Spanish-born American philosopher. *The Idea of Christ in the Gospels; or, God in Man* (1946) is a book-length essay in which Santayana describes the poetic, imaginative existence of Christ.

2. Devlin was at this time working on 'The Passion of Christ' (1957), one of his final long poems.

3. Camogli is a fishing village near Genoa in northern Italy.

To Robert Fitzgerald
5 August 1956

My dear Robert,

Thank you very much for the Pound number of 'Nuova Corrente'.[1] I much enjoyed your essay, which is penetrating on a poet about whom I'm unclear (I liked especially the sweep of the opening sections of Part II).[2] And on the personal miserable situation[,] your evident wish to be charitable and just comes through harmoniously.[3] The other American contributors are rather jejune; they are driving themselves to take a stand but you feel they had rather not.

It was extremely kind of you to send me Santayana's IDEA OF CHRIST IN THE GOSPELS, which I am just beginning to read. It will either help or totally befuddle me; if the latter, I'll just read the Gospel afterwards. We are in Ischia for August; I hope to get some things finished. You are doing your own poems as well as the Homer, are'nt [sic] you?

I hope Sally and the children are well and enjoying the sea. Caren and I send our love to you all.

Ever the best,
Denis

Typed letter signed. 1 leaf, 1 side. *Header:* Légation d'Irlande, Rome. Robert Fitzgerald Papers, Box 8, Folder 344, Beinecke, YU.

---

1. The Italian poet Alfredo Rizzardi commissioned contributions for a special Pound edition of *Nuova Corrente* (nos. 5–6, January–June 1956), a journal of literary and philosophical criticism.

2. Fitzgerald's essay was published as 'Gold and Gloom in Ezra Pound' in *Encounter*, vol. 7, no. 34, July 1956, pp. 16–22, and reprinted as 'A Note on Ezra Pound, 1928–56', *The Kenyon Review*, vol. 18, no. 4, Autumn 1956, pp. 505–18.

3. Pound was at this time in St Elizabeth's Psychiatric Hospital in Washington, having been spared a trial for treason after a series of anti-Semitic and anti-American radio broadcasts from Italy during the Second World War. Fitzgerald's article charts Pound's literary and personal decline from the 1930s.

To Eleanor Clark

[August 1956]

presso Capuana
3 Via Cesotta
Forio, Ischia

My dear Eleanor,

Everything, it seems, except will and affection conspires to prevent me from thanking you and Red for the wonderful weekend I spent with you.[1] In the week after my return, there was much to do in the Legation, including a great bother about myself; but it was a signal, a most fruitful bother for it ended in the almost certainty that I am not going to the Hague, I'm staying in Rome. What do youall [*sic*] think of that! We are highly gratified. And it means that we can see each other in the Fall after all, which is a most important part of th[e] affair. I did write to you as soon as I got to Ischia and gave the letter to Caren to post, who was going to Rome; but the misfortunate girl lost it. This is hiding under a woman's skirts with a vengeance. Caren however insists that I do so for once.

I had a beautiful time with you, in the air of friendship which it's true one breathes rarely. With good talk and poetry, by no means forgetting the sharp, delicate lobster and shiskabib [*sic*]. Nor the fine air when we had drinks at evening.

I hope your work is progressing, and Red's as well. Give my respectful bows to Ro'posy and a wink to Gabriel Penn.[2]

With love to you both.

Denis

Typed letter signed. 1 leaf, 1 side. *Header*: Legation d'Irlande, Rome. Header crossed out in typed slashes, Ischia address typed above. Eleanor Clark Papers, Box 28, Folder 363, Beinecke, YU.

---

1. Clark, Penn Warren and family were on an extended stay in Italy from June 1956 to March 1957, largely based at Porto Ecole in Grosseto. According to Penn Warren's letters, Devlin visited Porto Ercole towards the end of July 1956 (RPW to John Palmer, 15 July 1956, *SLRPW*, vol. IV, p. 125).

2. Rosanna Warren (b. 1953) and Gabriel Penn Warren (b. 1955), Penn Warren and Clark's children.

To Seán Murphy, Secretary, Department of External Affairs
6 May 1957

I have the honour to attach a translation of a letter dated 15 April, 1957, from the Secretary General of the BIENNALE di Venezia concerning the Exhibition of paintings from private collections which is to take place in the Dublin Municipal Gallery.

I am glad to support Prof. Pallucchini's request for an invitation to attend this Exhibition. He is a man of importance in Italian artistic circles and is undoubtedly in a position to give publicity to this Exhibition in the various magazines which he mentions in his letter.

I understand his letter to mean that he would expect to be the guest of whoever invites him to Dublin and this might involve providing him with hotel and subsistence.

I should be glad if you would be good enough to transmit this request to the competent authorities as soon as possible. If funds could not be made available to invite Prof. Pallucchini as a guest, may be [*sic*] an invitation could be issued to him in any event.

I should be glad to hear what action is taken on this subject at your earliest convenience.

[Denis Devlin]
Minister Plenipotentiary.

Typed letter unsigned (carbon copy). Handwritten corrections. 1 leaf, 1 side. Marked with departmental ref. no. 233/57/555A. Department of Foreign Affairs Papers, DFA/Rome Embassy/555A/1, NAI.

To Robert Greene, Arthur Guinness, Son & Co. Ltd.
17 May 1957

Dear Mr. Greene,

I attended the opening of the Milan Fair and saw the Guinness stand which, though small, was most attractively presented. Unfortunately, since it is never possible, and was not on this occasion, to predict the duration of the inspection tour by the President of the Republic, in whose wake we are obliged to follow, I missed seeing your agent the Marquis Peregrini.[1]

There was a serious, if understandable, error in the publicity whic[h] I pointed out, and which was, I was informed, rectified immediately afterwards. I shall tell you about it on your next visit.

Yours very sincerely,

(Sgd.) Denis Devlin

Irish Minister to Italy.

Typed letter stamp-signed. 1 leaf, 1 side. *Address:* R.W.S. Greene Esq., Director of Exports, Arthur Guinness Son & Co. Ltd., St James's Gate, Dublin. Marked with departmental ref. no. 1450/57/1909 (5) & 555D. Department of Foreign Affairs Papers, DFA/Rome Embassy/555D, NAI.

---

1. The Marquis Peregrini has not been identified.

To Seán Murphy, Secretary, Department of External Affairs
3 August 1957

Dear Sean [*for* Seán],

I have been meaning to write to you but prevented so far by forced rest & quietness. You will have seen from the medical certificate what's wrong with me. It happened suddenly with a haemorr[h]age followed by pneumonia when I was apparently in the best form. An old dead spot in the left lung (never previously active) was affected & the doctors gave, as the immediate cause, the heat wave – of which I had a week more than the Italians, and the worst, in Jugoslavia. I shall be in hospital for 2 or 3 weeks more, then convalescence in the mountains.

I'm sorry this has happened keeping me away so long from the Legation. But apparently it's quite curable if taken right from the start & the cure followed obediently.

I hope you are keeping well & that the United Nations won't be too hectic.[1] It looks as if it will be difficult though – all those incredible paynim states briefed up by unemployable lawyers.[2] Well, we have a nice mediator line.

My best regards – wishes & please remember me to your wife

Yours ever

Denis Devlin

Autograph letter signed. 3 leaves, 3 sides. *Header*: Légation d'Irlande, Rome. Department of Foreign Affairs Papers, PS 35/25 (Folder 2), NAI.

---

1. Ireland had joined the United Nations in 1955; the twelfth session of the United Nations General Assembly was opening in New York in September 1957. Frank Aiken (1898–1983), who succeeded Liam Cosgrave (1920–2017) as minister for external affairs in 1957, spearheaded an Irish representation at the United Nations that underlined Ireland's independence, and its commitment to supporting the rights of small nations to self-determination.

2. paynim (arch.): pagan, non-Christian.

To Thomas Woods, Department of External Affairs
14 March 1958

Dear [Thomas],

We have received your telegram n. 2 concerning participation in the Biennale di Venezia and you will by now have seen the not-too-optimistic terms of my reply in the Legation's telegram n. 4. I wish to confirm that at this stage it seems very unlikely that the Biennale authorities will be able to make any space available for an Irish exhibition. You will know of the associations which we have had in recent years with the Biennale and I do not think I am exaggerating when I say that they have not been very happy. You will also know that in November, 1951, I travelled to Venice in connection with the purposed participation of J.B. Yeats in the exhibition of the following year (1952) and, even at that stage, there was considerable difficulty in securing space for an Irish exhibition.

A further unfortunate step in our relations with the Biennale authorities was the démarche which Prof. Pallucchini made to me in April last year when he asked that he might be invited to attend the Exhibition of Paintings from Private Collections to be held in the Dublin Municipal Gallery.[1] In his letter of 15 April, a translation of which I attached to my official minute of 6 May, 1957, Prof. Pallucchini pointed out that he was Secretary General of the Biennale di Venezia (although he no longer is). It is unfortunate for us that we did not follow up his request for an invitation. I would ask you, therefore, not to be surprised if a visit to Venice does not produce a result, as hoped for.[2]

Yours sincerely,

(Sgd.) DENIS DEVLIN

Typed letter stamp-signed (carbon copy). 1 leaf, 1 side. *Address:* Thomas Woods, Esq., Department of External Affairs, Dublin. Marked "AIR MAIL", and with departmental ref. no. 132/58/555A. Department of Foreign Affairs Papers, DFA/Rome Embassy/555A/1, NAI.

1. See DD to Seán Murphy, 6 May 1957. démarche (Fr.): approach.

2. In a letter from John A. Belton on behalf of the secretary dated 11 April 1958, Devlin was urged to make every effort to secure space for Ireland despite the poor prospects, and travelled to Venice for a meeting with the Biennale secretary in April. The Irish Arts Council (under Sean O'Faolain) was once again determined to exhibit the paintings of Jack B. Yeats, who had died in March 1957. Aside from Devlin's reservations, correspondence suggests that the Biennale was particularly pressed for space this year, and not offering invitations to countries without their own pavilion. See DFA/Rome Embassy/555A/1, NAI.

To Con Cremin, Secretary, Department of External Affairs
11 July 1958

[*Extract*]

TURKEY AND CYPRUS

The Turkish authorities showed unusual concern over our opposition to their policy on the Cyprus question. For all the officials I saw, as well as for the country at large, it was the main topic; and they were at pains to explain and defend the Turkish point of view. They went out of their way to be pleasant and the Foreign Minister gave a large diplomatic lunch at which I was guest of honour; one can only suppose that their hospitality was a reflection of the effect of our Delegation's activities at the United Nations.[1]

The Secretary General, Mr. Esenbel, took up the Turkish argument on Partition which was put before the Minister by Mr[.] Esin, (your Office Note 7/5/1958) on the lines that Partition in Cyprus meant quite a different thing from Partition in Ireland.[2] Ireland was one nation culturally and ethnically – North and South were the same race. We were homogeneous and it was quite natural that we thought of Partition with abhorrence. In Cyprus the situation was different: there were two nations – the Greek and the Turk. They could live in friendliness side by side, but a State in which Turks would be ruled by Greeks would be utterly inconceivable.

If one turned to the claims advanced in the name of self-determination and applied this principle to Cyprus as a whole, as we were doing, the Turks rejected such an interpretation; they held out for self-determination for the Turkish minority. The principle of self-determination in a given geographical area had not always been accepted by the Greeks themselves: for, when in 1922, Venizelos took Western Thrace, he refused a plebiscite for the province because it had a Turkish majority.[3] The Turks put forward their plea of self-determination, but Venizelos rejected it arguing that the principle was not always and everywhere appropriate[;] that, in certain circumstances, strategic and geographical considerations must take first place. Well, said Mr. Esenbel, the Turks were now turning the tables on the Greeks and denying any absolute sanctity to the principle of self-determination as applied to Cyprus as a whole, because there were, apart from the ethnical arguments, broader strategical considerations involving the defence of Turkey; and these must, in this case, take first place.

Sir Hugh Foot's Cyprus plan had come out that same morning and the Secretary General said that Turkey would accept it as a Conference document because of the provisions guaranteeing free election rights to the Turkish minority; with this provision, the British were keeping a promise they had made to the Turks some time ago.[4]

Mr. Esenbel went on to say that the Greek policy on Cyprus was part of a wide[,] ambitious Greek expansionist plan, – which recalled the complaint of the Greek diplomat to Mr. Biggar in the latter's report from London [(]P.R.28/58[)]] about a resuscitated Turkish imperialism.[5] Any suggestion that an accommodation might be reached which would involve Turkish subjection to Greeks in Cyprus was out of the question. Mr. Esenbel wanted to impress on me in the most positive way that Turkey would never agree to handing over Turks to Greek sovereignty. Why should they be expected to celebrate the liberation of Turks from British sovereignty only to hand them over to Greeks? – "to free them from the British", – he said – "who are our friends and allies only to hand them over to the Greeks who …" Mr. Esenbel gestured that he was too polite to finish the sentence.

I had explained our attitude and intervened during the above ex-position at the appropriate points. Mr. Esenbel[,] who at the beginning of the conversation had demanded Ireland's sympathy, at the end asked me to urge you at least to adopt an attitude of neutrality.

Of the people I saw, Mr. Tuncel, Director-General of the Division of International Organisations, was the most forthright.[6] He wondered why Ireland had been so consistently anti-Turkish, on the Cyprus question; why, with our speeches, our voting and our influence, we had carried on what was an inimical campaign against them in the United

Nations. Beneath, or, rather, preceding his anger, he and the other Turks I met, seemed to be genuinely puzzled: I think their ideas about the correctness of political action are based on the zone-of-influence or zone-of-contiguity tradition; they wondered "ce que nous faisions dans cette galère".[7] I tried to explain to him, not only that we had the most practical reasons for objecting to Partition anywhere, since our public opinion felt that way, and our experience showed it to be a bad way out politically, but that, as a matter of principle, we would use our right to our opinion in the United Nations. Mr. Tuncel let this go, but said that Turkey would be counting heads and would know who were their friends in New York.[8] He said that ours was not the only Government to be upset at the idea of Partition; it was a pity that word had been adopted to describe Turkish policy on Cyprus; it did not carry the meaning ascribed to it abroad; the issue was quite simple: Turks would not live under Greeks. I hinted at the opinion which many foreigners have expressed that Turkey had never bothered about the liberation of their minority in Cyprus, until ENOSIS came up, according to which opinion, Turkish policy is inspired merely by anti-Greek spite. He denied this, saying that, in fact, the Turkish Cypriots had been quite content to live under the British, and the question of their liberation was then dormant.

[…]

>Denis Devlin
>Minister Plenipotentiary.

Typed memo signed. 4 leaves, 4 sides. *Header*: Légation d'Irlande. *Address*: Secretary, Department of External Affairs, Dublin. Marked: ROME Confidential, and with departmental ref. no. P.R. 8/58. Date-stamped 15 JUL 1958 for departmental receipt. Department of Foreign Affairs Papers, DFA/219/3/A, NAI.

---

1. Fatin Rüştü Zorlu (1910–61), Turkish foreign minister and former deputy prime minister. Ireland's commitment to the principles of self-determination and non-partition in its United Nations contributions led to an apparently pro-Greek stance in the dispute over the terms of Cypriot independence from Britain: Ireland supported *enosis* (the union with Greece).

2. Melih Rauf Esenbel (1915–95), secretary general of the Turkish ministry in Ankara. Seyfullah Esin (1902–82), permanent representative of Turkey to the United Nations.

3. Eleftherios Venizelos (1864–1936), served numerous terms as prime minister of Greece and led the Greek national liberation movement. Western Thrace is an area of north-east Greece, occupied by the Ottoman Empire until the Balkan Wars of 1912–13. Western Thrace was ceded to Greece in the Treaty of Sèvres (1920), which divided the Ottoman Empire; Venizelos had worked to gain diplomatic support from the Allies during the First World War, with a mind to expanding Greek territory. When Turkey proposed a people's vote in the largely Turkish-Muslim Western Thrace during the Treaty of Lausanne negotiations (1922), Venizelos (no longer prime minister) blocked the proposal and was assisted by the Allies.

4. Hugh Foot, Baron Caradon (1907–90), British diplomat and colonial administrator, the last governor and commander in chief in Cyprus from 1957 to 1960. After Foot had failed to reach agreement with the Cypriot president over a system of self-government, Harold Macmillan's government proceeded unilaterally, presenting the Cyprus Plan to the House of Commons on 19 June 1958. This proposal involved a joint administration of Cyprus by the United Kingdom, Greece and Turkey, and three separate parliaments.

5. Frank Biggar (see Correspondents' Biographies) was at this time a counsellor to the Irish embassy in London. DD inserts a departmental reference number for the report.

6. Necmettin Tuncel (1911–?), Turkish diplomat, was the director-general of the Ministry of Foreign Affairs at this time, and chairman of the Turkish delegation to the United Nations.

7. ce que nous faisions dans cette galère (Fr.): what we were doing in this mess.

8. The thirteenth session of the General Assembly of the United Nations was held in the New York headquarters from September to December 1958, and from February to March 1959.

To Eleanor Clark

[August] 1958

Dear Eleanor,

    – Are anxious to know what Red has been doing.[1] Got letter from him, sent on to me in Dolomites but have been travel[l]ing round. Now in Austria. Cld you send note of progress to Salzburg, Hotel Carlton, before 14[th] inst.? Hope you & children well. C & S[tephen] with me here.[2]

Love

Denis

[*in Caren's hand*:]

Join in the above. Most anxious for news [illeg.]. Did he have opera-tion? Much love to you and the children.

Caren

Co-authored postcard signed. Recto image mountainous picture of Hinterbichl, Austria. *Dating*: Postmark. Red postmark obscuring remain-der of Caren's second sentence. Robert Penn Warren Papers, Box 21, Folder 409, Beinecke, YU.

---

1. RPW had spent most of July 1958 in Zürich having specialist treatment on his shoulder; his letters suggest that he went to Zürich on the recommendation of Devlin and Ignazio Silone (see RPW to Albert Erskine, 12 July 1958, *SLRPW*, vol. IV, p. 16).

2. Stephen Devlin was born in 1953.

To Con Cremin, Secretary, Department of External Affairs
17 November 1958

With reference to your telegram n.[ ]56 regarding the question of possible visits by the Taoiseach to Italian political leaders during his recent visit to Rome as Head of the Irish Delegation at the Coronation of Pope John XXIII, the timing of any such visits could not be in doubt, as you said, in view of the purposes of the delegation and arrangements were, accordingly, not initiated until after the Coronation and the receptions by His Holiness and Monsignor Tardini of the national delegations.[1]

The Taoiseach, then, accompanied by myself and by Major de Valera, paid a courtesy call on the Prime Minister of Italy Mr. Fanfani at 7 p.m. on 7 November.[2] The two Prime Ministers talked for about twenty minutes on general subjects and the visit passed of[f] agreeably. Among other things, Mr. Fanfani recalled his academic life, when he was professor of Economic History at the University of Genova and at the Catholic University of Milan; he said that he had been a great admirer of Prof. B. [*for* G.] O'Brien and had quoted him in four or five places in his book on Reformation Economics, Catholicism and Protestantism.[3] I may say that the Italian Prime Minister had let me know unofficially beforehand that he was eager to meet Mr. de. Valera.

A call on the President of Italy was not considered necessary.[4] I consulted my French and German colleagues and found that they proposed to follow the same programme in this matter as did we.

(Sgd.) DENIS DEVLIN
Minister Plenipotentiary.

Typed letter stamp-signed. 1 leaf, 1 side. *Address*: Secretary, Department of External Affairs, Dublin. Marked "AIR MAIL" and with departmental ref. no. 511/58/142a) & 495B). Department of Foreign Affairs Papers, DFA/Rome Embassy/495B, NAI.

1. Éamon de Valera was at this time serving his third term as taoiseach. Domenico Tardini (1888–1961), diplomatic aide to Pope Pius XII in the Secretariat of State, made cardinal by Pope John XXIII in 1958, shortly after Devlin's letter.

2. Major Vivion de Valera (1910–82), Fianna Fáil TD for Northwest Dublin, and eldest son of Éamon de Valera. Amintore Fanfani (1908–99), at this time serving his second of five periods as prime minister of Italy.

3. Fanfani's *Catholicism, Protestantism and Capitalism* (first publ. 1934, trans. 1935), published shortly after his graduation from the Università Cattolica del Sacro Cuore, Milan, has been in print across the twentieth and into the twenty-first centuries. George O'Brien (1892–1974), an Irish senator and professor of political economy at UCD from 1930. O'Brien's *An Essay on Medieval Economic Teaching* (1920) is the work cited in Fanfani's study.

4. Giovanni Gronchi (1887–1978) was the president of the Italian Republic at this time.

To Allen Tate
18 November 1958

Dear Allen,

I'm grieved not to have been in Ireland for your first visit; after all these years it would have been so pleasant to have received you & taken you about. I hope you enjoyed it & the weather was not too gloomy. I hardly think that we shall be in London this winter but I hope we may see you &, of course, plans may change on both sides. I take it that, apart from your lecture trip home, you will be at Oxford till April?[1] We must keep in touch with a view to a visit from you after that.

By the way, a mysterious great package has arrived here addressed to you from Sicily, the Absender being <u>Ente Provinciale del Turismo</u> of Catania![2] Are you opening a travel bureau?

Yours ever,

Denis

Autograph letter signed. 1 leaf, 2 sides. *Header*: Ambassade d'Irlande, Rome. Allen Tate Papers, Box 25, Folder 27, PU.

---

1. Tate was a Fulbright professor in England in the academic year 1958–9; as well as two terms at the University of Oxford he spent the spring term at the University of Leeds.

2. Ente Provinciale del Turismo: Provincial Tourist Board. Catania is a port on the Sicilian coast. Absender (Ger.): sender.

To Shiela Healy (née Devlin)
2 April 1959

Dear Sheila [*for* Shiela],

 Even though it's so long since I got them, thanks for the Scotch records. You know it was curious but just then – January wasn't it? – I happened to be thinking of Scotland and of those songs and there they arrived beautifully at the right time.[1] He sings them in the right way too. It was very sweet of you. – Are the children well & Kevin? How is your migraine? You thought a while ago it was getting better. I hope so. We are all well here, though we had that miserable flu for months, and relieved after the festive & ecclesiastical boredoms of S[t] Patrick's Day – My decoration from H. H. is very handsome – a black & red sash ending in cross & a great star for the breast.[2] Well, all good things.

   All best to Kevin.
   Denis

[*postscript*:]
May be home Summer – depends on the Privy Purse – My medical experiences have ruined me. But cheer – domani [è] sempre domani.[3]

 Autograph letter signed. 1 leaf, 2 sides. *Header*: Ambassade D'Irlande, Rome. Postscript written above header on recto side. Private collection, Caren Farrell.

---

1. Devlin and his siblings spent their early years in the Lowlands of Scotland.

2. H. H.: His Holiness. In February 1959 Devlin was awarded the Grand Cross of the Order of Saint Sylvester by Pope John XXIII.

3. Domani è sempre domani (It.): tomorrow is always tomorrow.

To Robert Fitzgerald
5 May 1959

Dear Robert,

Caren is away but I'll be glad to lunch on V[ia] Appia on the 12th or 11th. I think Tuesday the 12th wld. be best. Ring me up when you get here.

I don't know about Allen. He only stayed a day here. I'll tell you.

Love to Sally.

Yrs

Denis

Autograph letter signed. 1 leaf, 1 side. *Header*: Ambassade d'Irlande, Rome. Robert Fitzgerald Papers, Box 8, Folder 344, Beinecke, YU.

To Brian Coffey

21 July 1959   3 Via Valle delle Camene

Dear Brian,

No, my failure to write to you did not mean that I did not like the poem.[1] In fact, I like it very much. I have been trying to get it published and "Botteghe Oscure" have now said that they would like to take [part] I for their number after the next: i.e. the one coming out in March, 1960.[2] The difficulty was they held on to the text for so long. I don't know whether you will think this too long to wait but, at any rate[,] the offer has been made (and I hope they won't let me down). There is a new editor whose name is Seán O'CRIADAIN.[3] The address is: "Botteghe Oscure" Palazzo Caetani, Via delle Botteghe Oscure 32, Rome. You might write to him direct.

I think your poem is out of the ordinary, in places very moving and, technically, interesting. I have put pencil notations against lines I think need revision. But, though I have no reserves about parts 2, 3 and 4, I think part 1 should be shortened considerably – though I do not agree with your shortening of the passage "how casual the fall of seed". I would not touch your Chinese philosopher who is very attractive.[4] Perhaps some of the lists cld. be shortened? I see you need Part 1 to set the scene etc.

I am going home at the beginning of August, and if I feel up to it I shall come through London & see you[.] If not, it means I take Aer[ ]Lingus direct Rome-Dublin. I am eager to get away from all this Italian screaming & really debilitating heat.

Sorry I didn't see the Pophams – I wonder if they called?[5] I have been away a lot on business this season.

Again, "increasings to you" (mórdha dhuit) on the poem.[6]

        Yours

          Denis

Typed letter signed. Handwritten amendments (text from 'Perhaps some of the lists …' written by hand). 1 leaf, 2 sides. *Header*: Ambassade d'Irlande, Rome. *Address*: Dr. Brian Coffey, 13 Elms Avenue, London N10. Brian Coffey Papers, Box 30, Folder 22, UDel.

---

1. The poem is 'Missouri Sequence', begun during Coffey's difficult period at St Louis University.

2. Coffey's poem did not appear in the Spring 1960 issue of *Botteghe Oscure* which was, in fact, the final issue. When it was published in its entirety in Ireland's *University Review* (vol. 2, no. 12, Winter 1962, pp. 29–46), the third section was dedicated to the memory of Denis Devlin.

3. Sean O'Criadain (1930–2004), Irish poet and editor. After his time as assistant editor at *Botteghe Oscure*, O'Criadain became publicity director at Simon & Schuster in New York.

4. Su Tung-Po (1037–1101), Chinese poet and statesman. The passage, at the beginning of section II, opens: 'It was, I think, in suchlike weather/Su Tungpo thanked God/his toil had worked the Eastern Slope/into fruitful soil', *BCPV*, p. 74.

5. The Pophams have not been identified.

6. mórdha dhuit (Ga.): 'power to you', or 'strength to your arm'.

Coda, 1959

CHRONOLOGY

1959

August	Devlins return to Ireland on a scheduled vacation. DD diagnosed with lung cancer and pneumonia, admitted to St Vincent's Nursing Home. He dies on 21 August. DD's funeral, at Dean's Grange Cemetery, Co. Dublin on 24 August, is attended by President de Valera.
Autumn	'Memoirs of a Turcoman Diplomat' is published in *Botteghe Oscure*, quaderno XXIV.

Caren Devlin to Eleanor Clark and Robert Penn Warren

6 August 1959   The Slopes, Dún Laoghaire

My dear Eleanor and Red,

I have very sad news. Denis is very ill with cancer, diagnosed as incurable, and will probably not live to see the year out. He is <u>unaware</u> of this, thank God. I am very desperate! We are in Ireland at home, and it is all very tragic. I wish you would write him, but <u>be careful</u> not to convey to him in any way that you think he is very ill.

I can say little more. You know what he is like, and what a loss he will be! It is all very sudden, and very tragic.

Excuse me if I write no more.

I am incapable of any thought –

       Much love to you both from both of us,

          Caren

Autograph letter signed. 2 leaves, 2 sides. Eleanor Clark Papers, Box 28, Folder 363, Beinecke, YU.

Caren Devlin to Robert Fitzgerald
14 August 1959

My dear Robert,

Denis is gravely ill, and is not expected to survive the next few days. If you want to see him for a few minutes come to Dublin[,] St Vincent's Nursing Home[,] 96 Lower Leeson Street, as soon as possible.[1]

I am there all the time. He has cancer of the lungs and pneumonia. He does <u>not</u> know that he is so ill, nor that he has cancer.

Forgive the shortness of this note. Please be <u>cheerful</u> when you see him, and pretend you were coming up <u>anyway</u> to Dublin – not for him!

All love from us both

Caren

P.S. He has received the Holy Sacrament you'll be glad to hear.

Autograph letter signed. 1 leaf, 2 sides. Robert Fitzgerald Papers, Box 8, Folder 344, Beinecke, YU.

---

1. Fitzgerald was in Limerick at the time.

Caren Devlin to Eleanor Clark and Robert Penn Warren

19 August 1959

Dear Eleanor and Red,

Just a hasty note to thank you for your letter. There is no point in your coming over. He is too ill to see anyone, and the end is near.

Much love to you both, and many thanks for your friendly and affectionate thoughts,

Caren

Autograph letter signed. 1 leaf, 1 side. Eleanor Clark Papers, Box 28, Folder 363, Beinecke, YU.

Caren Devlin to Brian Coffey
[September 1959]

My dear Brian,

It was Denis' last wish that you should look over some of his poems – the unfinished & published ones.

I am enclosing a few of the last ones, and a few others, that seemed fairly finished.

A review has asked me to send them a few for publication – let me know what you think.

I am fighting a flue [*for* flu] since a week!! Beastly weather. So sorry about last Sunday!

Ever yours

Caren

Autograph letter signed. 1 leaf, 1 side. *Dating*: letter unsituated, and dated "Tuesday". The content suggests it was written before Caren and Coffey began discussing the Devlin Memorial Award. It appears in Coffey's cuttings book next to a Devlin obituary. Brian Coffey Papers, Box 8, Folder 66, UDel.

Caren Devlin to Robert Penn Warren and Eleanor Clark

4 October 1959   40 Circus Road, London, NW8

My dear Red and Eleanor,

I have been meaning to write many a time, but then the move to London kept me so busy, it was impossible to get pen to paper. As you see from the above I have found a place to live in London, and Stevie is going to school. We are fairly happy here, but it is lonely after Denis' death! I am planning on staying here until x-mas.

You have asked me repeatedly if there is anything you could do! Well, yes there is – two things.

Firstly, I want to bring you a complete collection of Denis' poems (with reprints of poems in <u>Intercessions</u>, <u>Lough Derg</u>, and all his recent work) and I wonder[,] Red, if you could get Albert & Random House to publish this book in America.[1] There is great need of it, since D's work (as you know) is unfindable in printed form. Denis also asked me on his death bed to get Red to look over the poems he left (those that weren't published yet) for suggestions, corrections, etc. I'll send the manuscripts to Red in due course.[2] I am only beginning the whole job next week!

The second thing is, that some friends and admirers of Deni[s] want to start a collection around the world to institute a Denis Devlin Poetry prize, given every 3 years with the interest of the money collected, to an English speaking poet (that is to say Irish, English, American, or any Dominion) for a group of 12 poems, published or unpublished. We hope to get the Prize up to 500 pounds: (every 3 years) on the interest. There will have to be a Jury – and Honorary Committee, and 3 Honorary Treasurers.

For the jury we had thought of the following names:

     <u>America</u>:   Allen Tate
                    Robert Penn Warren

England: T.S. Eliot
            W.H. Auden
Ireland: Louis MacNeice
            Donagh MacDonagh

I haven't approached any of these people yet. Remember, it would be <u>only</u> every three year[s] that the Jury would have to select a likely candidate – and exchange the best poems from each country – I think it could be done by correspondence – do you?

There would be only <u>one</u> appeal for money – now. The checks would be made out to the Denis Devlin Poetry Award – and sent to the Honorary Treasurer in each country.[3] The Honorary Treasurer would then have to acknowledge receipt and forward the checks to a bank account opened in the name of the award.

As honorary treasurers we had thought of:

France: Sam Beckett
England: W.R. Rodgers
Ireland: Niall Sheridan
            or Mervyn Wall
America: Eleanor Clarke [*for* Clark]

Would Eleanor agree?

We have the following names for the honorary Committee:

Ireland: Seán O'Faolain
            Kate O'Brien[4]
            Elizabeth Bowen[5]
            Frank O'Connor
            Denis Johnston
            Austin Clarke
            Donagh MacDonagh
            Niall Sheridan
            Mervyn Wall
            Lord Longford[6]

                Lord Killanin[7]
                Monsignor Paddy Browne
                Mary Lavin[8]
                Conor Cruise O'Brien[9]
                Paddy Kavanagh[10]
                Louis MacNeice
                W.R. Rodgers
                Sam Beckett
                Val Iremonger[11]
       and   [É]amon [d]e Valera

England[:] T.S. Eliot
                John Hayward[12]
                W.H. Auden
                Kathleen Raines [*for* Raine][13]
                Cyril Connolly[14]
                W.H. [*for* W.S.] Graham[15]
                Bernard Wall[16]
                John Davenport[17]
                Editor of the Spectator[18]
                Paul Maguire [*for* McGuire] (Australian)[19]

France: St. Jean [*for* St-John] Perse
                René Char

Italy[:]   Ungaretti[20]
                Silone[21]
                Moravia[22]
                Elsa Morante[23]
                Piovere[24]
                Mario Praz
                Emilio Cecchi[25]
                Iris Origo[26]
                Princess Marguerite Caetani

America[:] Allen Tate
Robert Penn Warren
Robert Lowell
Theodore Roethke
Robert Fitzgerald
Ja[mes] Sweeney
[Richard] Wilbur[27]
Katherine Anne Porter[28]
Carolyne [*for* Caroline] Gordon
Elisabeth [*for* Elizabeth] Hardwick[29]
John Crowe Ransom[30]
Carson McCullers[31]
Huntington Hartford[32]
Eleanor Clarke [*for* Clark]
Karl Shapiro[33]
Randall Jarrell (?)
Vivienne Kock [*for* Koch] (?)

Subject[,] naturally, to refusal – but these
are all people who knew Denis (only Eliot &
Auden are doubtful because they knew him
very little) but Eliot is very keen (I hear) to
be on the Poetry Committee.

Do you think these committees are too big? On the other hand, honorary committee member[s] would take more interest in the fund.

I haven't approached anyone yet: Do you have any suggestions?
How should the circulars read? They will be printed by machine in
Rome. I will mail most of them myself, but would mail a number of
them to certain people to circulate. Have I forgotten anyone? Lon
Cheney [*for* Chaney]?[34] I don't think that there is anything Denis
would have liked better than to be remembered in this way. Do you?

We thought[,] first, of making it an only Irish prize, but there
would never be every 3 years a good enough poet.[35] And the prize[,]

if it comes to 400 or 500 pounds, would be the biggest Poetry Prize in England & Ireland – I don't know about America? It would give some young poet the chance of living and writing for about a year without worries of a material sort.

And Denis owed a great deal to America –

Do write me soon all you think. Stevie is well and sends love to Roposie + her brother.

All love to both of you.

Caren.

P.S. One important point: I think it should all be done as quickly as possible – after Denis' death.

[P.]P.S. I have[,] unfortunately, been left with very little money, and cannot do the fund on my own. In any case, I think it is the participation of a lot of peopl[e] that makes the thing.

> Autograph letter signed. 8 leaves, 8 sides. *Header:* Ambassade d'Irlande, crossed out. Telephone number 'Cunningham 0668' written beneath header on first leaf. Postscripts written at top of third and fifth leaves. Text beneath lists of possible honorary committee members ('Subject[,] naturally, to refusal …') written up right-hand margin of seventh leaf. Final greetings, from 'And Denis owed a great deal …', written up left- and right-hand margins of eighth leaf. Eleanor Clark Papers, Box 28, Folder 363, Beinecke, YU.

---

1. Albert Erskine (1912–93), vice president and editorial director at Random House. Erskine had worked with Devlin's publisher Frank Taylor at Reynal & Hitchcock until they both resigned in 1947.

2. Penn Warren and Tate brought out Devlin's posthumous *Selected Poems* with Holt, Rinehart & Winston in 1963.

3. Caren uses the American spelling for 'cheques'.

4. Kate O'Brien (1897–1974), Irish novelist and activist who challenged the Irish Censorship of Publications Act.

5. Elizabeth Bowen (1899–1973), Irish novelist and short-story writer, based in England for most of her working life.

6. Edward Pakenham, 6th Earl of Longford (1902–61), Irish peer, politician and translator, active in the Dublin literary scene.

7. Michael Morris, 3rd Baron Killanin (1914–99), Irish journalist and author, and head of the Olympic Council of Ireland.

8. Mary Lavin (1912–96), American-born Irish short-story writer and novelist.

9. Conor Cruise O'Brien (1917–2008), Irish politician, writer and historian, and Devlin's colleague in the Department of External Affairs.

10. Patrick Kavanagh (1904–67), Irish poet and novelist, active in Dublin journals such as *Envoy*.

11. Valentin Iremonger (1918–91), Irish poet and civil servant who joined the Department of External Affairs in the 1950s. He was at this time counsellor in the London embassy.

12. John Hayward (1905–65), English critic, anthologist and editor.

13. Kathleen Raine (1908–2003), English poet and critic, known for her work on William Blake and W.B. Yeats.

14. Cyril Connolly (1903–74), English writer and critic, founding editor of *Horizon* magazine.

15. W.S. Graham (1918–86), Scottish poet associated in his early career with the neo-romantic and New Apocalypse writers.

16. Bernard Wall (1908–74), English author, publisher and translator, part of an English Catholic intellectual movement.

17. John Davenport (1908–66), English critic and book reviewer associated with *The Observer* and *The Spectator*.

18. The editor of *The Spectator* at this time was actually the Irish historian, journalist and television presenter Brian Inglis (1916–93).

19. Paul McGuire (1903–78), Australian writer and diplomat, serving as minister to Italy in Rome at the same time as Devlin.

20. Giuseppe Ungaretti (1888–1970), Italian modernist poet and journalist, appointed professor of modern literature at the University of Rome during the Second World War.

21. Ignazio Silone (1900–78), Italian novelist, short-story writer and politician, one of Devlin's good friends in Rome.

22. Alberto Moravia (1907–90), Italian novelist and journalist, founder of the Roman literary magazine *Nuovi Argomenti*.

23. Elsa Morante (1912–85), Italian novelist, short-story writer and translator, at this time married to Moravia.

24. Piovere (It.): to rain. It is not clear who or what is referred to here.

25. Emilio Cecchi (1884–1966), Italian essayist, critic and cultural journalist.

26. Iris Origo (1902–88), English-born writer and biographer who lived in Italy for most of her adult life.

27. Richard Wilbur (1921–2017), American poet and translator, appointed professor of English at Wesleyan University in 1957.

28. Katherine Anne Porter (1890–1980), American journalist, essayist and short-story writer, a friend of Devlin's in Washington.

29. Elizabeth Hardwick (1916–2007), American literary critic, novelist and short-story writer.

30. John Crowe Ransom (1888–1974), American literary critic, editor and poet, whose teaching at Vanderbilt University helped to found the New Criticism. Ransom had retired from his professorship at Kenyon College this year.

31. Carson McCullers (1917–67), American novelist, short-story writer and playwright.

32. George Huntington Hartford (1911–2008), American businessman, stage and film producer, and patron of the arts.

33. Karl Shapiro (1913–2000), American poet and critic, consultant in poetry to the Library of Congress (1946–7) after Penn Warren.

34. Creighton Tull Chaney (1906–73), known by the stage name Lon Chaney Jr., American screen actor, known for his starring roles in horror films *The Wolf Man* (1941) and *The Ghost of Frankenstein* (1942).

35. Despite Caren's reservations, Penn Warren and Tate were both in favour of making this an Irish prize. The Denis Devlin Memorial Award was established in 1961 from the international fund and administered by the Irish Arts Council, largely owing to the efforts of Mervyn Wall, who had corresponded with Caren, Penn Warren and Tate (see Robert Penn Warren Papers, Box 21, Folder 409, and Allen Tate Papers, Box 25, Folder 27). The award has been granted triennially since 1964, for the best book of poetry published by an Irish citizen in the previous three years.

Caren Devlin to Robert Penn Warren
5 October [1959]   London

My dear Red,

I wanted to write to you myself (Eleanor will have given you all the rest of the news in my recent letter), to tell you how moved Denis and I were by your dedication of 'The Cave' to us[.][1] It is a truly splendid book, and I am so glad that it was nearly the last thing Denis saw before dying.

It has been very hard without him, and one does not know where to start. Stevie is great company and consolation, and seems very pleased with London. More so than I.

More soon.

Much love dear Red, and again a thousand thanks for this wonderful dedication.

Caren

Autograph letter signed. 1 leaf, 1 side. Robert Penn Warren Papers, Box 21, Folder 409, Beinecke, YU.

─────────────

1. *The Cave* (1959), Penn Warren's sixth novel, was dedicated 'To Denis and Caren Devlin'.

Caren Devlin to Thomas MacGreevy

[October 1959]   40 Circus Road, London, NW8

Dear Tom,

I am now writing to you about something else. Brian Coffey has suggested you be on the honorary committee of a Poetry Prize fund which is being started in memory of Denis. This is a <u>purely honorary function</u>, and the Committee will be made up of fifty writers, poets and art patrons. The prize will be awarded every three years to an Irish poet of Irish descendancy [*sic*]. There will be only one collection[,] the money will be invested, and it is the interest of this money, it is hoped about 400 to 500 pounds[,] that will constitute the Prize money. The award will be given by an international jury to the best group of twelve poems published or unpublished. The Prize is destined to help a poet to realise his poetic ambitions by freeing him of material worries temporarily. It is also destined to unite [poets] internationally[.] Something of this sort anyway. For Ireland it is hoped to have the following names on the Committee: Austin Clarke, Paddy Kavanagh, Donagh MacDonagh, Mervyn Wall, Sam Beckett, W.R. Rodgers, Louis MacNeice, Miles [*for* Myles] Dillon, Brian Coffey, Monsignor Paddy Browne, Denis Johnston, Frank O'Connor, Lord Longford, Lord Killanin, etc. Others for England, America, Italy and France. There will be a Jury of six writers, two American, two English, and two Irish. The circulars will be printed fairly soon so could you let me have an early reply about whether you agree to being on the Committee –[1]

All good wishes.

Most sincerely

Caren

Autograph letter signed. 1 leaf, 2 sides. *Dating*: MacGreevy's reply is dated 29 October 1959. Thomas MacGreevy Papers, 8112/17–22, TCD.

---

1. In MacGreevy's reply he states that he would rather be among the first subscribers to the memorial fund than be part of the honorary committee. His response betrays the ongoing antagonism MacGreevy felt towards 'literary' Dublin. See TM to Caren Devlin, 29 October 1959, Thomas MacGreevy Papers, 8112/17–22, TCD.

APPENDIX

Night of the Times

The father read the high life
in dirty novels
from neighbourhood libraries;
the pale, young mother
who hadn't laughed since her wedding day
performed a gentle death;
the seamstress on the landing
flooded with filthy sunsets
awaited the pleasure
of princes and upstarts;
the snow fell
on Père-Lachaise;
the pimps in silk hats
gathered under the gas hose
shuffled the Kings and Queens;
the athlete told the butcher
of a night in Amsterdam
he had seen the troop pass
with fifes and drums.
It was a year of plenty:
the wheat had sprouted
on the earth of France,
we went on the ramparts
to remember the war,
the young men who had kissed
pink corsets and black stockings,
often to die in the villages
of girls in the odour of sanctity.

from Jean Follain, 'Soir d'époque'

CORRESPONDENTS' BIOGRAPHIES

Frank Biggar (1917–74)

Irish civil servant and diplomat, joined the Department of External Affairs in 1941. In the 1950s he served in Dublin, London and Portugal, and in the early 1960s was ambassador to Belgium and Luxembourg, and head of mission to the European Economic Community.

Amy Bonner (1891–1955)

American poet and journalist, served as the eastern business representative for Chicago's *Poetry* magazine between 1937 and 1947.

Cesare Brandi (1906–88)

Italian art critic and historian, specialist in conservation theory. Brandi was the founding director of the Istituto Centrale del Restauro (the Central Institute for Restoration) in Rome, which he led for two decades.

Ernest Brooks (?1908–84)

American law graduate, worked in arts and educational philanthropy. Brooks was legal adviser, assistant secretary and treasurer of the Bollingen Foundation, and president of the Old Dominion Foundation (which became the Andrew W. Mellon Foundation) from 1956 to 1969.

Hugh Chisholm (1913–72)

American poet, translator and editor, worked as assistant editor at the Bollingen Foundation in New York in the late 1940s and early 1950s.

Eleanor Clark (1913–96)

American novelist, travel writer and translator. Clark was publishing in left-wing political magazines such as *The Partisan Review* during her time at Vassar College; in 1937 she became one of Trotsky's translators on a trip to Mexico. She moved to Washington during the Second

World War to work for the Office of Strategic Services, and met both Devlin and her husband Robert Penn Warren through their mutual friend, the novelist and short-story writer Katherine Anne Porter.

Austin Clarke (1896–1974)

Irish poet, playwright, novelist, journalist and broadcaster. Clarke taught English at UCD after graduating in 1917; he then moved to London to work as a critic and editor from 1921 to 1937. On his return to Dublin he founded the Dublin Verse Speaking Society which performed at the Peacock and Abbey Theatres, and presented a weekly poetry show on Radio Éireann.

Brian Coffey (1905–95)

Irish poet, Devlin's closest friend and collaborator at UCD and during their postgraduate years in Paris, where Coffey was studying physical chemistry before taking up a doctorate in philosophy. Teaching in England during the war, Coffey moved his large family to Missouri to take up a lectureship in philosophy at St Louis University in the 1940s. He moved back to England in the early 1950s to teach mathematics, and returned to publishing poetry.

Cornelius (Con) Cremin (1908–87)

Irish diplomat, joined the Department of External Affairs at the same time as Devlin, working on the League of Nations portfolio. He was assistant secretary from 1949 to 1950, and secretary from 1958 to 1963.

Clarence Decker (1904–69)

American literary critic and editor, president of the University of Kansas City from 1938 to 1953, and founding editor of *The University Review* (later *The University of Kansas City Review*, and *New Letters*).

Shiela Devlin (see Shiela Healy)

George H. Dillon (1906–68)

American editor, poet and Pulitzer Prize winner, succeeded Harriet Monroe as editor of *Poetry* magazine in 1937.

Brian Durnin (1912–?80)

Irish diplomat and radio broadcaster, moved from Radio Éireann to the Department of External Affairs in 1949. Secretary to the Cultural Relations Advisory Committee before taking up positions in Washington, as permanent representative to the Council of Europe, and ambassador to Australia.

William P. Fay (1909–69)

Assistant secretary to the Department of External Affairs in 1954, shortly to be appointed Irish ambassador to Paris. Devlin mistakenly addresses Fay as 'W.G. Fay' in one letter, with good reason: Fay was the nephew of Frank and Willie G. Fay, co-founders of the Abbey Theatre.

Robert Fitzgerald (1910–85)

American poet, critic and translator. Fitzgerald and his family spent a decade in Italy from 1953, while he was working on translations of Sophocles' *Oedipus at Colonus* (1954) and Homer's *Odyssey* (1961), the latter of which won the Bollingen Award and became a standard text for classics students. Fitzgerald became Boylston professor of rhetoric and oratory at Harvard in 1965, preceding Seamus Heaney in the role.

Kimon Friar (1911–93)

Greek-American poet and translator, edited anthologies of modern American, British and Greek poetry. Friar translated Nikos Kazantzakis' *The Odyssey: A Modern Sequel* into English in 1958.

Robert Greacen (1920–2008)

Northern Irish poet, literary critic and editor, lived and worked in Belfast, Dublin and London across his career. After publishing two volumes of poetry in the 1940s, and assisting Valentin Iremonger in editing *The Faber Book of Contemporary Irish Poetry* (1949), Greacen took a long break from publishing, returning with a new volume in the 1970s.

Robert Greene (dates unknown)

Irish businessman, worked for Arthur Guinness, Son & Co. as export manager and assistant trade manager.

Richard Francis Hayes (1878–1958)

Irish politician, historian and director of the Abbey Theatre. He was Irish film censor from 1941 to 1954, and member of the Cultural Committee established in 1949 to advise the minister for external affairs.

Shiela Healy (*née* Devlin) (1918–94)

Devlin's sister, the seventh child of Liam and Margaret Devlin. Healy attended Kylemore Abbey convent school while Devlin was in Dublin in the early 1930s, and showed special promise as a pianist, winning a medal from the London College of Music. In 1938 she spent a year studying at a Catholic lycée in Amiens. Her musical ambitions were cut short by the start of the Second World War, and Healy worked as an assistant in her father's confectionery manufacturing business until her marriage in 1947.

Joseph Hergesheimer (1880–1954)

American novelist, author of decadent society novels that were very popular in the 1920s, and identified with the 'aesthetic' school of F. Scott Fitzgerald and Sinclair Lewis. His popularity declined in the 1930s. In 1962 Samuel Beckett claimed that Hergesheimer's *Java Head* (1919) was 'the best [American novel] I ever read'.

Vivienne Koch (1914–61)

American literary critic with expertise in modern poetry, taught at Mount Holyoke College and New York University and published studies of William Carlos Williams and W.B. Yeats. Koch co-founded the James Joyce Society of New York in 1947, and headed the NYU Poetry Center.

James Laughlin (1914–97)

American poet and publisher, friend and admirer of Ezra Pound and William Carlos Williams. Laughlin founded the influential modernist publishing company New Directions in 1936, after visiting Pound in Rapallo, and while still a student at Harvard.

Alexis Leger (1887–1975)

French poet and diplomat who wrote under the pseudonym Saint-John Perse. Leger was general secretary to the French Foreign Office until his citizenship was revoked under the Vichy government during the occupation of France. He lived in exile in Washington DC from 1940, and Archibald MacLeish arranged for his appointment as poetry consultant at the Library of Congress. Devlin met Leger in Washington, and began working on collaborative translations of his poetry in 1944.

Patrick Little (1884–1963)

Irish solicitor, journalist and Fianna Fáil politician. Little was the first editor of republican magazine *An Phoblacht*, and was chairman of the Irish Arts Council from 1951 to 1956.

Máire MacEntee (See Máire Mhac an tSaoi)

Thomas MacGreevy (1893–1967)

Irish poet, translator, critic and art historian. MacGreevy was Beckett's predecessor as *lecteur d'anglais* at the École Normale Supérieure, at a time when a lively expatriate community was forming around Joyce.

He introduced Beckett to Joyce, and eventually introduced Devlin and Coffey to Beckett. After many years as a literary and art critic in Paris, London and Dublin, MacGreevy was made director of the National Gallery in Dublin in 1950.

Norman Macleod (1906–85)

American poet, novelist and editor, established the Poetry Center at the 'Y' in New York's 92nd Street. Macleod founded and served as editorial director of the *Maryland Quarterly* and the *Briarcliff Quarterly* while he was teaching English at the University of Maryland and Briarcliff Community College.

Raymond McGrath (1903–77)

Australian-born architect and interior designer, principal architect in the Office of Public Works, Dublin (1948–68).

Victor Mallet (1893–1969)

British diplomat and author, ambassador to Italy in the first years of Devlin's posting in Rome (1947–53).

Máire Mhac an tSaoi (born Máire MacEntee) (1922–)

Irish poet, writer and diplomat. Mhac an tSaoi joined the civil service in 1947, was the Irish representative on the UN Humanitarian, Social and Cultural Committee in the 1950s, and resigned in 1961. She became an influential voice in Irish-language poetry and scholarship.

Niall Montgomery (1915–87)

Irish writer, critic and architect, a few years behind Devlin at UCD, but made known to his circle through his precocious talents. In the 1930s Montgomery collaborated with Devlin on translations from modern French poetry into Irish; he occasionally collaborated with Brian O'Nolan on the 'Cruiskeen Lawn' columns in *The Irish Times*, under the pseudonym Myles na gCopaleen. He achieved great success as an architect, establishing a private practice in 1946, and was committed to the preservation and restoration of Dublin's architecture.

Ria Mooney (1904–73)

Irish actress, a director at the Abbey Theatre, and a director of both the Abbey School of Acting and the Gaiety School of Acting. Devlin's sister Moya was also an Abbey actress, who had performed with Mooney in Brinsley MacNamara's *Margaret Gillan* in February 1937 (Moya in the title role); Devlin most likely met Mooney through Moya.

Seán Murphy (1896–1964)

Irish barrister and diplomat, assistant secretary to the Department of External Affairs during Devlin's early years as a cadet (1927–38). After serving as ambassador to Canada from 1950, Murphy became secretary to the department in 1955.

Sheila Murphy (1898–1983)

Irish civil servant and diplomat, and Ireland's highest-ranking female diplomat during her career. She joined the civil service in 1921, became Joseph Walshe's private secretary (1926) and departmental archivist (1936), before taking up an ambassadorial role in the Vatican in 1946. Murphy was first secretary to the Irish embassy in Paris (1956–61), and assistant secretary to the department two years before her retirement in 1964.

John Frederick Nims (1913–99)

American poet, editor and academic. Nims was on the editorial staff at *Poetry* in the 1940s and '50s, while teaching at the universities of Notre Dame, Toronto, Florence and Bocconi University in Milan, becoming editor in 1978.

Seán Nunan (1890–1981)

Irish diplomat, fought in the Easter Rising as a member of the Irish Volunteers. Became minister to the United States of America (1947–50), assistant secretary (1950), and secretary (1950–5) to the Department of External Affairs.

Brian O'Nolan (1911–66)

Irish novelist, columnist and civil servant, another of Devlin's UCD contemporaries. O'Nolan joined the civil service in the same year as Devlin, in the Department of Local Government. He published fiction under the pseudonym Flann O'Brien, and a satirical *Irish Times* column, 'Cruiskeen Lawn', under the pseudonym Myles na gCopaleen.

Rodolfo Pallucchini (1908–89)

Celebrated Italian art historian, appointed general secretary of the Venice Biennale in 1947. Devlin had sat alongside Pallucchini on the selection committee for the Biennale in 1950.

John Palmer (1913–2009)

American literary editor, managing editor of the *The Southern Review* (1940–2), and editor of *The Sewanee Review* (1946–52) after serving in the US Navy during the war.

George Reavey (1907–76)

Russian-born Northern Irish poet and publisher, a friend of Devlin and Coffey's in Paris in the early 1930s. Reavey established the Bureau Littéraire Européen in Paris, which became the Europa Press when he transferred to London. Europa issued the first solo volumes of poetry by Beckett, Devlin and Coffey.

William Robert Rodgers (1909–69)

Northern Irish poet, critic, radio broadcaster and Presbyterian minister. Rodgers moved to London after the Second World War to concentrate on writing and, through Louis MacNeice, secured a post as scriptwriter at the BBC in 1946. He became a freelance broadcaster and was elected to the Irish Academy of Letters in 1951.

Selden Rodman (1909–2002)

American poet, editor and critic of art and literature. Rodman co-founded the socialist magazine *Common Sense* in 1932, and was committed to the promotion of Haitian and African-American folk art in America.

Theodore Roethke (1908–63)

American poet and critic, taught English, composition and creative writing at Lafayette College, Michigan State College, Penn State University, Bennington College and the University of Washington. In the 1950s Roethke spent time teaching and travelling in Europe on grants from the Ford Foundation and Fulbright. He met Devlin in Rome in 1953, and wrote a poem, 'The Dancing Man', in Devlin's memory.

William Matson Roth (1916–2014)

American publisher, trade ambassador and shipping executive. A literature graduate, Roth set up the Colt Press with printer Jane Grabhorn in San Francisco in 1941. The press ceased operations during the Second World War, and Roth joined the Office of War Information, serving in Alaska, India and Burma.

Aloysius Michael Sullivan (1896–1980)

American poet, magazine editor and radio broadcaster, served five terms as president of the Poetry Society of America and as president of the Catholic Poetry Society of America in the 1950s.

Allen Tate (1899–1979)

American poet, novelist and literary critic. Tate was part of the Fugitive group of poets led by John Crowe Ransom at Vanderbilt University, and co-founded *The Fugitive* magazine, which heralded a Southern American literary renaissance. When Devlin met Tate in the 1940s he was consultant in poetry at the Library of Congress. He went on to edit *The Sewanee Review*, and held academic appointments at the University of New York and the University of Minnesota.

Mervyn Wall (1908–97)

Irish playwright and novelist, Devlin's contemporary at UCD. Wall entered the civil service shortly before Devlin, worked for Radio Éireann from 1948, and became secretary of the Arts Council in 1957.

Joseph P. Walshe (1886–1956)

Irish diplomat, served as acting secretary to the Department of External Affairs shortly after the establishment of the Irish Free State in 1923, secretary (1927–46), and ambassador to the Holy See (1946–54).

Robert Penn Warren (1905–89)

American poet, novelist and literary critic. Penn Warren was roommates with Allen Tate at Vanderbilt, and contributed to *The Fugitive* magazine. While teaching English at Louisiana State University in the 1930s, Penn Warren and his colleague Cleanth Brooks co-authored the influential textbook *Understanding Poetry* (1938), exemplifying what was becoming known as New Critical reading practice, and helped to establish *The Southern Review*. Penn Warren became Tate's successor as consultant in poetry at the Library of Congress, and probably met Devlin in Washington through Tate. From 1950 he held a professorship of playwriting at Yale University.

Marcella Comès Winslow (1906–2000)

Washington-based American portrait painter, whose sitters were predominantly American writers. Winslow's Georgetown home was an informal literary salon in the 1940s and '50s.

Thomas Woods (1923–61)

Irish diplomat and writer, joined the department in 1943, became first secretary in 1949, and served as Irish permanent representative to the Council of Europe until his death (1957–61). Woods wrote a literary and cultural column in *The Irish Times* called 'Private Views', under the pseudonym Thersites.

BIBLIOGRAPHY

Archives Consulted

Bollingen Foundation Records, Library of Congress, Washington DC

Amy Bonner Papers, Special Collections Research Center, University of Chicago Library

Marguerite Caetani Papers, Fondazione Camillo Caetani, Rome

Eleanor Clark Papers, Yale Collection of American Literature (MSS 315), Beinecke Rare Book and Manuscript Library, Yale University

Austin Clarke Papers (MS 38,651-38,708), National Library of Ireland, Dublin

Brian Coffey Papers (MSS 382), Special Collections, University of Delaware Library

Correspondance particuliere de Saint-John Perse (Alexis Leger) et Dorothy Leger, Les Collections Patrimoniales, Fondation Saint-John Perse, Aix-en-Provence

Colt Press Records, *c.* 1941–70 (MSS 94/15c), Bancroft Library, University of California, Berkeley

Department of Foreign Affairs Papers, National Archives of Ireland, Dublin

Denis Devlin Literary Papers (MSS 33,747-33,810), National Library of Ireland

Robert Fitzgerald Papers, Yale Collection of American Literature (MSS 222), Beinecke Rare Book and Manuscript Library, Yale University

Kimon Friar Papers (C0713), Department of Special Collections, Princeton University Library

Robert Greacen Papers (MSS 7940), Manuscript Department, The Library of Trinity College Dublin

Joseph Hergesheimer Collection (MS 1921), Harry Ransom Center, University of Texas at Austin

Thomas MacGreevy Papers (MS 7985-8190), Manuscript Department, The Library of Trinity College Dublin.

Norman Macleod Papers, Yale Collection of American Literature (MSS 718), Beinecke Rare Book and Manuscript Library, Yale University

Niall Montgomery Papers (MS 50,118), National Library of Ireland, Dublin

Ria Mooney Papers (MS 49,603), National Library of Ireland, Dublin

New Directions Corp. Records (MS Am 2077), Houghton Library, Harvard University

Brian O'Nolan Papers (1/4/MSS 051), Southern Illinois University Special Collections Research Center

Papers of the magazine *Transition* (MS Am 2068), Houghton Library, Harvard University

Poetry: A Magazine of Verse. Records 1895–1961, Special Collections Research Center, University of Chicago Library

David Ray Papers 1936–2008, Special Collections Research Center, University of Chicago Library

George Reavey Papers (MS 3430), Harry Ransom Center, University of Texas at Austin

W.R. Rodgers Papers (D2833), Public Record Office of Northern Ireland, Belfast

Selden Rodman Papers (Collection No. 4259), American Heritage Center, University of Wyoming

Theodore Roethke Collection (0418–001), University of Washington Libraries Special Collections

The Southern Review Records, Yale Collection of American Literature (MSS 694), Beinecke Rare Book and Manuscript Library, Yale University

A.M. Sullivan Papers, Special Collections Research Center, Syracuse University Libraries

Allen Tate Papers (C0106), Manuscript Division, Department of Rare Books and Special Collections, Princeton University Library

Mervyn Wall Collection, Harry Ransom Center, University of Texas at Austin

Robert Penn Warren Papers, Yale Collection of American Literature (MSS 51), Beinecke Rare Book and Manuscript Library, Yale University

Marcella Comès Winslow Papers, 1915–82 [and undated], Reel 2424, Archives of American Art, Smithsonian Institution

Literary Works

Beckett, Samuel, *Disjecta: Miscellaneous writings and a dramatic fragment*, ed. Ruby Cohn (London: John Calder, 1983)

———— *The Letters of Samuel Beckett*, vols 1–2, ed. Martha Dow

Fehsenfeld, Lois More Overbeck, Dan Gunn and George Craig (Cambridge: Cambridge University Press, 2009–11)

Clark, Eleanor, *Rome and a Villa* (Garden City, NY: Doubleday, 1952)

Coffey, Brian, *Third Person* (London: Europa Press, 1938)

————— 'Missouri Sequence', *University Review*, vol. 2, no. 12, December 1962, pp. 29–46

————— *Poems and Versions, 1929–1990* (Dublin: The Dedalus Press, 1991)

Daiken, Leslie, *Good-bye Twilight: Songs of the struggle in Ireland* (London: Lawrence & Wishart, 1936)

Devlin, Denis, *Intercessions* (London: Europa Press, 1937)

————— *Lough Derg and Other Poems* (New York: Reynal & Hitchcock, 1946)

————— *Selected Poems*, ed. Allen Tate and Robert Penn Warren (New York: Rinehart & Winston, 1963)

————— *Collected Poems*, ed. Brian Coffey (Dublin: The Dolmen Press, 1964)

————— *The Heavenly Foreigner*, ed. Brian Coffey (Dublin: The Dolmen Press, 1967)

————— *Collected Poems of Denis Devlin*, ed. J.C.C. Mays (Dublin: Dedalus Press, 1989)

————— *Translations into English: From French, German and Italian poetry*, ed. Roger Little (Dublin: Dedalus, 1992)

Devlin, Denis and Mathews, Jackson, Translations from the poetry of René Char, *Botteghe Oscure*, quaderno X, 1952

Eliot, Thomas Stearns, 'Tradition and the Practice of Poetry', *The Southern Review*, no. 21, 1985, pp. 873–8

Eluard, Paul, *Thorns of Thunder*, ed. George Reavey, trans. Samuel Beckett et al. (London: Europa Press and Stanley Nott, 1936)

————— *Oeuvres Complètes*, vol. 1, ed. Marcelle Dumas and Lucien Scheler (Paris: Gallimard, 1968)

Finlay, Lilian Roberts, *Always in My Mind* (London: Collins, 1988)

MacGreevy, Thomas, *Collected Poems of Thomas MacGreevy: An annotated edition*, ed. Susan Schreibman (Dublin: Anna Livia Press, 1991)

————— *Jack B. Yeats: An appreciation and an interpretation* (Dublin: Victor Waddington, 1945)

Macleod, Norman, *Calendar: An anthology of 1940 poetry* (Prairie City: Press of James Decker, 1940)

Mallarmé, Stephane, *Collected Poems and Other Verse*, ed. & trans. E.H. Blackmore and A.M. Blackmore (Oxford & New York: Oxford University Press, 2006)

O'Brien, Flann, *The Collected Letters of Flann O'Brien*, ed. Maebh Long (Victoria, TX, McLean, IL and Dublin: Dalkey Archive Press, 2018)

Perse, Saint-John, *Letters*, ed. and trans. Arthur J. Knodel (Princeton: Princeton University Press, 2014)

————— *Exile and Other Poems*, trans. Denis Devlin (New York: Pantheon Books, 1949)

Read, Herbert, *Reason and Romanticism: Essays in literary criticism* (London: Faber & Gwyer, 1926)

Roethke, Theodore, *Selected Letters of Theodore Roethke* (London: Faber, 1970)

Stevenson, Robert Louis, *The Letters of Robert Louis Stevenson*, vols 4–5, ed. Bradford Booth & Ernest Mehew (New Haven: Yale University Press, 1994–5)

Warren, Robert Penn, *Selected Letters of Robert Penn Warren*, vol. 4, ed. Randy Hendricks and James A. Perkins (Baton Rouge: Louisiana State University Press, 2008)

Memoir and Biography

Coffey, Brian, 'Of Denis Devlin: Vestiges, sentences, presages', *The Poetry Ireland Review*, no. 75, Winter 2002/3, pp. 82–100

Cronin, Anthony, *No Laughing Matter: The life and times of Flann O'Brien* (New York: Fromm International, 1998)

Dennett, Laurie, *An American Princess: The remarkable life of Marguerite Chapin* (Montréal: McGill-Queen's University Press, 2016)

Devlin, Denis, 'St-John Perse in Washington', *Les Cahiers de la Pléiade*, no. X, Eté–Automne 1950, pp. 86–9

Gordon, Lyndall, *T.S. Eliot: An imperfect life* (London: Vintage, 1998)

Montgomery, Niall, 'Farewells Hardly Count', *Éire-Ireland: Weekly bulletin of the Department of External Affairs*, no. 494, 5 September 1960, pp. 8–9

Mooney, Ria, 'Players and the Painted Stage, Part One', *George Spelvin's Theatre Book*, vol. 1, no. 2, Summer 1978, pp. 3–120

Roth, William M., *The Colt Springs High: A publishing memoir of the Colt Press, 1939–1942* (San Francisco: The Book Club of California, 2004)

Silone, Ignazio [untitled tribute], *Éire-Ireland: Weekly bulletin of the Department of External Affairs*, no. 494, 5 September 1960, pp. 4–5

Critical and Historical Works

Brearton, Fran and Gillis, Alan (eds), *The Oxford Handbook of Modern Irish Poetry* (Oxford: Oxford University Press, 2012)

Brown, Terence, *Ireland: A social and cultural history, 1922–79* (London: Fontana Paperbacks, 1981)

Cahill, Alex, *The Formation, Existence, and Deconstruction of the Catholic Stage Guild of Ireland* (Newcastle upon Tyne: Cambridge Scholars Publishing, 2017)

Coughlan, Patricia and Davis, Alex (eds), *Modernism and Ireland: The poetry of the 1930s* (Cork: Cork University Press, 1995)

Crowe, Catriona, Fanning, Ronan, Kennedy, Michael, Keogh, Dermot and O'Halpin, Eunan (eds), *Documents on Irish Foreign Policy*, vols IV–IX (Dublin: Royal Irish Academy, 2004–14)

Daly, Selena and Insinga, Monica (eds), *The European Avant-Garde: Text and image* (Newcastle upon Tyne: Cambridge Scholars Publishing, 2012)

Davis, Alex, *A Broken Line: Denis Devlin and Irish poetic modernism* (Dublin: UCD Press, 2000)

Gillis, Alan, *Irish Poetry of the Thirties* (Oxford: Oxford University Press, 2005)

Kennedy, Michael, *Ireland and the League of Nations, 1919–46: International relations, diplomacy and politics* (Blackrock, Co. Dublin: Irish Academic Press, 1996)

Little, Roger, 'Saint-John Perse and Denis Devlin: A *compagnonnage*', *Irish University Review*, vol. 8, no. 2, Autumn 1978, pp. 193–200

McKeown, Edwina and Taaffe, Carol (eds), *Irish Modernism: Origins, contexts, publics* (Oxford: Peter Lang, 2010)

O'Dowd, Ciara, 'The On and Off-Stage Roles of Abbey Theatre Actresses of the 1930s', unpublished thesis submitted for examination at NUI Galway in May 2016

Smith, Stan, 'Frightened Antinomies: Love and death in the poetry of Denis Devlin', *Advent VI: Denis Devlin Special Issue* (Dublin: Advent Books, 1976)

Reviews

Boulton, Inez, 'Celtic Nova', *Poetry*, vol. 69, no. 1, October 1946, pp. 169–71

Colum, Padraic, 'The Irish Are Still Poets', *The Saturday Review of Literature*, vol. XXIX, no. 12, 23 March 1946, pp. 18–19

Devlin, Denis, 'Twenty-four Poets', *The Sewanee Review*, vol. 53, no. 3, Summer 1945, pp. 457–66

Kavanagh, Patrick, 'Letter from Ireland', *Poetry*, vol. 74, no. 5, August 1949, pp. 286–91

Koch, Vivienne, 'Poetry Chronicle', *The Sewanee Review*, vol. 54, no. 4, Oct–Dec 1946, pp. 699–716

MacGreevy, Thomas, 'Reason and Romanticism', *The Irish Statesman*, 25 December 1926, pp. 879–80

MacManus, M.J., 'Denis Devlin's Poems', *Irish Press*, 19 October 1937, p. 7.

Quidnunc, 'Irishman's Diary', *The Irish Times*, 7 December 1935, p. 6.

Random, Roderick [Review of George Reavey's *Nostradom*], *Time and Tide*, vol. XVI, no. 22, 1 June 1935, p. 823.

Rodman, Selden, 'Daemonic Poet', *New Republic*, vol. 115, no. 4, July 1946, pp. 106–7

Online Resources

The Abbey Theatre Archive (Abbey Theatre/Amharclann na Mainistreach): https://abbeytheatre.ie/about/archive/

Chasing Aideen: Encounters with Women in Irish Theatre History (blog by Ciara O'Dowd): https://chasingaideen.com

Irish Newspaper Archives: https://archive.irishnewsarchive.com

The Irish Times Archive (via Proquest Historical Newspapers)

The New York Times Archive (via Proquest Historical Newspapers)

The Washington Post Archive (via Proquest Historical Newspapers)

INDEX